Literacy and Democracy

Literacy and Democracy

Teacher Research and Composition Studies
in Pursuit of Habitable Spaces

Further Conversations from the
Students of Jay Robinson

Edited by

Cathy Fleischer
Eastern Michigan University

David Schaafsma
Teachers College, Columbia University

National Council of Teachers of English
1111 W. Kenyon Road, Urbana, Illinois 61801–1096

Staff Editor: Kurt Austin

Interior Design: Tom Kovacs for TGK Design

Cover Design: Pat Mayer

Cover Photograph ©Mark Harris/Tony Stone Images

NCTE Stock Number: 29773–3050

It is the policy of NCTE in its journals and other publications to provide a forum for the open discussion of ideas concerning the content and the teaching of English and the language arts. Publicity accorded to any particular point of view does not imply endorsement by the Executive Committee, the Board of Directors, or the membership at large, except in announcements of policy, where such endorsement is clearly specified.

Library of Congress Cataloging–in–Publication Data

Literacy and democracy: teacher research and composition studies in pursuit
    of habitable spaces: further conversations from the students of Jay
    Robinson/edited by Cathy Fleischer, David Schaafsma.
          p.   cm.
       Includes bibliographical references and index.
       ISBN 0-8141-2977-3 (pbk.)
          1. Literacy. 2. Sociolinguistics. 3. English language—Rhetoric—
    Study and teaching. 4. Critical pedagogy. 5. Robinson, Jay L., 1932–   .
    I. Fleischer, Cathy. II. Schaafsma, David, 1953–   . III. Robinson, Jay L.,
    1932–   .
    LC149.L4957   1998
    302.2'244—dc21   98-39385
                                                                          CIP

Contents

Foreword

Jacqueline Jones Royster
Ohio State University

Literacy and Democracy pays tribute to the scholarship and teaching of Jay L. Robinson in two specific ways. From one point of view, the types of engagement with language that are chronicled here celebrate his work as a researcher and scholar in historical linguistics and sociolinguistics and in English education. From another perspective, by the very collectivity of the essays, this volume demonstrates that the professional lives of many have been positively touched by Jay's incredible intellect, his vision of language and literacy, and his view of the work that we should do both inside and outside of the university. This collection encourages us to notice that the measures of this professor's success are most evident in the work of the women and men whose professional lives have been shaped and nurtured under his aegis. Within the sound of his voice, we committed ourselves to a critical exploration of theories and methodologies in context, to a conscious consideration of our own habits as teachers and researchers, and to an envisioning of the fields of rhetoric, composition, and literacy studies as sites for both knowledge making and action.

As a tribute, this volume has a particular resonance with two of Jay's earlier publications: *English Linguistics* (1970), which he edited with Harold Hungerford and James Sledd, and *Varieties of Present-Day English* (1973), which he edited with Richard W. Bailey. *English Linguistics* is an anthology on English grammar, English dialectology, and the history of English. On the surface it seems to be, as its title indicates, a very interesting collection of essays on English linguistics. On closer examination, however, what is most striking is that Hungerford, Sledd, and Robinson made central to their organizational scheme the needs of "the teacher of teachers." They brought together articles that demonstrated either a particular excellence or a representativeness of kind. They sought to bridge the gap between what linguists know about the English language and what teachers need to know to be prepared to teach it. They included pieces that in their view were professional and well-rooted in the knowledge of the discipline (i.e., English linguistics) but that at the same time were written not only for linguists but for what they called "a wider audience of intelligent readers" (ix).

In making these decisions, they acknowledged the day–to–day challenges that teachers face in classrooms, laying out knowledge and issues in language studies in a way that was accessible and instructive for those of us—i.e., their students at both undergraduate and graduate levels—who would choose careers as teachers of English. At the time, this collection was not only an opportunity for English majors across the nation to become well-informed about classic and current scholarship in the history and developments of English. It was also an opportunity, sparked by the study questions at the end of each essay, to think about the implications of such knowledge for action in contemporary educational enterprise.

This concern for future teachers and for the teachers who teach them emerges as a vibrant thread in Jay's work, perhaps always, but certainly from that public moment forward, such that in his next co-edited book, *Varieties of English*, the teaching of English became even more obvious as the raison d'être for his research and scholarship. The essays were divided into three sections: "English in the Modern World," "English in America," and "English in the Classroom." This type of ever-sharpening viewpoint signaled unmistakably that Bailey and Jay were suggesting provocative relationships between knowledge broadly conceived, its implications, and the programs and strategies that might be implemented on a local level in response. This schema action, as encoded specifically by the section "English in the Classroom," became co-equal with concerns about English as a world language and about language as a variable phenomenon in a multiethnic society.

The collection was eye-opening. In the preface, Bailey and Jay raised the questions that framed the collection:

> Variety in English is the subject of the readings contained in this book; among questions addressed in separate essays are these: What has caused this variety? Why does variety persist in spite of standardizing forces in society? How widely do national, local, and social varieties of English differ from one another? How should variety be confronted by the teacher of language use who must formulate teaching strategies and make daily decisions on how to implement them? (ix)

These questions as they were addressed in this collection made a case for language as more than autonomous expression. The questions helped to clarify in historical and in present-day terms that language is also ideological, i.e., that it has social, economic, political, and historical consequences. What still stands out about *Varieties*, however, even after more than twenty years, is how dynamic their questions were, how responsive the essays in the collection were to them, and how such concerns are continuing to occupy us as we have developed considerably more knowledge and expertise about the nature and implications of viewing language within the sociocultural contexts of its use.

In this regard, *Literacy and Democracy* is a response to good teaching. The contributors to this volume obviously feel well taught by Jay L. Robinson, and, I venture to say, that we also feel privileged to have this opportunity to show our gratitude in a way that feels so appropriate. In my own case, this moment of reverie takes me to the spring of 1971 when as a graduate student at the University of Michigan I had the good fortune of entering Jay's office. Another professor, his co-editor Richard Bailey, had suggested to me that a conversation with Jay might help me to clarify a question (which I have long since forgotten) that I had about American English. What I remember now about that meeting is that Jay interrupted whatever he was doing that day to take my question seriously. He treated me and my curiosities with respect, and I walked away thinking that the time had been very well spent. Ultimately, I enrolled in courses with him, and I was fortunate to have his advice and counsel as a member of my dissertation committee.

Throughout this process of intellectual and professional growth, I was inspired by the calm and gentle way that he shared insights in class, by the way that he modeled strategies for probing linguistic concerns, and by the way that he pushed his students and himself to question interpretive boundaries. His questioning helped me to come to my own sense of how language works, while simultaneously anchoring this vision in the language practices of real people. He encouraged me always to be imaginative, but he also pressed me to keep my claims about literacy development clear and manageable and to consider the inextricable connections between theoretical insight and classroom action.

Given such memories of my own growth and development, the sense of *Literacy and Democracy* that resonates most for me is how from writer to writer this collection suggests that over the decades more than one of Jay's students has received the kinds of messages from him that I received. His legacy, then, as inscribed by this collection is a legacy of action. At this point in time, there exists a cadre of his students from over the decades who form a network of English teachers across institutional sites—in schools, colleges, universities, and community organizations. By the indications of this collection, we are a group who see the work that we should do in our classrooms and communities in ways that demonstrate, in the language of my cultural home, "the laying on of hands," acknowledging in our various and sundry ways the influence of Jay L. Robinson: researcher, scholar, teacher of teachers.

Acknowledgments

We proposed editing a volume in tribute to Jay Robinson with equal parts excitement and trepidation, honored to take on the task of making public the continuation and expansion of his ideas through the work of his former students, but well aware of the horror stories surrounding the putting together of edited collections. Luckily, our task has been—for the most part—both delightful and inspiring, triggered by the important work our friends have been doing over the past few years, tied in some obvious and some subtle ways to our common starting point. Obviously, we thank all the authors of this volume: for conducting themselves so ethically with those they teach, for sharing their reflections on that work so honestly with those who will read these pieces, and for responding so positively (and quickly) to the suggestions made by us and by each other—making this a truly collaborative volume.

We'd like to thank a number of people whose work is not represented in this volume, but whose words have been inspiring to those of us who have authored pieces: Patricia Lambert Stock, Kathleen Dixon, and Randall Roorda in particular. We'd also like to thank all of the students and colleagues who attended the symposium in honor of Jay's retirement in June 1996, and especially Anne Ruggles Gere for organizing the event. Our colleagues at NCTE have helped us a great deal as well: Michael Greer, who has enthusiastically shepherded us through the project; Kurt Austin, who helped in the final stages; and the NCTE Editorial Board and reviewers who gave us a number of helpful suggestions.

We'd like to thank our families for providing just the right balance of encouragement and distraction: Lori Weiselberg and Sam Schaafsma, and Andy Buchsbaum and Seth and Jesse Fleischer Buchsbaum. And, finally, we thank Jay Robinson—our mentor and friend—who, we hope, can recognize through these essays just how much he matters to both a new generation of literacy workers and those with whom we work.

Introduction: Further Conversations: Jay Robinson, His Students, and the Study of Literacy

Cathy Fleischer
Eastern Michigan University

David Schaafsma
Teachers College, Columbia University

Talking about Literacy

> Democracy begins in conversation.
>
> —John Dewey

One September morning just over a decade ago, the two of us, along with some of the authors in this volume, tentatively climbed the stairs of the School of Education Building at the University of Michigan, peering at room numbers as we searched for the classroom that would hold our introductory seminar for the doctoral program in English and Education. As we entered and found seats, we stared at the other students, all of whom, we would soon discover, were coming from situations much like our own: experienced teachers who had paused in that other life to pursue graduate studies, some interested in rhetoric and composition, some in English education, some in both; some committed to teaching at the college level, some planning to return to secondary or elementary schools. As we sat there, nervously wondering just what we had done to our lives by uprooting our spouses and significant others, leaving our secure jobs, and moving to an unknown city, wondering if we were up to the challenges of a competitive doctoral program, our professor, Jay Robinson, entered.

"Good morning," he said, a slow smile spreading on his face. "Let's start off by writing for a few minutes. Can you write about this: What do you think we mean by the word *literacy*?"

Silence. A few smiles and sighs of relief. This wouldn't be so hard, we thought. We were, after all, experienced teachers of reading and writing; we knew what literacy was about. We had been in classrooms for years and felt we could pretty easily distinguish between those kids who were literate and those who were not. And so, as we wrote our responses, freewrites focused on literacy as reading and writing and doing those skills well enough to survive, we recall feeling just a little smug. If this was the kind of question our professors would pose, how hard could graduate school be?

We began that day by talking about our own definitions, taken from our lives as teachers. And as the semester progressed, Jay opened that discussion to voices beyond the walls of our School of Education classroom, asking us to immerse ourselves and our experiences in the words of various theorists and teachers whose names we couldn't always pronounce and whose discussions of literacy stretched both our disciplinary narrowness and our individual understandings: Maxine Greene, Raymond Williams, Terry Eagleton, Paulo Freire, James Boyd White, John Dewey, and Shirley Brice Heath; and over the next few years, Lev Vygotsky, Mikhail Bakhtin, Richard Rorty, and Michel Foucault, to name but a few. But on that first day, after talking about our own definitions, Jay shared with us a take on literacy that struck chords immediately and has continued to resonate over the years. It began with a quote from James Boyd White, a professor of law, English, and classics at the University of Michigan:

> I start with the idea that literacy is not merely the capacity to understand the conceptual content of writings and utterances but the ability to participate fully in a set of social and intellectual practices. It is not passive but active, not imitative but creative, for it includes participation in the activities it makes possible. (72)

This quote was startling to some of us, a stretch for our more limited definitions, and—most of all—a promise of what was to come in our new education. Our subsequent discussions of how that quote might apply to real classrooms with real students, informed by our sharing of experiences and readings of other authors, increasingly complicated any simple definition of literacy, especially for those of us who initially had felt so confident in our understandings. The emerging talk in which we engaged challenged us to reconsider what we thought we had known well—the realities of kids in classrooms. And as many of us who were not already Michigan public school teachers found ourselves invited by Jay to work with teachers in the schools over the next few years, to participate in classrooms filled with students whose experiences with literacy were much different from our own, we began to uncover even more questions: If a literate person was someone who could read and write well enough to survive, what about those who couldn't read or write well, but who were surviving (at least in economic terms) just fine?

And what about those who could read and write, but found those abilities meaningless in their struggle to survive? What did it really *mean* to read or write well? What if, for example, you could read and interpret your tax form but not Shakespeare? Or Shakespeare but not Toni Morrison? What did it mean if you could read those authors but *chose* not to? Did we mean by literacy E. D. Hirsch's notion of "cultural literacy," a version of literacy that insists on a shared cultural heritage? Or did we mean James Gee's idea of an "essay-text literacy," a form-based literacy created by and for schools? Or the ability to sign one's name? The ability to score 50 percent on the reading section of a state-administered proficiency test? Or the ability to listen to a political debate on the voucher system for public schools and write a letter to the editor to express our beliefs?

As that semester progressed and gave way to other courses, other conversations, other shared experiences in classrooms, the original question—what is this thing named literacy—remained central. We began to reconsider literacy at least in part in terms of our own continuing practices as teachers, recognizing it as a term that gets defined within particular historical moments, depending on various social circumstances. Literacy, we slowly realized, is not an unproblematic—"you're literate or you're not"—concept; literacy, as Cy Knoblauch and Lil Brannon remind us, "is and must always be ideologically situated . . . qualified by the context of assumptions, beliefs, values, expectations, and related conceptual material that accompanies its use by particular groups of people in particular sociohistorical circumstances" (15). "Literate," then, might be better understood as a representation of something, a naming of an individual or a group of individuals that reflects as much about the namer's beliefs and values as it does about the person being named. For many of us, this realization of *our* complicity in defining literacy, in the resultant naming of people as literate or illiterate, and in the very real consequences of that naming, became the impetus for thinking about what Knoblauch and Brannon call "the explosively simple question, 'Why do it this way?'" (11).

How we might do it a different way is in large part what we have learned from Jay Robinson since that day, reflective of what decades of students, undergraduate and graduate, have learned from him as well: important lessons about imagining new ways into conceiving literacy, new ways of recreating ourselves as teachers and learners. How we might do it a different way is what drives the professional and personal lives of many of Jay's former students—and is what drives the essays these former students have written for this book. More than merely a collection of writings composed to honor the work of our mentor, this volume serves as a series of concrete enactments of how we might do it a different way, written by authors whose methodological assumptions and practices vary, whose contexts and circumstances vary, whose composing styles and genres of expression vary—but whose underlying concepts of what literacy might mean reflect striking similarities—and which may, in fact, offer some insights as to what a democratic vision of literacy looks like in practice.

A Life in Literacy

> To study literacy and its uses is to commit oneself to the study of contexts and relations.
>
> —Robinson, *Conversations on the Written Word*

Doing his graduate work at the University of California, Berkeley, preparing to be a medievalist, Jay first wrote about the importance of contexts in the understanding of texts in his dissertation on Chaucer, entitled *The Context of* The Prioress's Tale. But as his own contexts changed, Jay's studies began to change also. Teaching from 1961 to 1965 at Northwestern University, Jay began to make a transition from medieval studies to linguistics, both areas of interest that would have an impact on his later work in literacy studies. Coming to the University of Michigan in 1965, Jay solidified his transition to language scholar considerably, writing a number of articles about lexicography and phonetic interpretation and editing several volumes with a growing group of collaborators: *English Linguistics: An Introductory Reader* (with Harold Hungerford and James Sledd), *Varieties of Present-Day English* (with Richard Bailey), and the *Real World English* series (with Bernie Van't Hul).

While maintaining his presence in the world of medieval language studies as Executive Director of the Middle English Dictionary, and after chairing the English Department from 1974 to 1981, Jay came to co-direct the Ph.D. Program in English and Education in 1982, first with Steve Dunning and later with Anne Ruggles Gere. In 1984, Jay became the founder and Director of the Center for Educational Improvement through Collaboration, where many literacy scholars began to know him for his groundbreaking work in school-university collaborations and specifically for his redefinitions of literacy and the role of English departments in supporting that redefinition. During that time, Jay and Associate Director Patricia Lambert Stock worked extensively in public schools around the state of Michigan and developed a cadre of professors and graduate students from across the university to join them in collaboration with K–12 teachers and students, to think together about issues of vital importance: assessment and its connection to curriculum development, student voices and their connection to schooling, narrative depictions of classrooms and teacher research, the political and ethical responsibilities of all those involved in literacy work.

The process of exploring the nature of literacy and rethinking the role of English departments within that process began to intensify for Jay through his collaborative work with public school teachers in Ann Arbor and Saginaw: "My thoughts in my own study, at Northwestern and Michigan, and my words in my own classroom, were shaped by the words of teachers," he explains (1990, 4). At the same time, Jay began to write extensively about this work from his own perspective as university professor and visitor in these classrooms. As we in his classes began to read these essays, some written for journals in the field and some written as "conversation papers" for us, his doctoral students, we—like others around the country—found ourselves challenged to examine carefully our own commitments; such pieces as "Literacy in the Department of English" and "The Politics of Literacy" (co-authored with Patti Stock) forced us to confront some unpleasant realities of how institutional definitions of literacy impact the lived worlds of students and teachers. These essays and other of his writings on literacy were collected in the 1990 volume *Conversations on the Written Word: Essays on Language and Literacy*, a book which serves to exemplify the metaphor of conversation in its very structure; in addition to the pieces written by Jay, the book includes both essays co-authored with Patti Stock and essays composed by two of his students, Carol Winkelmann and Cathy Fleischer. Maxine Greene wrote the foreword for the book, introducing it in this way:

> [The authors] allow us to experience the necessity of conversation because they engage in it themselves. Moreover, they make us feel intensely the existential importance—as well as the political importance—of liberating persons to find and use their own voices . . . It is not simply a question of right or equity. It is a question of the culture's articulate life, as it is of the health of our public space. (x)

Jay's own Introduction to *Conversations on the Written Word* lays out in broad outline some of the guiding principles for the collaborative ventures he and many others embarked upon for those years, principles that we contend have been central as well in the work that continues in this book. Jay explains:

> In our work . . . we are trying to understand how literacy develops, when it does, in the adolescent years of schooling. We are trying to understand how members of a school class come to constitute themselves (if they do) into a social community of a particular kind: something Stanley Fish might call an interpretive community. And we

> are trying to understand how social and sociointellectual interac-
> tions among members of the forming community both effect and
> affect individual development of those competencies and the enact-
> ment of them that we comprehend with the term "literacy." We are
> trying to understand and describe not so much the peculiar culture
> of *the* classroom as the particular cultures of particular classrooms
> as these are shaped by personal and institutional histories and as
> they take shape in anticipation of future, perhaps possible worlds. (7)

Important to observe here is Jay's attention to social and interpretive
issues in learning, with particular focus on the ways communities are
most productively formed in school settings. For Jay, community—with
its focus on human beings with lived lives who converse together, learn
from each other, and create understanding together—is essential before
anything like literacy can be realized. Integrally tied to this is his resistance to totalizing descriptions of teaching and learning. As he says elsewhere, "I think we need to put aside efficient languages for 'inefficient'
ones—well-ordered languages that serve like newly cleaned-up desks
in neatly ordered studies" (1990, 320–21). The often too "well-ordered"
languages of various comprehensive "Grand Narratives" of schooling
he resists as limiting and closed, ignoring the differences between and
among us. Talking about *the* classroom ignores what's most important:
individual kids and teachers who bring to specific classrooms a plethora
of experiences too often left unexplored by both those who run schools
and those who do research into them.

Since the publication of that book, Jay has remained an important
voice in our field. He was one of the founders and is now on the Editorial Board of *On Common Ground*, a journal devoted to the work of university-school collaborations which brings together the voices of university scholars and classroom teacher-researchers to discuss and
problematize their work. He also was one of the co-directors—with Patti
Stock, Janet Swenson, and David Schaafsma—of the Write for Your Life
Project, a national university-school project focusing on literacy, health,
and social change.

Constitutive Literacy

So what is this literacy of which Jay speaks in his writing and through
his work? What are its dimensions and parameters? What are the conditions under which it might best flourish? To fully understand Jay's uses
of the term literacy, one must begin with his notion of a constitutive
rhetoric: a rhetoric in which meaning is necessarily *constituted* in the
context of one's interactions with others. Because reading, writing, speak-

ing, and listening are purposeful human actions which take place in specific and local circumstances, they "are made meaningful by the contexts in which they occur" (1990, 95). Whenever we use language, we are constituting meaning; in order to do that, we are always constituting other things as well: our own character, the character of others, the intentions we bring to the interaction, the community that surrounds us, the cultural mores which help define that community. Because we are "rhetorical animals" Jay tells us, "we have no other choice" (1990, 111). And because language interactions rely upon multiple parties, meaning becomes constituted within the contexts of the interactions of those who participate. Rhetoric is then a social construction, constituted through the institutional, historical, and individual constructions which occur when human beings share a language. Jay explains,

> We use language to make meanings, of course, but we make meaning in language only when our intent in doing so is perceived by those whom we address, or is at least perceptible to them. To know my meanings, my reader or my listener must know what to do with them; and to know what to do with my meanings, my reader or my listener must know me—or at least that particular construction of me that functions and counts in the community I am trying to constitute with my audience through my saying of what I am saying. (1990, 102)

Such a constitutive rhetoric requires an active role on the part of its participants. It is not enough merely to recognize that language use is a social construction; Jay reminds us that understanding can be created most fully only if language users are wide awake both to the voices of others and to their own part in that construction. When we are aware of our own ability to choose how we constitute ourselves and how we constitute others, the nature of the conversations in which we participate becomes a kind of negotiation with others; in these circumstances, both our language and our understandings of one another change and grow.

The creation of meaning, then, relies upon multiple parties, the intentions of those parties, the selves that are created through and in the conversation, the community constraints upon such conversation, the cultural beliefs which determine the parameters of the conversation. Such a rhetoric is, in Jay's terms "an art that helps us sustain human freedom" (1990, 111). Because we have choices about how we constitute ourselves, because we have some impact on the communities and cultures we constitute, Jay tells us, our role in a constitutive rhetoric relies on our artfulness as language users and teachers as we purposefully and vitally come to "understand what freedom is and how it is constituted through the ways we use language to talk with one another and to write for one another" (1990, 111).

The essential components of a constitutive rhetoric set the stage for a complex notion of literacy, a literacy for which the constructions of self, other, intent, community, and culture are essential. In Jay's understanding, these various constructions create contexts, contexts which rely upon a language user's present circumstances, of course, but that also reach both into her past—what Jay calls a sociohistorical process—as well as into her future. As he explains,

> [Literacy is], in essence, sociocultural development, not merely cognitive development, a notion that seems to imply an isolated learner and not one who lives and learns as a social being in conversations with others. Learning, we are trying to say—and especially language learning—is a particular kind of sociohistorical process. Becoming literate, we think, crucially involves a glimpse of some future—a sight, however blurred, of what Nelson Goodman or Jerome Bruner might call a possible world; but it also involves, as crucially, some sense that one may find habitable space in that future as a self who can speak and act meaningfully. (1990, 7)

The kind of literacy of which Jay speaks here is social, cultural, and historical in nature. Because it is in part determined by such dynamic factors, it is also a literacy which envisions possible futures, the creation of selves speaking and acting meaningfully. What is crucial to the fostering of such a conception is the development of a "habitable space," a common place, a safe place, where conversation can begin and where meanings might be negotiated to create communities in which literacy might flourish. In an essay co-authored with Patti Stock, Jay cautions us to remember that participation in the kinds of social and intellectual practices called for by James Boyd White cannot happen without opportunity—and opportunity depends upon these common spaces for all students. Such an emphasis necessarily demands a rethinking of terms like "marginal," terms that push students to the edges of those common spaces with no hope of coming to center.

Jay asks us to think about these habitable spaces in at least three ways: first, as teachers in classrooms, in order to create more openings for kids to read, write, speak, and listen; second, as university professors, in order to rethink our connections to the literacy habits of the adults and prospective teachers we instruct; and third, as collaborators involved in university-school partnerships, in order to negotiate new ways of understanding issues of concern to all parties. In our striving to create habitable spaces for these others, we must first consider the purposes of our own roles, our own constructions: "What is the usefulness of our thoughts and theories?" Jay asks us. "What is the reach toward students in classrooms, toward students whose differences from one another and from us test the comprehensiveness and humanity of any thoughts we think, any theories we manage to construct?" (1990, 5). His beliefs encourage us to begin our journey into understanding literacy by critically examining our own practices—For what reasons do we teach? What changes are we trying to effect? And for whom do we speak and write? Whom do we represent in our literate renderings of the students and classrooms we encounter?—and to do so with an awareness of our own roles in constituting the literacy that will arise from those encounters.

In a more recent article exploring the dimensions of habitable space as we work with others, Jay cautions us to recognize our own positionality:

> In collaborative projects, participants always meet in a *borderland*, a space that has recently been named by scholars who are interested in examining new structures of interaction that emerge when members of separate cultures find themselves, for whatever reason, living together and working together. Trying to find one's way in a borderland, old maps help some, but new maps must be drawn. Walking on unfamiliar ground, people have to find new ways to talk together if they are not to get hopelessly lost. . . . (1996, 15)

In this reminder, we see that if we strive toward full collaboration, no one participant can occupy the center; all begin at the edges. As we work with each other to determine new ways to talk and act together, though, we might begin to meet on more common ground.

Vital to any notion of habitable space, of course, is the theme of human agency, another recurring image in Jay's writing. When teachers metaphorically (and at times not so metaphorically) reimagine the spaces of their classrooms in order to create opportunity, they necessarily open a world to student voices, inviting students to be heard through their reading, writing, and speaking, and "to become critical about their presences" in the worlds they see depicted (312). In the essay from which these words are taken, the now classic "Politics of Literacy," Jay and Patti Stock analyze the writing of one student they name Charles Baldwin, a real student whose texts have become emblematic for many of us, in part because they are defined by an absence of self. Charles Baldwin's words, taken from a series of essays he composed for a teacher-designed assessment, depict a chilling world of violence in which he and his friends emerge as pawns, acted upon by outside forces, a world described matter-of-factly by Charles as he weaves stories of gangs and guns and explosive anger. Jay and Patti argue here that we can't talk about literacy for a student like Charles without speaking as well about his apparent lack of agency. "Given a world in which he lives as marginal," they ask, "can he become literate?" They claim not, or at least not until he sees a glimpse of his own connection to, his own reason for, participation in another kind of world. In language reminiscent of White's call for literacy's definition to be "not passive but active, not imitative but creative, for it includes participation in the activities it makes possible" (1990, 72), Jay and Patti explain what they mean:

> In the world we inhabit with our students, one is not made literate or taught to become so; one chooses to become literate in circumstances where choice is made available. . . . No one becomes literate who does not see some opening, however small, toward active participation in a literate world that is part of the reality in which he or she lives. No one becomes literate who does not glimpse, and then come to feel, some possibility, no matter how tightly constrained, to shape the meanings that inevitably control one's life. (1990, 313)

To become literate, then, individuals must see themselves, even for a moment, as actors in/creators of their worlds. Basic to the development of this kind of literacy is

> the empowerment of individuals to speak freely in such voices as they have about matters that concern them, matters of importance, so that conversation may be nourished. The most debilitating suggestion in our dominant metaphors for literacy is this one: that a language must be learned, a voice acquired, before conversation can begin. . . . (1990, 284)

This metaphor of conversation and the exercise of voice, human voices replete with agency, are central for both students and teachers to achieve understanding, to effect change. Neither is possible, though, unless the kind of language used by teachers and scholars radically changes to what Jay calls "a common language." Jay makes it clear that the creation of a common language is essential for the building of literate communities, necessary if we have any hope of creating a just society. As he says, "To find a common language—to found a common language—is to make it possible for writers to write and for readers to read and for all to learn together in community in order to achieve some larger common end, to act together in community to build a better world" (1990, 284). Jay cautions us about the difficulty of such an act, of the danger of coercive actions intended on the surface to create a common discourse but which instead recreate authoritarian positions: "To achieve community through a common language, we cannot impose our language on those others; to find a common language those others' languages will have to change, of course, but so will our own" (1990, 266).

For Jay, this metaphor of conversation, with its emphasis on common language, is a necessary component of what he and Patti define as critical pedagogy, an essential approach to the kind of literacy he imagines:

> A critical pedagogy opens out only in a classroom where authorship can flourish, only in a space where students may learn that

> words have some potential for changing worlds. A critical peda-
> gogy needs a classroom in which starts might be made toward a
> multivoiced literacy in which all might speak, no matter what lan-
> guage, to reach toward responsive understanding of deeper mean-
> ings of language and of the word as they shape worlds we must
> inhabit. (1990, 285)

This notion of a critical pedagogy, arising as it does from a critical literacy, rejects the kind of coercive approaches and dualistic assumptions
common to many of the current discussions of critical pedagogy and
speaks for understandings more complex, more shaded, without clo-
sure. We are cognizant as we read some others' renditions of critical
pedagogy, that our work with Jay has immersed us in a very different
definition from the "confrontational pedagogy" Fishman and McCarthy,
for example, critique. They speak of the created dichotomy between those
teachers who see critical pedagogy in monolithic ways, unsatisfied with
their classes unless powerful emotions erupt and who see other less confrontational teachers as being "non-progressive" (1990, 343–44). Similarly, Knoblauch and Brannon argue convincingly that critical pedagogies
cannot, must not, become another form of "political correctness" in which
a certain way of thinking is what becomes valued. Like Elizabeth
Ellsworth, we realize that those approaches, well-intentioned as they
are, just don't "feel empowering" for us or our students. For those of us
steeped in a different understanding of critical pedagogy, one which
always is based in conversation,

> The literate communities we build . . . must substitute an authority
> gained through experience or through learning shared in conversa-
> tion for an authoritarianism that can only be gained through the
> exercise of coercive power and be sustained through having the
> powerful speak and the powerless listen quietly (Robinson 1990,
> xx).

Authority and power issues are central to a conception of literacy focusing on multiple voices and perspectives. And what those of us who are
the authors of the essays which follow have learned from Jay Robinson
is that working with others to achieve literacy is inevitably tied to the
political and ethical considerations of what it means to be literate, of
what it means to be a teacher and researcher of literacy, of what it means
to live in a society based on conversation rather than coercion—in our
minds, to connect literacy to the kind of democracy envisioned by Dewey
and others. For us, such a society begins in the microcosm of the classroom, but in a classroom that has invoked some radical changes in order to meet the challenge of creating a community that is so in more
than name only. Creating such a literate classroom involves more than
the seemingly inevitable writing and perfecting of a new canon, a new

curriculum. Jay tells us, "If classrooms are communities, curricula become much less important than pedagogies: the ways students and teachers communicate among themselves—the sets of relations they establish among themselves—are the crucial issues in language development"
(1990, xx).

Further Conversations: Honoring Jay's Work

When we learned that Jay would be retiring from the University of Michigan in 1996, we approached him with the possibility of putting together
some sort of Festschrift in order to honor his work, intending initially to
invite contributions from some well-known scholars who clearly respect
his work and refer to him in their own: Shirley Brice Heath, Maxine
Greene, Cy Knoblauch and Lil Brannon, among others. But as we began
thinking and talking about Jay and his influences, we realized that one
of the most important embodiments of his work lies in its continuation
among those he has taught. And thus our goal in this book has been
twofold: first, to collect a series of essays that might have some impact
on the field of literacy education, something that would be useful to us
in our own teaching and research, but which would speak to English
educators and teachers of literacy everywhere; and second, to show the
widespead influence one man has had—on his own students, on their
students, and on the people with whom/on whom they research. Over
the summer of 1995 we met several times with Jay (who was encouraging, but characteristically resistant to essays *about* him and his work) to
discuss some broad themes about which essays could be written, and to
discuss which of his former and current students might speak to those
themes because of the research and teaching they are undertaking. These
themes were intended as merely a starting point for what we hoped
would be rich conversation among authors, what we dreamed might be
a sort of continuation of the many seminars these authors had taken
over the years with Jay. And so, we asked the authors to start thinking,
and we met at several conferences over the following year to talk about
ideas, to share drafts, and to come together (at a retirement gathering
for Jay in May 1996) for an intensive day of talk about the issues raised
by the drafts of these essays. The original themes we proposed to the
authors were these:

1. Critical Literacy

   What are we promoting when we talk about "critical literacy"?

   - What does critical literacy mean in practice?
   - What are the contexts for a critical literacy?
   - What are the politics of a critical literacy?

2. Representation

How do we talk to/with people about our understandings of critical literacy, i.e., What are our roles and responsibilities as scholars and researchers?

- What genres do we use? What languages do we use?
- How do we provide access for others?
- How do we encourage others to participate?

3. Social and Educational Change

What changes can we make in our worlds with our understandings of critical literacy? What kinds of reforms can we/should we promote and encourage?

- In what ways can we contribute to educational reform movements?
- In what ways might we feel those reforms may be limiting?
- Are there contradictions between the goals of a critical literacy and some notions of education reform?

Although we asked the authors to have these questions serve only as a very loose structure, you will see, we hope, the nuances and implicit considerations of them in the work of each. And you will see other themes as well, many of them reflective of Jay's work and of the multiple understandings we have gleaned through our conversations with him over the years. As Jay has told us, "We read our pasts to shape them into our futures" (1990, 2). As editors of this volume, we are not surprised then to see the ways Jay's voice and commitments are echoed in his students' essays; at the same time, we are struck by their own strong voices, by the work they are doing in diverse and sometimes unusual settings, and by the expansive contributions they are making to our understanding of what literacy and pedagogy might mean for the democratic society Jay has helped us to imagine.

Underlying all these essays is their central commitment to the creation of that kind of society, first introduced to us through the words of Dewey and made concrete for us through Jay's words and work. Jay's dream of a just and democratic world relies in part on the elements basic to his notion of literacy: the creation of habitable spaces for all citizens which in turn allows for the development of human agency; the establishment of participatory communities in which students can move their private understandings into public settings, connecting their pasts with their presents, anticipating their futures. In a newly written essay included in this volume, Jay speaks specifically of two components necessary to this democratic vision: a civic and a civil literacy. For Jay, the notion of a civic literacy is similar to the teachings of a number of progressive educators: an engaged and engaging literacy which involves students (and others) in practicing the acts of citizenship and languages of critique which help them to recognize and enact changes in their immediate and future lives. It's what Maxine Greene calls "wide-awakeness," what Hannah Arendt calls "enlarged thinking"—ways of viewing and acting upon the world which result from the kinds of critical pedagogies mentioned earlier. A civic literacy would have students

> extend beyond a language of critique to languages of construction and of possibility, to ways of thinking and speaking that are adequate to the complexities of collective living and problem solving, to modes of listening and of responding that are sensitive to the multiple voices and minds of those who have stakes in civic issues and those who are affected by the solutions that are proposed for difficult problems. ("Literacy and Lived Lives")

But Jay talks as well in that essay of a second kind of literacy necessary for a truly democratic society to work: a civil literacy, a literacy that he says

> has to do with the character of the relations we seek to establish with our words and in our engagements with other members of our literate communities. . . . Its essence is a willingness to listen—especially to others whose voices often go unattended; its exercise is the courtesy and the courage to listen responsively. . . .

A civil literacy relies on politeness, of course, but is never merely that. Linked to a civic literacy, it asks us to be sensitive to the voices that develop when we ask students to bring their experiences and pasts into the school environment, but it asks us also to be seriously responsive, to engage students in true conversations in order to help those voices grow stronger.

For Jay, for us, and for the authors of these essays, the literacy we envision is at once civic and civil in nature—intended to help individuals read, write, speak, and listen thoughtfully, courteously, and yet critically about their own lives and the lives of their communities in order to help effect the kind of change that is essential to achieve these democratic ideals. And like a true democracy, the authors included here speak to these issues not in a singular voice, but ever cognizant of their own circumstances and commitments.

All of the essays, of course, focus on problematizing any easy definition of literacy, a return to that question of our first day with Jay, a concern that obviously continues to haunt all of these authors. There is no easy agreement, though, among these authors as to the parameters or confines of literacy—or even any agreed-upon definition of the term. But we do recognize certain recurring themes reflective of the connection between literacy and democracy. The first is that there are passionate human concerns addressed in these writings—from Carol Winkelmann's work in a women's shelter to Roberta Herter's Detroit night school class to Laura Roop's poetry writing with students and teachers to help them make sense of their lives—concerns which focus on real people in real circumstances. We see such concerns at times raise questions for the authors about their preformed definitions of literacy and about the political stances toward particular methods of literacy instruction that often arise from those definitions. But what we notice even more is the level of compassion expressed here—about the people and contexts in which these authors have worked, indicative of the strength of commitment these authors bring to their circumstances.

We are struck as well by the ways in which these passions are tempered with a kind of humility, an openness to other perspectives, that is not always characteristic of academic essays. As Jay taught us, through his words and actions, these essays are respectful: of students, of teachers, of theory, of new understandings, enactments of what Jay calls "literacy as listening." There is what we will call a useful tentativeness in most of these essays, reflective of the tensions these authors sometimes feel both within their own understandings and also in the new kinds of understanding that have emerged for them through their work with others. Reminiscent of Gadamer's call for a fusion of horizons, only as these authors have immersed themselves in the horizons of others, critically looking together with those others to become enough a part of another's world, have they begun to achieve some kind of understanding.

Such awareness leads these authors toward what we might call a pedagogy of ethics—a stance toward their work which seems to us present explicitly or implicitly in every essay. The writers here are people who constantly question not only *what* they do in these dual roles of teacher and researcher, not only *why* they do it, but also *how* they do it: the ethics and politics of the choices we teachers make every day in curriculum and method; the ways we represent others in the research process; the roles and responsibilities we take on when, as researchers, we talk about ourselves and others. As Todd DeStigter tells us in his essay in this volume, "[T]he question asked by, say, an ethnographer desiring to be useful becomes not so much 'What can I do to/for others?' but 'What is the nature of my relationship with this person? How can/should we *be together?*'" In the authors' efforts to determine how to be together with the teachers and students with whom they have worked, they have placed a strong emphasis on the voices of students and teachers. We admire how these voices are never taken for granted nor treated in any kind of simplistic fashion. And in terms of Jay's own call for "inefficient" instead of "well-ordered" languages to describe various classrooms, most of these authors engage in the "messy" language of narrative, choosing to tell complex stories of their own and others' practices, replete with occasional contradictions, constant questioning, and self-awareness about their roles as the shapers of the texts you read.

Most of these authors, then, seem to demand for themselves a critical self-reflection, but not in the way popularly dismissed these days as "navel-gazing." Instead, the authors see self-reflection as inevitably tied to Freire's notion of *praxis*: "the action and reflection of men upon their world in order to transform it" (66). Freire tells us there can be no action without reflection; as these authors write about the worlds in which they work, they conscientiously and carefully research their own presence in those worlds, recognizing—and studying—the inevitable effect of their presence, both for themselves and others. As Tom Philion explains in the introduction to his piece, "I hope to teach myself through my writing: that is, by describing and reflecting. . . , I hope to obtain a better understanding of who I have been and who I may yet be as a literacy educator." Consistent, critical reflection upon what we do keeps us honest, we believe. Recognizing our own commitments and desires; questioning our own positions of power and authority; understanding our own multiple purposes and audiences all serve to strengthen our work. Recognizing our sometimes implicit roles as change agents demands our sincere efforts to be cognizant of what change might mean for ourselves and for those with whom we are working—and forces us to be much more careful about our actions in those settings and our representations of those settings in other worlds.

Democracy and Literacy: Jay's Students' Essays

As Jay's questions have become our own, they have been reshaped and reconfigured within our specific contexts. All of the authors here have taken their own driving questions about literacy and followed them into a variety of settings and contexts. Essays run the gamut in style and methodology: from the carefully footnoted and documented anthropological approach typical of ethnolinguistics to the turn-by-turn discussion of conversation practiced by discourse analysts to the intertwined personal stories of teachers and students common to teacher researchers. And much like the conversation in a typical "Jay seminar"—which attracted linguists, rhetoricians, teacher-researchers, and even one memorable term, a musicologist—the variety of the work represented here shows the wonderful hybrid of approaches we have increasingly come to see as "normal" for composition studies and which grace all of our learning in vital ways.

For the first essay in the collection, a piece entitled "Literacy and Lived Lives: Reflections of the Responsibilities of Teachers," we asked Jay Robinson to continue his conversation with us one more time by writing of his vision for the future of literacy education. For those of you less familiar with Jay's previous work, this piece will serve as a brief introduction, as he reflects on some of the contexts in which he has participated over the past decades. He speaks specifically in this writing to the responsibilities we teachers must take on when we engage with students whose real-life circumstances are often challenging (for them and for us). Admonishing us to be reflective as we attend to the lives of these students, Jay reminds us of the importance of listening, of caring, of practicing civil literacy if we have any hopes of helping young people negotiate the worlds in which they (and we) live.

The next two essays, Todd DeStigter's "Good Deeds: An Ethnographer's Reflections on Usefulness" and Tom Philion's "Three Codifications of Critical Literacy" follow Jay's admonition, as each author studies in some depth his approach to and motivation for his own teaching and research—each one problematizing what he means when he talks about such issues in critical ways. Todd's essay, based on three years of ethnographic research among Latino students at a predominantly Anglo rural high school, explores the delicate epistemological and ethical issues that arise when privileged researchers—and Todd includes himself—presume to represent the experiences of "the other" in their own terms, which are inevitably subject to particular cultural, perhaps even colonial, biases. Specifically, he discusses the ways in which his evolving relationships with individual students who served as his "subjects" led to his reformulating his understandings of how he might be "useful" to these students on *their* terms rather than his own.

Tom's piece traces his own development as a critical pedagogue over a number of years, first as a graduate student and course assistant at the University of Michigan, later as a collaborative teacher in an urban elementary school, and finally in his present position as an English education professor at an urban university. Throughout the piece, Tom uses Freirian codifications as ways to represent his experiences; within his analysis of each codification, he rejects any simple explanations for the term *critical literacy,* instead situating his developing definitions within the local circumstances of his own teaching.

The next three essays continue this theme of reflection, situating that reflection in part in their authors' social and political commitments. Researching and writing from the varied methodological perspectives which characterize this book, these authors attempt to understand what others, given habitable spaces and opportunities, can tell us about their own literacy. In her essay,"Not a Luxury: Poetry and a Pedagogy of Possibility," poet and educator Laura Roop, parallels her uses of poetry writing and reading in her personal life, in professional development opportunities with practicing teachers, and in coaching invitations to students in classrooms. Laura argues that poetry is not a luxury but an essential component of being wide awake, as she urges educators to heed the words of poet Audre Lorde: "(Poetry) forms the quality of the light within which we predicate our hopes and dreams toward survival and change, first made into language, then into idea, then into more tangible action." In this piece, Laura analyzes what role poetry might take in lives: in her own, in the lives of her students, in the lives of two exemplary educators, Sharon Galley and Laura Schiller, with whom she has collaborated.

In "Unsheltered Lives: Battered Women Talk about School," linguist, composition professor, and community activist Carol Winkelmann also explores the power of writing to effect personal and social change. In her essay, Carol examines the memories of schooling which the women she has encountered in her ethnographic research at a local shelter shared when given the opportunity to talk and write. For shelter women, according to Carol, "school" concerns relationship, not location. They recall institutional relationships as marked by power struggles and class/race/gender inequities; they believe violence begins in the schools. Carol's conclusion is that girls survive school because they transform and transcend its institutional meanings, in part, by seeking out dialogic mentor relationships with sister-kin in families, communities, and sometimes school.

In "Imagining Neighborhoods: Social Worlds of Urban Adolescents," English educator Colleen Fairbanks looks at work she did with the Saginaw Public Schools while working with Jay for the Center for Educational Improvement through Collaboration. Colleen calls for an interactive theory of learning that might better serve a culturally diverse society, one that, as Anne Haas Dyson suggests, talks "less of 'empowering' and more of recognizing the power that exists in a . . . child." Fairbanks looks at how a group of ethnically homogeneous students talk and write about various moral dilemmas to their white teachers; she then analyzes how the students use both the languages of school and community to formulate their own evolving concepts of self.

Colleen looks at these issues from the perspective of a university professor committed to working sensitively with public school teachers and students. In "Conflicting Interests: Critical Theory Inside Out," Roberta Herter examines issues of collaboration and political commitment from her perspective as a high school English teacher engaging in such a collaborative project, a night school collaboration between a University of Michigan English professor's Theater and Social Change students and her own Detroit Henry Ford High School students. The collaborative work ostensibly provides habitable space and opportunity for both sets of students involved, but questions arose for Roberta about the success of the project: questions about the portability of Freire, the self-perpetuating nature of theory, perhaps especially "critical" theory, and the social change aspects of service learning courses from an inside-the-school perspective.

The next two essays look closely at their authors' own college classrooms, addressing the role English departments and English professors play in defining and practicing literacy in a democratic society. Sylvia Robins's "Writing Back: The Research Writing of a Freshman College Composition Student" examines the evolution of a text of one of the community college students she teaches. The student essay, one defending the practice of deer hunting, is one in which the student struggles with academic discourse. This struggle, which Sylvia admits is not unlike her own struggle as a busy, classroom-focused community college professor to write within the scholarly discourse tradition, is about the importance of finding one's own "voice" within an often foreign discourse community. Reminiscent of the ways in which Jay and his colleagues sympathetically and critically engage student voices in *Conversations on the Written Word*, Sylvia gives us a model of critical, reflective teaching upon which to ponder as she engages with her student in his struggle to construct an academic essay.

"Time, Talk, and the Interpretation of Texts in a Teacher Education Seminar" by John Lofty touches upon another of Jay's lifelong concerns: that of the connection between oracy and literacy. In his essay, John explores the discourse of small groups, which have become a common learning format in composition, literature, and education classes at every level. If the full potential of learning through talk is to be achieved, John argues, teachers will need finely grained descriptions not only of the different kinds of talk that occur, but also an understanding of how one kind of talk prompts and relates to another. In a seminar discussing approaches to teaching, Lofty observes how one group of teacher education students achieves topic continuity, maintains conversational coherence, and negotiates the purposes of the task to meet personal and academic needs. Such observations provide a basis for Lofty to raise issues and questions for how teachers might explore the oral, literate, and temporal dimensions of conversations that promote a wide range of learnings.

If Mikhail Bakhtin is correct, and "any utterance is a link in a very complexly organized chain of utterances," (Robinson 1990, xx) then Jay, and the voices of the vast numbers of students and teachers who have worked with Jay over the years, are speaking through us, and through these essays and stories. As we read through them, we hear Jay's voice in the background of all of them, telling us, "In matters of teaching, in matters of learning—and especially in matters of the teaching and learning of language—all choices are inevitably contingent, all findings inevitably tentative. If we admit that, conversation becomes possible, and as Dewey said, 'democracy begins in conversation.'" (1990, 3). We invite you to enter the conversation as well as you read these essays and think about the stories their authors tell.

Works Cited

Ellsworth, Elizabeth. 1989. "Why Doesn't This Feel Empowering? Working Through the Repressive Myths of Critical Pedagogy." *Harvard Educational Review* 59: 297–324.

Fishman, Stephen M., and Lucille Parkinson McCarthy. 1996. "Teaching for Student Change: A Deweyan Alternative to Radical Pedagogy." *College Composition and Communication* 47: 342–66.

Freire, Paulo. 1981. *Pedagogy of the Oppressed.* Trans. Myra Bergman Ramos. New York: Continuum Books.

Gee, James Paul. 1986. "Orality and Literacy: From *The Savage Minds* to *Ways with Words.*" *Tesol Quarterly* 20: 719–46.

Knoblauch, Cy, and Lil Brannon. 1993. *Critical Teaching and the Idea of Literacy.* Portsmouth, NH: Boynton/Cook.

Robinson, Jay. 1990. *Conversations on the Written Word: Essays on Language and Literacy.* Portsmouth, NH: Boynton/Cook.

———. 1996. "University-School Collaboration and Educational Reform." *On Common Ground* 6 (Spring): 14–15.

Robinson, Jay, and Patricia L. Stock. 1990. "The Politics of Literacy." *Conversations on the Written Word: Essays on Language and Literacy.* Jay L. Robinson. Portsmouth, NH: Boynton/Cook. 271–317.

White, James Boyd. 1985. *Heracles' Bow: Essays on the Rhetoric and Poetics of Law.* Madison: University of Wisconsin Press.

1 Literacy and Lived Lives: Reflections on the Responsibilities of Teachers

Jay Robinson
University of Michigan

For the most part, we have profited—as have our students—from re-imagining ourselves as teachers of literacy rather than as teachers of English, or even as teachers of writing and reading. Doing so has led us to read, and become professionally responsible for, a body of scholarship and writing that has changed and advanced our thinking about our tasks as teachers and as scholars. These readings, and the practices that follow from them, have encouraged us to do at least these three things:

First, to expand the domain of texts that might be thought of as "literature," including in our reading lists texts authored by people whose works and very lives were never considered canonical; even to include texts penned by students, which when invited by imaginative assignments and then read sensitively, can prove to be much more than schoolroom exercises. Second, to remember always that writing and reading are practices carried on purposefully by human beings in contexts that are material and changing: that in teaching reading and writing, we are always teaching and encouraging *uses* of language—not, as earlier conceptions (and some nostalgic ones) would have us do: teach *language,* as if our students had none, teach *language* as a set of forms and usages sanctioned by custom and the preferences of certain social classes. Third, when teaching language *use,* always to be attentive to the contexts in which humans use language, both those that exist in our society and those we seek to create in our own classrooms.

In sum, as teachers of literacy, we have to think constantly and critically about the category "literature," wondering what voices are excluded from the canons we establish for study and emulation. As teachers of literacy, we have to be attentive to the connections among written and oral uses of language, as well as to similarities among the texts produced by established authors and those produced by apprentice ones.

1

And as teachers of literacy, we have to be aware of the shaping contexts that affect the utterances and texts our students produce.

It is always helpful, when talking about literacy, to remind oneself that writing is only one of the media through which language is and can be employed, as our contacts with talkative students should always confirm. Such a reminder guards against the seductions of some claims for literacy's instrumental power to effect favored forms of cognitive, historical, cultural, political, and social development. Written language is, or can be made to be, a powerful instrument; or, if the term serves better to suggest the limits of its potential, a powerful technology. But as an instrument, as a technology, its potential can only be realized through human actions: its effects, its consequences, can only be understood or talked about by talking about what humans do (or don't do) when they employ the technology. Language use—human uses of language—are what we are after when we seek to understand the consequences of literacy. The uses of language are what teachers of literacy teach (or should teach), which means that how we teach is at least as important as what we teach—maybe, in fact, more important. It means too that we can never limit ourselves only to teaching technique—the forms and skills involved in employing the technology—but must explore as well with our students the ethical, political, and social values that are inevitably involved in the employment of written language.

David Olson, in a well-known and influential early article, separated text from utterance in talking about some of the powers and consequences of literacy: the first a mode of shaping written language, the second a mode of talking meaningfully (if sometimes superficially).[1] Bakhtin, of course, prefers the term *utterance* for any intentional and meaningful use of language, which enables him to talk about a conversational gambit or a nineteenth-century novel in ways that illuminate both their roots in the universal human possession of language and their similarities and differences as uses of language.[2] What differentiates modes of utterance from one another, in this way of thinking, are both human intentions and the social and cultural webs of meaning that form and surround human uses of language. In this way of thinking, it makes no sense to attribute an essence to such a human thing as language, no sense to attribute an essence to such a human thing as literacy; neither does it make any sense to talk about either texts or utterances without asking questions about their human uses and about the shaping social and intellectual contexts of those uses. To adopt this way of thinking makes certain arguments about language or about education appear quite groundless, as in the recent national flap about Ebonics; or, more significantly, shows those arguments to be what they really are—arguments about attitudes and values that attach themselves to race and socioeconomic status, arguments whose grounds are ultimately both social and political. That is what Patricia J. Williams argues so cogently in her *New York Times* Op-Ed piece "The Hidden Meanings of 'Black English'":

> Causing further confusion in this debate is the apparent treatment of illiteracy as if it were black speech. Black children are crowded into remedial education classes and are disadvantaged in finding jobs because too many of them have never been taught *any* variation of the printed word, whether phonics, ebonics, or Esperanto. Some young children learn more of the alphabet on "Sesame Street" than they can in overtaxed and overcrowded inner city schools.
>
> Moreover, the very conflation of illiteracy and the reasoned, rich and expressive complexity of most forms of black speech is based on a peculiarly freighted symbolism in the American lexicon. While accent prompts many levels of discrimination in the United States, there is no greater talisman of lower or underclass status than *the* black accent . . . , no greater license to mock than with some imitation of black speech. Whether in the Dartmouth Review or "The Lion King," black English is the perpetual symbolic code for ignorance, evil and jest, the lingo of hep cats and hyenas.
>
> Even solidly middle-class blacks with strings of higher degrees and perfect command of standard grammatical structure can face discrimination if their accents are deemed in any way identifiably "black." (9)

Language always reveals its complex meanings—both cognitive and affective—in the multiple and variable contexts of its human uses. Language holds the power, when used in certain ways, to connect us to other human beings in conjoint attempts to make meaning and to act upon the meanings we make. But in certain of its human uses, language can also hold potential to divide and to exclude. As teachers of literacy, our largest responsibility is always to promote expansive and inclusive uses of language, always to resist conceptions of language or attitudes toward language use that oversimplify and demean, as do the attitudes Williams points to.

In their introductory essay to this volume, Fleischer and Schaafsma cite James Boyd White's definition of literacy as one that is expansive and at least potentially inclusive:

> I start with the idea that literacy is not merely the capacity to understand the conceptual content of writings and utterances but the ability to participate fully in a set of social and intellectual practices. It is not passive but active, not imitative but creative, for it includes participation in the activities it makes possible. (72)

As Fleischer and Schaafsma note, participation of the kind White finds essential to the full exercise of literacy demands that teachers provide opportunities for students to become participants. So too does it demand that the practices in which we engage our students be accessible and meaningful to them so that in fact they can participate in active ways. As teachers of literacy, it is within our competence to provide such opportunities if we are committed, imaginative, and in some cases courageous enough—as have been several of the authors of this volume, several of whom, Winkelmann and DeStigter, for example, have found themselves teaching and researching in settings that bear little resemblance to conventional classrooms. They have learned from the late Paulo Freire that work on the word requires work both in and upon the world. As scholars and teachers of language use, we must be willing to leave the academy, when doing so will enable us better to understand how social realities shape language uses, when we test out our sense that words can be used to reshape realities.

To those conversant with current best thinking about literacy, as are the authors in this volume, these opening paragraphs will seem merely to restate the obvious: there is consensus among many who have read to inform their ways of thinking and writing about language and about literacy. And yet, we have not recognized always how radically such conceptions must change our practices, not just as scholars and researchers, but especially as classroom teachers. And when we see, as we do, the persistence of skill-and-drill practices, not just in pre-collegiate but in college classrooms; when we read off-the-mark public debates about Ebonics or about whole language pedagogies or about the teaching of grammar and logic—we need to recognize that one of the urgent responsibilities of informed and committed teachers is to engage in public debate, to work—as Cathy Fleischer would have us do—as advocates.[3] The issues that are central in the pedagogies of literacy are too complex, far too important, to be left to editorial writers and to politicians. Those of us who find our work (perhaps deliberately) misrepresented in public media, usually by conservative pundits, as mine was recently,[4] will know the urgency of speaking out in advocacy for our best thinking and our best practices.

But in this essay, I want to suggest other, if related, responsibilities than advocacy for teachers of language use. I'll try to get at these responsibilities concretely, through anecdotes: stories that bring to mind my own still-pressing questions, even as they remind me of places I have been and of things I have and haven't done. Although my quest is not so ambitious as hers, I'd like to borrow words from my friend Maxine Greene as she reflects, in her introduction to *The Dialectic of Freedom*, upon her own aims in writing about texts and their uses:

> This book arises out of a lifetime's preoccupation with quest, with pursuit. On the one hand, the quest has been deeply personal: that of a woman striving to affirm the feminine as wife, mother, and friend, while reaching, always reaching, beyond the limits imposed by the obligations of a woman's life. On the other hand, it has been in some sense deeply public as well: that of a person struggling to connect the undertaking of education, with which she has been so long involved, to the making and remaking of a public space, a space of dialogue and possibility. (1988, xi)

I will suggest in this essay that this is the greatest promise of literacy, if such promise can be realized through human endeavor: to offer means for students to connect what is deeply personal with what can be made deeply and meaningfully public in attempts to make and remake public spaces of dialogue and possibility—places where we can meet one another, perhaps, as friends, even as we act out in words and actions our own peculiar identities, obligations, and responsibilities.

Literacy and Loneliness: Creating Literate Communities

Much of my own work for more than a decade involved me (with Colleen Fairbanks, Cathy Fleischer, David Schaafsma, and Patricia Lambert Stock as colleagues) in collaborative literacy projects with high school students and their teachers (most conspicuously among them, Jane Denton, Sharon Floyd, and Kathie Smith, also colleagues).[5] Most of that work was done in Saginaw, Michigan, a mid-sized mostly industrial city (when there is work) that serves as the inner-city core for a sprawling population area in Michigan's midsection. A river runs through this city, and on either side of that river there's a high school. The west-side high school is racially mixed, with whites predominating. The east-side high school, at last count I know about, numbered 98 percent of its students members of minority groups, very predominately African American. In fact, in local parlance, the east-side high school is talked about as "the black school."

Coming from the University of Michigan, some eighty-five miles south of Saginaw, our work was to take us university participants into both high schools, but on a very early trip, we visited "the black school" first. Leaving classrooms there, we had left little time to get to the west-side school to make our appointments, and at that point in our work, we didn't know the city very well. We stopped in the office to get directions and were greeted by a very tall and warmly polite African American student aide who asked if he could help us.

"Can you give us directions to the [west-side] high school?" we asked.

He seemed startled, but then uttered words that remain with me: "I don't think I can; it's a long way from here."

As measured in the usual manner, the "long way" is, in fact, less than five miles. But to get there, you do have to cross that river, and in that city, as Fairbanks notes in her essay in this volume, the river is a well-defined boundary line. In the late sixties, when parts of Detroit burned and Saginaw suffered a "riot" that existed more in the minds of its white citizens than in violent acts, the police and their auxiliaries closed and guarded the bridges that cross the river to prevent the "wrong" kind of people from passing east to west. We were there, in the eighties and nineties, in that city, to assist good and committed teachers in their attempts to devise more effective ways to teach reading and writing. But this young man, and so many other students we came to know, challenged us to see our work in other, more demanding ways, to imagine, as we could, more ambitious aims. His words helped us to begin to see what we needed to do to re-imagine ourselves as teachers of literacy, responsible for encouraging uses of written language that might work to help young people become aware of circumstances that constrained them, to re-imagine their sometimes too limited and limiting lives in ways that would open possibilities.

Could we help students, even modestly, to reach out to one another across that dividing river? With their help we tried, by involving students from both high schools in book publishing projects—reading and revising one another's work, more importantly, reading (if not revising) one another's lives, as authors from both sides of the river met together, listening and reacting to stories told in neighborhoods that were not always familiar to them. One of our aims in the book publishing projects was to teach the technologies of written language: to help students learn to employ the language forms (including those of so-called nonstandard dialects when students needed them to give expression to their own experiences) that readers expect to find in published works, to learn to serve as editors of their own and others' written products. But our wider aims were to encourage students to engage in a common project in which they might come together as members of a literate community, writing and reading together to explore their backgrounds, common and particular, to critically examine the lives they were leading and to imagine lives they might lead—to offer, as authors, to those who would read their work, accounts of their lives, sharing pains and joys, reading responsively so that adult readers might join with adolescent authors in identifying obstacles young people confront and must overcome in order to live lives more satisfying to them.

We wanted these publishing projects, these introductions into the uses of written language, to serve as antidotes to debilitating forms of separation, isolation, and loneliness; to serve as means to help students realize that the distance between two high schools—the kind that enforces separation and social isolation—is more often psychological than a matter of geography. We wanted students to learn that written language can be used both to recapture pasts, lives they and other authors have lived, and to imagine futures—futures against which present realities can be tested. We were seeking to make and remake a public, through engagement in a common project, in which language could be used to translate the deeply personal, which can only be deeply felt, into the public character words can achieve as readers open their minds to worlds authors can shape for them. We remembered a comment of Dewey's: "Communication is a process of sharing experience till it becomes a common possession" (1916, 12).[6]

In *The Bridge: Linking Minds: Growing Up in Saginaw*, published in 1988, the authors—all members of two twelfth-grade classes for "at-risk" students (the label was neither their teachers' nor ours)—wrote essays and stories about their experiences growing up in the neighborhoods in which their lives were shaped. Publication of the volume was recognized as a community event at an upscale local inn at which authors and their families, coming from both sides of the river, celebrated together and with representatives of local media (print and electronic) the lives these young authors had led and the accounts they had written about them. Seeking other audiences for these students' work, fellow students from Saginaw's Center for the Arts and Sciences—affected by these stories—produced a play based on the accounts in *The Bridge*, which showed in two performances to packed houses in the district's Center for Lifelong Learning— a fitting setting for the community's glimpse into the lives these young authors were leading. Scenes in the play enacted the pleasures young people take in coming together in play and at work, the joy they find in loving relationships with adults who care about them, the pain they feel when caring adults are lost to death or to imprisonment, the attractions of alcohol and drug use as well as the terrible consequences, to persons and families, of chemical dependency and participation in drug trafficking, the ways domestic violence and sexual abuse tear into and deform young lives that are in formation, the fears young people face each day they walk to school when they have seen brutal attacks or witnessed drive-by shootings, the humiliation young people feel when in encounters with prospective employers or clerks in stores—when in occasional and chance encounters on the street—they are made to know that their skin color defines them more certainly than their character or their abilities.

In writing and in acting together, these young student authors and actors learned they were not alone in their fears and hopes, that others of their age and in their and other neighborhoods faced obstacles that were similar if not identical to their own. And in writing and acting for adult audiences, familiar and unfamiliar members of their larger community, they learned that their voices and actions could matter if others could be persuaded to read and to listen, to be moved with them in joint efforts to change both attitudes and the material conditions that inevitably shape growing up. For a time, in Saginaw, a new literate public was in the making: one attentive to the expressible feelings and hopes of students who were learning to become literate—students who were participating in sets of social and intellectual practices that they were helping to create.

In a subsequent project, again involving whole classes in cross-school, cross-river publishing, students produced *Footsteps: Looking Back, Moving On*, an even larger collection of multigenred, multinuanced explorations of their own lives and of the lives of others whose examples had touched or might influence their ways of making sense of the world.[7] These authors' attempts to imagine lives were always rooted in concerns that were their own—were deeply personal. This, for example, from a short story about a young woman caught in slavery, was written by DeMetra Jackson:

> "Goin' once, goin' twice—sold to Mr. Smith for two hundred fifty dollars." I stood next in line waiting hurriedly to get this done. A white man called me, "Come on up here gal!"
>
> "Yes sir," I said. My heart was beatin' so fast and my mind was a wonderin' where was I gonna end up? Why is my freedom being sold? I just stood there with only a piece of sack covering my frail, dark body. I thought back to the night when them men tore me away from my family. Yeah, they came in and took me as if I were a stray pup. They hit my pappa over the head and told my mamma they would kill her if she looked at them. I heard her cryin' out for me, but I said to myself, "I was gonna be strong." I turned her way and said, "Mamma, don't worry. I'm gonna make it and, when I become free, I'm gonna set my family free."
>
> The man holdin' me just laughed and said, "Gal, you ain't gonna be free. Niggers ain't born to be free!!!" (20)

Other authors wrote stories, essays, and personal accounts that deal more directly with the effects of racism on their young lives, but only a reader with tin ears could fail to be moved by DeMetra Jackson's evocation of a past that still lives in the memories of many African Americans; only the insensitive could fail to know that "the man's" assertion, put in blunt and offensive words, echoes in the minds—calls to mind everyday experience—for those who live, as we all do, in cities divided by rivers or by like barriers. And those who care rather more about code than content might note that Jackson, a young author, is learning to employ the conventions of standard written English, even as she appropriately makes use of the "rich and expressive complexity of . . . forms of black speech" that Patricia Williams alludes to.

Once again, a deeply personal concern may be read in a poem a young author, Sarah Edwards, published in *Footsteps*; she may well be thinking about her own future as she nears graduation from high school, though her work also reflects deep empathy for another's plight:

> In his abandoned room,
> a man lies shivering,
> forgotten in the silence,
> of a nation otherwise preoccupied.
>
> After two decades
> at Dawson Tool and Die,
> he reads his name
> on the layoff list.
>
> Canvassing the one-industry
> town, he finds only empty words.
> "Sorry pal, I'd like to help,
> but you know how the
> recession is."
>
> Near the broken window,
> a sieve for February wind,
> a man lies rigid,
> shrouded in a silence,
> where even nature's elements
> refuse compassion. (98)

In these publishing projects, we always sought to teach young authors what they needed to learn about the technologies of the written word so that their writings could find fitting audiences (some basics, in fact, do matter). But we felt a deeper responsibility to listen to and learn to understand the languages these young authors brought to the tasks of becoming literate—to encourage them to use such language as they had in their attempts to make meanings for themselves and for the audiences they chose to address. To do otherwise—to disparage or demean languages that are close to heart and home—is to invite silence: to force those students we should be most eager to hear and help into isolation and loneliness. The well-intentioned and informed among those in Oakland, California, who sought to recognize and validate Ebonics as a form of language in daily use among their students were merely saying that their students' usages should be heard and appreciated: more, perhaps, that the "reasoned, rich and expressive complexity of most forms of black speech" should find place among the diverse languages that comprise American English. Our ablest authors are, of course, multivoiced: able to command a range of dialects and registers. If we are to teach our students basics that are worth anything, we do them a great disservice to settle for anything less.

Writers who write well and with purpose know themselves to be members of literate communities which shape their words even as their words reshape the communities of which they are members. To encourage our students to learn—to learn how to enrich and purposefully employ their linguistic resources—we had to enlist these young writers into literate communities, to help them find voice, to enable them to discover that their own experience, when made into words, can count and matter in worlds outside classrooms. Even though ultimately there may be little we can do, as teachers of literacy—and literature—to alter the powerful forces that shape and sometimes misshape young lives in our often uncaring society, in a nation all too often "otherwise preoccupied," the little we can do can often count for much. We can ask students to write as authors do, not just as students do. And we can ask our students to read as writers do—to compare their words and worlds and lives with worlds and lives figured by other authors, inviting them to articulate their own experience and to read, as models and material, other articulations. We can ask our reader/writers to imagine themselves into others' experiences: What did it feel like to be sold into slavery? What does it feel like to be told by a shopkeeper that only two of your group can come into his store at any one time? What does it feel like to be unemployed, perhaps unemployable? What worries attend getting an education when a future looks like a succession of minimum wage jobs?

To ask our students to read literature and to compose their own may enable our students—at least some of them—to glimpse realities in their own worlds and to identify obstacles that stand in their way; more importantly, to glimpse possible worlds and then, perhaps, to imagine possibilities in their own neighborhoods, possibilities that might be made real through individual or, more likely, collective action. Communities can be fashioned and changed through inclusive uses of the written word, and communities so fashioned can sometimes be made into publics acting in concert to bring about social change. Democracy can perhaps begin in conversation, and conversation can be extended to recover pasts and to fashion futures when conversants deliberately employ the technologies of literacy for such purposes. In literate communities, which invite connection to past and future in an ever-changing present made through language, there is no need ever to feel isolated, ever to find oneself completely alone, ever to feel the despair of powerlessness that accompanies isolation and loneliness.

Maxine Greene cogently describes a mental set all too easy to find among the students who currently populate our classrooms—one it is our responsibility to recognize and attend to: "I am suggesting," she writes in an essay titled "Wide-Awakeness and the Moral Life:"

> that for too many individuals in modern society, there is a feeling of being dominated and that feelings of powerlessness are almost inescapable. I am suggesting that such feelings can to a large degree be overcome through conscious endeavor on the part of individuals to keep themselves awake, to think about their condition in the world, to inquire into the forces that appear to dominate them, to interpret the experiences they are having day by day. Only as they learn to make sense of what is happening, can they feel themselves to be autonomous. Only then can they develop the sense of agency required for living a moral life. (1978, 43–44)

In authorship there can be some degree of autonomy; through authorship, one can feel a sense of agency. Reading attentively, writing to probe one's own experience of being in the world, we can find means to keep ourselves awake.

There are signs of wide-awakeness and of agency in the pages of the books Saginaw's students produced: *The Bridge* and *Footsteps*. These students did not read the following words of Maxine Greene's, but they seemed, in their acts of authorship, to sense their import:

> To be aware of authorship is to be aware of situationality and of the relation between the ways in which one interprets one's situation and the possibilities of action and of choice. This means that one's "reality," rather than being fixed and predefined, is a perpetual emergent, becoming increasingly multiplex, as more perspectives are taken, more texts are opened, more friendships made. (1988, 23)

Those who use words for their own purposes, to explore the worlds they live in and to imagine worlds that just might come into being, need never feel powerless, need never be entirely lonely. Those who do might glimpse some possibilities for "action and choice," might even learn that the psychological distance between two high schools can be shortened, even when physical distances can't, might even learn that bridges are in fact built to be crossed. Words can be bridges we can build with our students to lead them from the deeply personal to the meaningfully public, to help them find friends, to help them locate voice and place in literate communities they help form. It is our responsibility to help them learn to use words to just these ends.

Literacy and Citizenship: Creating Public Spaces

It was while working on another, quite complex collaborative project linking literacy and environmental education, that we began to speak of our work as aimed at promoting both a *civic* and a *civil* literacy. Again, this project—which came to be known as "the Saginaw River Project"— was an attempt to form a literate community that would use words to promote action. The University of Michigan team, whose membership is named above, was joined by William B. Stapp, Professor (now Emeritus) of Resource Planning and Conservation in the School of Natural Resources; the school team was joined by too many elementary and secondary teachers to name, save for Jo Pelkki, Science Coordinator for the Saginaw Public Schools. Jo's work was so influential and enduring that the project is now known, appropriately, as "Jo's Project." In the project, students from most of Saginaw's schools— elementary, middle, and secondary—monitored water quality in that river some of them couldn't comfortably cross; they then wrote up their findings, exploring not just the quality of the river's water but the uses, values, and meanings of the river in the city's history and in its present. Students engaged in the project forged a community—a public—that grew to include the city's water control engineers, members of the city council, environmental engineers from Dow Chemical and from General Motors (who helped fund the project and whose factories border the river), the editor of the city's newspaper (who published the students' findings and whose readership thus joined the expanding public), and producers from the regional public television station which broadcast programs that were student produced. Today, students in Saginaw's schools constitute the agency that monitors water quality in the Saginaw River, Michigan's largest, reporting regularly to the State's Department of Natural Resources.

Perhaps, from this very brief report, it is obvious why we came to think of our work as an engagement in *civic* literacy: these students were engaged in acts of citizenship as they sought to learn about and take actions to ameliorate threats to the community's immediate environment. But again, anecdotes may better capture what the term came to mean for students and their learning and why we chose to link civic with something we called *civil* literacy.

At the first River Congress—a city- and districtwide meeting in which students reported their scientific and other findings to the public—a fourth-grade boy, call him Ricky, reported to assembled students, teachers, administrators, parents, and environmentalists from community agencies and local industries the results of his class's water testing: tests done to assess the relative health of the Saginaw River. One of the tests they had done was for fecal colloforms—the presence of biological organisms in the water that is evidence of pollution from animal and human wastes. News about this test is a hot item because of the direct relation between fecal colloforms and human diseases like hepatitis.

Ricky faced an audience of people mostly older than he; in fact, though as tall as he should be for his age, he had to be helped up onto an empty milk crate to reach the microphone. With great seriousness, Ricky announced that he would tell us the test results not for fecal colloforms but for "fetal cauliflower" in the Saginaw River. He got a few laughs, but of course that is not what he intended to do. What he did do, if unintentionally, was help us think about why we should add the modifier *civil* to our work to promote a civic literacy. More about that after another anecdote.

On that same occasion, during the afternoon session in which small groups formed to discuss particular topics, a city council member, Roosevelt Ruffin, joined a group of students who were exploring avenues for activism aimed at improving water quality in the river and who wished to enlist his help. Ruffin listened attentively, especially to a very intense and articulate eighth-grade girl, but he did more than listen. When he had heard her expressions of concern, he responded with some of his own. In proposing solutions to poor water quality, were these young activists aware of the unemployment rate in the city? Were they considering the economic impact of their various proposals? And did they know, he asked, that the infant mortality rate in the city was higher than that of other Michigan cities? Could there be any connection between the students' concerns and this one? How should one conceive the term "environment," and what other factors than water quality ought to be considered in addressing so serious a problem as infant mortality? As a responsible politician, he asked them, how do I make decisions, knowing that resources are limited, especially in this community? How do I set priorities in seeking to respond to the many problems that plague our community, water quality among them?

Civic literacy, it seems to me, is exemplified in this engagement of an eighth-grade student with a city council member. This young student has conducted a serious inquiry into a topic of public consequence, has written about it, and then, in a public forum, submitted her findings to public scrutiny by others who have convergent if not identical concerns. Ruffin, whose elective position requires him to become informed about and take action to correct conditions that affect the health of Saginaw's citizens, learns from the student's findings, takes her concerns seriously not merely by accepting but by probing them, talking from his own wider

knowledge and experience to help this young citizen understand link-
ages of her concerns to others that affect her community, to encourage
her to think realistically about resources, priorities, competing claims
upon a community's attention and funds. A civic literacy must make
use of the languages of critique that Marxist oriented theorists have urged
upon literacy workers. But civic literacy must extend beyond a language
of critique to languages of construction and of possibility, to ways of
thinking and speaking that are adequate to the complexities of collective living and problem solving, to modes of listening and of responding that are sensitive to the multiple voices and minds of those who
have stakes in civic issues and those who are affected by the solutions
that are proposed for difficult problems. Exchanges of this kind demand
an intellectual stance that Hannah Arendt describes as "enlarged thinking":

> The more people's standpoints I have present in my mind while I
> am pondering a given issue, and the better I can imagine how I
> would feel and think if I were in their place, the stronger will be my
> capacity for representative thinking and the more valid my final
> conclusions, my opinion. (241)

Enlarged thinking is the kind we should encourage as we seek to help
our students to attain a civic literacy; it is the kind we should encourage
as we guide our students through their encounters with texts, their own
and others. Civic literacy implicates and is made possible by activities
of the sort Shirley Brice Heath identifies in this characterization of literate acts:

> Being literate means being able to talk with and listen with others to
> interpret texts, say what they mean, link them to personal experi-
> ence and with other texts, argue with them and make predictions
> from them, develop future scenarios, compare and evaluate related
> situations, and know that the practice of all these literate abilities is
> practical. (298)

Being literate, to again stress the obvious, demands opportunity if
these abilities are to form and be exercised. To become literate, our students will have to reach audiences formed and forming outside their
classrooms, will have to find opportunity—as this eighth grader has—
to talk with and write for adults who will take their words seriously and
then join with them in practical actions: the acts citizens can take that
might in fact result in remediation of intolerable conditions. This eighth
grader, through her literate acts, has received a lesson in citizenship; so
too has Roosevelt Ruffin.

Civil literacy, a complement to civic literacy, has to do with the character of the relations we seek to establish with our words and in our

engagements with other members of our literate communities—with the modalities of conversations and contacts. Its essence is a willingness to listen—especially to listen to others whose voices so often go unattended; its exercise is the courtesy and the courage to listen responsively, as Ruffin did in the encounter I have sought to characterize, when he honored a young woman's words by asking her to think more deeply about what she was saying and proposing—to become willing to modify her thinking if reflection convinces her that she needs to think more complexly and more practically. Civil discourse must be both tough minded and critical, lest it become merely polite, merely an exercise of empty tolerance. Civil literacy may be thought to reside too in the afterthoughts that come to us when we have recovered from laughter at a mistake a nine- or ten-year-old boy makes when, standing on a milk crate, he substitutes "fetal cauliflower" for "fecal colloform;" captured too in the responses we make—as members of a literate community, especially as teachers—to all nonstandard uses of language, all nonsanctioned ways of engaging in literate activities. Since one encounters it all the time, it is not necessary to imagine a view of literacy that equates "proper" pronunciations of hard words, "proper" spellings of them, with understanding of the concepts those sounds and spellings record. Better to imagine what damage one can do if one were to call a child illiterate when he makes a childlike mistake, even though he has struggled with his feet in the sand and his hands in the Saginaw River, with his mind in a lab, to say to people who should be caring what in the world he thinks he has found out.

There are dangers in our time, of course, in using modifiers like *civic* and *civil* to describe literacy: in our time and in our society such terms are all too often used to urge accommodation and assimilation to hegemonic values, to a patriotism that borders on xenophobia, to conceptions of family values rooted in the preferences and biases of class and religious persuasion, to a politics imagined only as the operations of a marketplace. The terms *civic* and *civil* can resound with unfavorable overtones when used in societies that are dominated by voices from the top: white, male voices mainly, speaking with authority and speaking only to and with other members of privileged classes. As John Dewey taught us, consensus can be deadening when the search is for something that can be held in common to forge a working public. We did not want to exclude conflict or controversy as our students struggled with tough issues of serious social concern; and yet, troubled by the violence we could see in the neighborhoods in which these young men and women lived, often depressed by the divisive and arrogant character of too much public discourse, appalled when discourse extends to the sanctioning of acts of destruction—the bombing of abortion clinics, the wanton murder of workers and visitors to a federal building—we wanted our students to employ humane and respectful modalities of representation and argument as they contended with one another. In working with students to help them employ such modalities, we tried to remember these words of Dewey's as he thought about "creative democracy":

> To take as far as possible every conflict which arises—and they are bound to arise—out of the atmosphere and medium of force, of violence as a means of settlement, into that of discussion and of intelligence, is to treat those who disagree—even profoundly—with us as those from whom we may learn, and in so far, as friends. (1940, 226)

Roosevelt Ruffin treated an eighth-grade student as Dewey's kind of friend, one with whom he could disagree, and thus teach; one from whom he had something to learn, even as he taught her.

Literacy begins and ends, as Maxine Greene tells us, always in the same place: in a believable end—that is, it always has to do with how we are made, with what worlds we would make, and with how we make and remake both self and world. Along the way toward any believable end, certain things have to happen: a fourth-grade child—an eighth-grade child—has to find out that she has some voice, some place in the world for her to speak her piece, even if the words don't always come out right. And for that to happen, this must too: someone has to listen and, in listening, speak back—not always to correct, but to help young speakers get from here to there, from childlike sayings to more adult ones. To learn to become citizens—active participants in civic projects intended to improve and enrich collective life and individual lived lives—students must be allowed and encouraged to make use of such experience, knowledge, and language as they have. It is then that democracy can begin in conversation; it is then that civic literacy, and a civility that might sustain it, can flourish.

Literacy as Listening: Attending to the Lives of Others

I'll try in yet another anecdote to capture other of those troubling and "perpetual emergent(s)" that seem always to characterize our lives as teachers. This story, which I will tell after a preamble of sorts, was told to me by a secondary school teacher whose classes were comprised of a rich diversity of students. Her story came to memory forcefully as I prepared, in my last term of formal teaching, to offer a first-year seminar to what turned out to be a similarly diverse group of students. I had titled my seminar (maybe insensitively; I thought then courageously) "Voices from Other Neighborhoods;" as I faced my students, I struggled to find means to attend to the voices I was hearing in my own classroom.

In addition to remembering, I read for my seminar, re-reading—as I do now—Clifford Geertz's important essay, "The Uses of Diversity." In this essay, Geertz likens present living "to living more and more in the midst of an enormous collage," inhabiting, as we now do, a world whose distances are overcome and whose differences of discourse and belief are made that much more apparent as the eyes and ears of electronic media penetrate neighborhoods once known only by natives and by the occasional ethnographer. But what interests Geertz more in this essay are the distances and differences that may be observed in our everyday lives and in our own neighborhoods, with special attention to the emergent social and ethical problems that are created when

> . . . the person we encounter in the grocery store is as likely, or nearly, to come from Korea as from Iowa, in the post office from Algeria as from the Auverne, in the bank from Bombay as from Liverpool. Even rural settings, where alikeness is likely to be more entrenched, are not immune: Mexican farmers in the Southwest, Vietnamese fishermen along the gulf coast, Iranian physicians in the Midwest. (121)

What to do, is Geertz's question, when cultures rub shoulders so intimately: how to choose and act when inevitably contrasting, often conflicting, sometimes contradictory and apparently irreconcilable differences of moral and ethical outlook emerge in our contacts (as we now inevitably have them) with "the other." And of course Geertz's questions have become even more impelling as American attitudes toward immigrants darken, reflecting fears and hatreds that have characterized our past; when California leads a now national movement to dismantle programs of affirmative action that have sometimes worked to bring about a diversity that characterized, thanks to my University's admissions policies, the makeup of my students in that first-year seminar.

But now to my anecdote, with Geertz's questions, and my own, as background and challenge:

Some years ago I had occasion to work, though only occasionally, with teachers in another district than Saginaw who were facing problems of the kind Geertz writes about. Into that district, once rather uniformly white and middle- or upper-middle-class, had come large numbers of working-class children, both white and African American, sizable numbers of recent Russian immigrants (most from devout or nearly so orthodox Christian backgrounds), and larger numbers of Chaldeans (also mostly from orthodox Christian backgrounds that were, however, sharply different from those of the Russian students and their families). These students, of course, brought their own stories, their own ways of acting, their historically constructed ways of making and validating meanings into the predominately liberal democratic culture of schooling in Michigan: a culture that sometimes promotes, more often at least valorizes, reason and discussion as means toward truth, principled (if sometimes and unfortunately only polite) modalities of discussion as means toward equitable distribution of power and authority.

A teacher from this district told me about a young Chaldean woman, a very good and dutiful student with a near straight-A average, who one day disappeared from her class and who reappeared some two weeks later. The teacher, a caring one, asked for a story that would explain the absence; the student, though a dutiful one, refused to offer one. It took some checking, some conversations with others, for the teacher to make a story into which the absence, and the student's refusal to talk about it, might fit: it seems that the teacher had given this near straight-A student a C on a particular assignment, and in a marginal comment suggested that the student, who of course had the ability to do better, had been lazy—had not lived up to her teacher's image of or expectations for her. The student's father, reading the grade and the comment, confined the young woman to her room, on reduced rations, for two weeks. For him, a teacher's assessment and words were authoritative, maybe even authoritarian; and as he read her words, he fit them into a narrative of authority and its uses that were not those the teacher would tell to explain her own uses of means of authority like grades and comments. The teacher's actions and words were judgmental in the parent's and her own readings of them; but the judgments held different meanings in their contrasting systems of values—their own ways of thinking about power and authority, their own historically constructed ways of validating the accuracy and consequences of judgments.

Out of this story, out of this parable, so many questions emerge for me as I try to grasp responsibilities I have as a teacher of language use: to get a handle on possibilities and dangers as meanings are differently apprehended in the complex settings our classrooms have become. For one, whose story is this anyway, and who gets to tell and interpret it? Is it the father's, who can tell a perfectly coherent story whose moral is the need for firm authority and for practices which enforce it—a story about discipline and enculturation in which the young learn from the old through punishment? Is it the teacher's, who has other narratives to explain and validate her own practices involving discipline and enculturation, her own uses of grades and comments, her own culturally and professionally sanctioned notions about how the young learn from the old? Is it the young woman's, who at the point I lost track of this story, still remained inarticulate? For another, how can we reconcile—or perhaps better, negotiate among—obviously conflicting systems of values as these reveal themselves in the stories people tell to make sense of and justify their actions.

Other questions may make the dilemma more concrete: what if we called the father's actions, as many of us would and as legal and professional codes of conduct would have us do, an instance—perhaps an indictable one—of child abuse? What if we named any unwillingness on the part of the teacher to name it as such—to tell the story in that way— an instance of unprofessional behavior for which she could be fired (as Michigan codes for teachers who ignore child abuse require)? What room would names of these kinds, stories of this sort, uses of language like these, leave for a young Chaldean woman to tell her story, should she ever choose, or be allowed, to do so? As a young person living in a collage—caught in systems of incommensurate values—what stories would she, what stories must she, both listen to and tell as means to understand her experience? And for us as teachers, welcoming as we do students with stories different from our own, wanting them to hear ours even as we listen to theirs—how might we fashion our classrooms to make them work as forums in which meaningful conversations—those that change things—can take place between a liberal democratic teacher, a traditional Chaldean father, and a young woman more or less caught in a web of meanings not yet of her own making?

Writing about dilemmas of just this kind, Geertz offers answers that are by no means easy or easily made comfortable: living in a collage, we must learn to see and to discern patterns in the various stories we hear, in the varied shapes of beliefs and actions that present themselves to us. For Geertz, life in a collage, living with conflict, must not take place in the dark. For him, to enlighten shapes and patterns not easily seen, imagination can help: we must, he says, strengthen "the power of our imaginations to grasp what is in front of us . . ." (123). "To live in a collage," he writes,

> . . . one must in the first place render oneself capable of sorting out its elements, determining what they are (which usually involves determining where they came from and what they amounted to when they were there) and how, practically, they relate to one another, without at the same time blurring one's own sense of one's own location and one's own identity within it. Less figuratively, "understanding" in the sense of comprehension, perception, and insight needs to be distinguished from "understanding" in the sense of agreement of opinion, union of sentiment, or commonality of commitment . . . We must learn to grasp what we cannot embrace. (122)

If we cannot embrace what may appear, at least in one telling of the story, as cruelty to a child, what upon examination may in fact *be* cruelty to a child—as we must not—we must yet determine "what [such actions] are" and "where they came from," for only then can stories of difference be told and then contested, if they need be. And as Geertz, drawing from Arthur Danto, so persuasively reminds me of how I must act as a teacher of my diverse collections of students:

> It is the asymmetries . . . between what we believe or feel and what others do, that makes it possible to locate where we now are in the world, how it feels to be there, and where we might or might not want to go. (114)

Denying difference, seeking to erase it—even relaxing into an easy tolerance that accepts all difference without judgment, "is to cut [ourselves] off from such knowledge and such possibility: the possibility of quite literally, and quite thoroughly, changing our minds" (114).

My young seminarians in that first-year class read together Alex Kotlowitz's *There Are No Children Here.* When I asked those readers, not all of whom had come from backgrounds one could call "privileged," though most had, to indicate whether or not they were surprised to learn that American children had to live lives of the kind Lafeyette and Pharoah lived in Chicago's Henry Horner Homes, all but two, if hesitantly, raised their hands. In our time and place, living in a collage, living as David Zucchino tells us we do "during the dying years of the American welfare state" (14) in his attempt to explode the "myth of the Welfare Queen" (as he titled his book), we have to help our students look into the lives of children like Lafeyette and Pharoah, examining the values that keep them living as well as the circumstances that make it so difficult for them to do so. So too must we open our own and our students' minds to lives even less like ours, those of Chaldeans who may well become our students, our neighbors, our fellow citizens, those Koreans or Palestinians we may meet in the grocery store, the Algerians we may meet in the post office—Mexican farmers, Vietnamese fishermen, Iranian physicians, Latino physicists. It is this sort of mix we must learn to address through a civil literacy; it is in communication and cooperation among a multivoiced and differently-minded population that a workable civic literacy will have to be forged if we are to realize the potential our democracy, in its best moments, can offer us.

What Geertz would have us do to reach toward larger social responsibilities is within our competence, lies well within our responsibilities as teachers of writing and of reading. There are texts to be read that can help our students imagine and feel with the lives that others lead; there are modes of reading and ways of conducting class discussions that will invite our students to examine their own experiences and to test their understandings against the experiences of others, the meanings others have derived from them, and the systems of value that have determined others' choices of belief and action.

The first book I required my young seminarians to read in "Voices from Other Neighborhoods" was Carl Nightingale's complex and sometimes difficult book, *On the Edge: A History of Poor Black Children and Their American Dreams*—a book about the forces that shape the lives of young people growing up in one of Philadelphia's more troubled neighborhoods. The students chose the topic for our opening discussions about the book: Nightingale's examination of different modes of rearing and disciplining children and his recommendation that discussion replace physical punishment as one means of combating the violence that characterizes the lives of the children he writes about. My students were quickly telling each other stories about their own family relationships and the ways they were disciplined; and it did not take them long—in discussions that were often heated—to connect their accounts of individual experiences to deeply seated cultural values that reflect America's separations of race and class. They were doing what Geertz would have us do as we live in a society that is multicultured: sorting out elements of beliefs and behaviors that on first glance seem alien, learning where these came from, weighing them against their own experiences and beliefs, doing so in ways that did not blur their "own sense of [their] own location and [their] own identity within it." They were learning to grasp, at least, what they could not necessarily embrace, differently storied and historied as they were. And maybe in the process, some of them were beginning to learn how to change their minds as they opened themselves to reflective, responsive, and critical consideration of the experiences of others. The deeply personal can become the *deeply* public.

In learning about others, in learning how to live with others, I think we must learn to be caring in ways Nel Noddings would have us be: only in caring can we hope to see that others with labels in fact have proper names; only through feeling with a young Chaldean woman, or with Lafeyette or with Pharoah, can we think past stereotypes to find, with them, solutions for problems that will better individual lives. In our society, Noddings says,

> We establish funds, or institutions, or agencies in order to provide the caretaking we judge to be necessary. The original impulse is often the one associated with caring. It arises in individuals. But as groups of individuals discuss the perceived needs of another individual or group, the imperative changes from "I must do something" to "something must be done." (25)

In seeking to promote a civic literacy—one that offers hope of finding pattern and meaning and purpose for life in a collage—each author of its texts must start and end with the imperative "I must do something." Listening, although a beginning, is finally not quite enough.

Community, Contingency, and the Current: Final Words

Maxine Greene is one of our profession's most articulate advocates for the power of literature—the power of art—to spur examination and re-examination of our lives: of lives that can become mechanical as they are caught up in daily routines, of lives whose patterns can seem predetermined by forces beyond one's control, of lives lived in inarticulated silence and the desperations of powerlessness, of lives lived in loneliness. In naming her own aim in *The Dialectic of Freedom*, Greene articulates a hope that might rather be taken as a statement of the most pressing responsibility of teachers who live and work in a collage:

> My hope is to remind people of what it means to be alive among others, to achieve freedom in dialogue with others for the sake of personal fulfillment and the emergence of a democracy dedicated to life and decency. (1988, xii)

The terms *civic literacy* and *civil literacy* are meant to name capacities for the uses of the written word that promote certain ways of communicating "to achieve freedom in dialogue," to enable both "personal fulfillment and the emergence of a democracy dedicated to life and decency." The first names collectively the responsibilities of citizenship in a democracy; the second names a mode of conducting dialogue that holds some promise of achieving decency in our conversations, in our dialogues, as we inevitably encounter conflicts that can threaten to separate us.

Perhaps we never could, certainly we cannot now, insulate our classrooms from the problems outside school walls that trouble our students—problems that must be confronted and acted upon if anything like a civic literacy is to be practiced. A civic literacy must be a critical literacy: critical always because we cannot leave our students content, in these times, with the content of their lives, influenced as they are by the powerful voices of consumerism issuing from public media of all kinds; critical always because too many young lives are being deformed by the forces of racism and sexism, of class bias, of economic inequity, of a politics of division that would separate still more widely rich from poor, people of color from those who imagine themselves as having no color, immigrants from citizens who imagine themselves as native, no matter how recently their ancestors may have emigrated. The obstacles to self-development and to the emergence of a nourishing democracy must be identified, named, and faced.

So too must a civic literacy be an engaged and active literacy: we promote citizenship and democracy when we invite our students to practice "enlarged thinking," when we encourage them to read widely and critically, to raise their voices and use their pens as agents with the capacity to do something practical and useful in collective work aimed at solving difficult and persistent problems. Studying and writing, making choices and taking action, student citizens can inform their community of their findings and thus do something that may reverse generations of inattention, or worse, to the quality of water in the Saginaw River; writing from their own experience, they can act to combat the corroding effects of racism on their own and others' young lives; becoming informed, writing up and publishing their reflections and understandings, they can join other authors and actors who seek to remediate the devastating consequences of domestic and social violence, of drug use and alcohol abuse.

When as teachers we engage in work to promote a civic and a civil literacy, it is all too easy for us to become discouraged if not dispirited. The problems that torment our students' lives, the forces and conflicts that threaten to deform our collective living, can appear overwhelming to those whose tools can seem *merely* words. And the literate communities, the publics, we manage to bring into formation seem always to be so temporary, so nearly ephemeral, when we are caught up in daily routines and always constrained by the structures of lives lived both inside and outside school walls. School terms come to an end, students graduate, educational and social priorities shift, teachers get tired and administrators get pressed to have their schools take on yet other responsibilities. Some promising, and even some successful, projects will, alas, come to an end.[8]

When they do, it is well to remember how John Dewey characterized a central aim in teaching and learning: in working with students, he said, we are or should be always striving to modify and educate *dispositions*—emotional and intellectual inclinations that under the right conditions just might become habitual. The student authors who produced *The Bridge*, those who recorded their experiences in *Footsteps*, will never come together again as a group working on a common writing project, but they may well remember the pleasure and power of single voices raised in chorus and feel themselves disposed to sing in other choirs. The student scientist/authors who studied and wrote about the ecology of the Saginaw River may find themselves inclined to undertake, with others, similarly important community projects, similarly amenable for solution to an application of commitment and intelligence with the aim of making things better for those who will come after. We are educating, Dewey tells us, always for growth, always seeking to foster what he calls a human capacity for adaptation, for "plasticity," which he takes as the essence of growth. Plasticity in humans, he says, is not "the plasticity of putty or wax."

> It is not a capacity to take on change of form in accord with external pressure. It lies near the pliable elasticity by which some persons take on the color of their surroundings while retaining their own bent. But it is something deeper than this. It is essentially the ability to learn from experience; the power to retain from one experience something which is of avail in coping with the difficulties of a later situation. This means power to modify actions on the basis of the results of prior experiences, the power to develop dispositions. (1916, 49)

In discouraging moments, we must always remind ourselves too that words are never *mere*, that others' uses of words are never *merely*. We are, to some large extent, coterminous with what we say, and our selves and worlds are themselves verbally constituted. Dewey says this better in his philosophizing about the relations of education and democracy:

> Society not only continues to exist *by* transmission, *by* communication, but it may fairly be said to exist *in* transmission, *in* communication. There is more than a verbal tie between the words common, community, and communication. Men [and women] live in a community in virtue of the things which they have in common; and communication is the way in which they come to possess things in common. What they must have in common in order to form a community or society are aims, beliefs, aspirations, knowledge—a common understanding—like-mindedness as the sociologists say. Such things cannot be passed physically from one another, like bricks; they cannot be shared as persons would share a pie by dividing it into physical pieces. The communication which insures participation in a common understanding is one which secures similar emotional and intellectual dispositions—like ways of responding to expectations and requirements. (1916, 7)

It would be quite inaccurate, bordering on insult, to tell the young authors of *The Bridge: Linking Minds: Growing Up in Saginaw* or *Footsteps: Looking Back, Moving On* that their words were *mere*, their acts of authorship *merely*. The very titles of their books accurately capture their self-conscious awareness of what they were about: that there were and are barriers in their city, divisions that can be both seen and felt, obstacles to their appropriate self-development and to the civil functioning of their civic lives; but that in building bridges to one another and to others in their community, in walking ahead while looking back, barriers and obstacles can be removed, overcome, to combat isolation and loneliness. The titles, and their stories, poems, and essays, show these adolescent authors' sure sense that their lives are rooted in personal histories that are meaningful, that future growth can develop from these roots in ways that are in no way stunted as they find means to change and develop the minds that they have, to enrich the languages in which they speak. In seeking to build community with us their readers, they say to us clearly that they can "move on" if their aspirations are read as counting for something in the worlds they inhabit—worlds they can to some measure change if they find words and will enough and if we find courage and intelligence enough to work with them. Given opportunity, their words tell us—opportunities to tell their own stories—they can, as their words find range, author worlds they might more profitably and more willingly inhabit.

Words and worlds are intimately connected, and teachers of literacy must work in and upon the world, as many do. Working in our own classrooms, trying to open them to the worlds we and our students must live in; working out in the world in classrooms not our own, in communities and community centers, in shelters for battered women, in nursing homes and homeless shelters, we might take it as our responsibility to make sense of and respond to a challenge offered by John Dewey almost a century ago in his still seminal work, *Democracy and Education*:

> Men [and women] have long had some intimation of the extent to which education may be consciously used to eliminate obvious social evils through starting the young on paths which shall not produce these ills, and some idea of the extent in which education may be made an instrument of realizing the better hopes of men. But we are doubtless far from realizing the potential efficacy of education as a constructive agency of improving society, from realizing that it represents not only a development of children and youth but also of the future society of which they will be the constituents. (1916, 85)

Perhaps as students of literacy, as teachers of literacy, working with our students, we can find ways with words—modes of teaching language use—that will promote and sustain multiple-voiced and open communication: the kind that makes community possible to achieve, the kind that creates and then nourishes development and maintenance of a just and democratic society.

A Postscript

To offer thanks to the authors in this volume: to Cathy and to Dave for imagining it in the first place and then taking on the duties, sometimes thankless, as editors. To Laura, Carol, Colleen, Roberta, Sylvia, John, Tom, and Todd for writing things that are well worth reading. You have all been my students, and have taught me; you have been and are valued colleagues: more than that, you have taught me the values of friendship and civility—especially when we have disagreed. How comforting to leave Dewey's challenge in your hands.

Notes

1. Olson, David. 1977. "From Utterance to Text: The Bias of Language in Speech." *Harvard Educational Review* 47: 257–81.

2. The best introduction to these notions of Bakhtin is his *Speech Genres and Other Late Essays* (1986).

3. Fleischer, Cathy. 1997. "Taking It to the Streets: Teachers as Advocates." Presentation at the National Council of Teachers of English Spring Conference, April, Charlotte, North Carolina.

4. The reference is to an article by John Leo, "The answer is 45 cents," which appeared in *U.S. News and World Report,* April 21, 1997, p. 14. The article, an attack on an "anything goes movement" that is more in Leo's head than in American classrooms, unfortunately spawned similar scurrilous misrepresentations and caused some harm to my own institution, the University of Michigan.

5. It is not possible to say enough about the commitment and courage of these three teachers, and of several of their colleagues, to the education and well-being of inner-city students. Two administrators share these qualities: Foster B. Gibbs, Superintendent of Schools, School District of the City of Saginaw, and Burris Smith, Director of K–12 Education in that district.

6. The best available account of this publishing project and of the curricula associated with these experiments in literacy education is Patricia Lambert Stock's *The Dialogic Curriculum: Teaching and Learning in a Multicultural Society* (1995)— a must-read for anyone interested in the kinds of schooling and literacy argued for in this essay. Stock was Director of Projects in the formative and most active years of work for the University of Michigan's Center for Educational Improvement through Collaboration (CEIC). Her intelligently guiding hand and warm spirit had most to do with success of the Saginaw projects.

7. Colleen Fairbanks, who reports in this volume on some of her work in Saginaw, succeeded Patti Stock as Director of Projects for the CEIC, and lived and worked in Saginaw for two years. Hers was the guiding hand in the publication of *Footsteps;* she was responsible as well for work on other projects—a successful student-to-student tutoring project, for example, bringing high school and elementary students together, and for development of aspects of the Saginaw River Project.

8. I am indebted to Aaron Schutz for some of the ideas about community in this section (and its suggestions about the limits of "caring"). Schutz, a graduate student in Michigan's Joint Program in English and Education now working on his dissertation, is doing important theoretic and empirical work on the formation of educational and professional communities. Two important essays on this subject are now in press: "Creating Local Public Spaces in Schools: Insights from Hannah Arendt and Maxine Greene" (*Curriculum Inquiry*) and "Caring in Schools Is Not Enough: Community, Narrative, and the Limits of Alterity" (*Educational Theory*).

Works Cited

Arendt, Hannah. 1977. *Between Past and Future: Eight Exercises in Political Thought.* New York: Penguin.

Bakhtin, M. M. 1986. *Speech Genres and Other Late Essays.* Trans. Vern McGee. Eds. Caryl Emerson and Michael Holquist. Austin: University of Texas Press.

The Bridge: Linking Minds: Growing Up in Saginaw. 1988. Saginaw, MI: School District of the City of Saginaw.

Dewey, John. 1940. "Creative Democracy: The Task Before Us." In *The Philosopher and the Common Man.* Ed. Sidney Ratner. New York: Putnam's.

———. 1985. *Democracy and Education* [1916]. In *The Middle Works, 1899–1924,* Vol. 9. Ed. Jo Ann Boydston. Carbondale and Edwardsville: Southern Illinois University Press.

Footsteps: Looking Back, Moving On. 1991. Saginaw, MI: School District of the City of Saginaw.

Geertz, Clifford. 1986. "The Uses of Diversity." *Michigan Quarterly Review* (Winter). Ann Arbor: University of Michigan.

Greene, Maxine. 1978. *Landscapes of Learning.* New York and London: Teachers College Press.

———. 1988. *The Dialectic of Freedom.* New York and London: Teachers College Press.

Heath, Shirley Brice. 1990. "The Fourth Vision: Literate Language at Work." In *The Right to Literacy.* Eds. Andrea A. Lunsford et al. New York: Modern Language Association.

Kotlowitz, Alex. 1991. *There Are No Children Here: The Story of Two Boys Growing Up in the Other America.* New York: Doubleday.

Leo, John. 1997. "The answer is 45 cents." *U.S. News and World Report,* 21 April, 14.

Nightingale, Carl Husemoller. 1993. *On the Edge: A History of Poor Black Children and Their American Dreams.* New York: Basic Books.

Noddings, Nel. 1984. *Caring: A Feminine Approach to Ethics and Moral Education.* Berkeley: University of California Press.

Olson, David. 1977. "From Utterance to Text: The Bias of Language in Speech." *Harvard Educational Review* 47: 257–81.

Stock, Patricia Lambert. 1995. *The Dialogic Curriculum: Teaching and Learning in a Multicultural Society.* Portsmouth, NH: Boynton/Cook–Heinemann.

White, James Boyd. 1985. *Heracles' Bow: Essays on the Rhetoric and Poetics of Law.* Madison: University of Wisconsin Press.

Williams, Patricia J. 1996. "The Hidden Meanings of 'Black English'." *The New York Times,* Late Edition—Final, Sunday, 29 December, Sec. 4, Editorial Desk, 9.

Zucchino, David. 1997. *Myth of the Welfare Queen.* New York: Scribner.

2 Good Deeds: An Ethnographer's Reflections on Usefulness

Todd DeStigter
University of Illinois at Chicago

We have in America a fast-growing number of cultivated young people who have no recognized outlet for their active faculties. They hear constantly of the great social maladjustment, but no way is provided for them to change it, and their uselessness hangs about them heavily. Huxley declares that this sense of uselessness is the severest shock which the human system can sustain, and that if persistently sustained, it results in atrophy of function.

—Jane Addams, *Twenty Years at Hull-House*

There is no substitute for the vitality and depth of close and direct intercourse and attachment.

—John Dewey, *The Public and Its Problems*

The Problems of Usefulness

It is a long way from Ann Arbor to Addison, Michigan, almost an hour even if the roads are clear of snow. But one morning in December of 1992, as I edged my Honda through the fog at thirty-five miles per hour behind a Ford pickup, I knew the trip would take even longer than I had expected.[1] A few years before that first drive to what would become my research site, at ten past eight in the morning I would have been in a classroom at the Ohio State University, sipping coffee at the feet of the eminent rhetorician Edward P. J. Corbett. I would have been marveling at how he could recite from memory entire paragraphs from Richard Whately's *Elements of Rhetoric* or scribbling in my notebook his explanations of the nuances of Aristotle's original Greek that are lost in even the best translations. I might also have been considering the project due the following week in my composition theory course, the one in which I was evaluating responses instructors had written on the essays of students I had never met. In either case, I would have been thinking about how rhetoric might help me become a better English teacher.

That morning, though, as I left a world of fashionable coffee shops and the stately silence of the graduate school reading room and entered a landscape of expansive corn fields and pale, listing barns, I listened to the instructional tape in my car: *"En qué clase de concurso participó Alberto, un concurso de inglés o un concurso de matemáticas?"* I knew that I must try to think in Spanish again, that I must attempt to cross into another world that was, in many ways, very far away.

Since that initial trip to Addison, I've become comfortable with the drive. I have exchanged my good shoes and sport jacket for sneakers and a cotton shirt, the tails of which I sometimes leave hanging out of my jeans. This morning I glance at my watch as I slow for a curve that passes an abandoned church, its windows shrouded by sheets of weathered plywood. If I'm there by 8:15, I know I'll be on time for school. When the two-lane blacktop straightens out, I coax a bit more speed from the Honda, remembering to drift to the center of the road to avoid the pot holes that wait just beyond the big white house where a rusted Buick sulks in the front yard, the hand-painted sign propped inside its windshield inviting passers-by to "Make offer." I especially enjoy the drive in early autumn, when, if I turn up the heater and roll down the window, I can smell the crops lying heavy and ripe in their rows. I turn into the school driveway just in time to hear the bell calling the students to class. Downshift and swerve to the left so as to hit the speed bump with only the right wheels. Pull into the space to the left of the science teacher's Toyota. Grab my blue and white Addison High School parking permit from the glove compartment and toss it onto the dashboard. I've grown accustomed to this ritual.

Twice each week for three years, I have traveled to Addison High to conduct ethnographic research focusing on the literacy practices of the school's Latino students, especially those who are called "limited English proficient" (LEP).[2] Attending classes with these students, helping them with their homework, listening to their stories, I try to understand the many challenges they face and how I might use my background as a writer and teacher to improve their experiences at school and to increase the number of options available to them both now and later in life. I seek, in other words, to be useful. Among the many things I have learned in the course of my research, however, is that "usefulness" is difficult to define and effect when confronted by the kind of profound cultural differences that stand between me and my research "subjects." For although the place and the people are by now familiar, when I sit face-to-face with Juan, a sixteen-year-old migrant worker from the *barrio* of Brownsville, Texas, it is impossible to ignore the *frontera* between us. His hands alone—the tomato-field dirt worked under the skin, the gang insignia tattooed in the loose flesh where the forefinger meets the thumb—testify to the distance separating his life, his *cultura,* from mine.

My work in Addison has in part been a struggle to find ways to understand and then to narrow such distances—a process which I believe holds the best promise that I may be useful in helping Juan and other Latino students improve the quality of their lives. In this essay, I discuss experiences and ideas that have contributed to my understanding of what it means for me to be useful in my role as an educational researcher. More specifically, I explain how I have come to think of my responsibility as an ethnographer as going beyond (though it certainly includes) being meticulous in my research methods. Instead, I suggest that we ought to view ethnography as a relationship—a way of being with other people—that will enable us to critique the potentially colonialistic ways our privileged positions allow us to intervene in people's lives. My project here, therefore, is not to explicate a method but to urge researchers to foster a disposition that I hope will enable us to make our work more humane and mutually productive than it often is now. Insofar as the relationships we ethnographers form with others may ultimately influence the way we think about classroom practices, this, too, is a story about how rhetoric might help us become better English teachers.

Located about fifty miles southwest of Detroit and with a population of over twenty-two thousand, Addison relies on an economic base of agriculture and small industry that attracted large numbers of Latino workers to the area in response to war-time labor demands in the 1940s. The children and grandchildren of these workers now form the base of Addison's Latino population, which accounts for over 16 percent of all Addison residents—the second highest percentage of all Michigan cities. Though many of Addison's Latinos are long-time residents, others are recent arrivals who often work in small factories supplying parts to automobile assembly plants in Detroit, Pontiac, and Flint. Still others are temporary migrant workers who, after the northern harvest of tomatoes, pumpkins, or sugar beets, move on to solicit work from growers operating along the Eastern seaboard from Maryland to Florida.[3] In Addison, where much of the quality of life is tied directly to working-class jobs, the struggle for sustained employment is one Latinos are clearly losing. According to the 1990 census, the median annual family income for Addison Latinos is approximately nineteen thousand dollars, compared to twenty-nine thousand dollars for whites. Over 30 percent of these Latino families live below the poverty line (twice the percentage of whites), and Latino households receiving some type of public assistance income is roughly 27 percent, compared to 12 percent for whites.

Although the myth of public education is that it affords political and economic power to the dispossessed, writers like Martin Carnoy, Henry Giroux, and Penelope Eckert have shown that schools contribute to perpetuating the socioeconomic disparity represented in these statistics by reproducing the cultural privilege and class relations of the broader society. Addison High, I have found, is no exception. One morning last fall when I arrived in the second-period English as a Second Language class in which I served as a tutor, Alice Martinez, who at the time was the only ESL teacher in the entire district, looked at me with dark, angrily narrowed eyes and jerked her thumb toward a message written in bold letters on the chalkboard: "ESL, DO NOT MOVE THE FURNITURE." I shook my head, annoyed by this latest instance of the school's alienating its Latino students, but knowing that we would have to comply. Because Martinez was in the high school just one period per day, this room was on loan, a space normally reserved for teaching history and U. S. government.

When all the students had settled into their seats, we began to work our way through the oral sections of a test. That day we talked a bit louder than usual, our voices having adjusted to the sputtering whine of a dot-matrix printer on which the history teacher had begun printing a review sheet for his class next period. I pulled a chair alongside Claudia, a fifteen-year-old Puerto Rican who speaks English and Spanish fluently but struggles to read or write in either language.

"Todd, you're not supposed to move the chairs," she said.

"I'll put it back," I said. The history teacher looked up from his computer but did not say anything. Before Claudia would focus on her test, she insisted on showing us photos of her recent birthday party. The first was of Claudia herself, wearing a Mickey Mouse T-shirt, smiling beside her Mickey Mouse cake. Other pictures showed her sisters with arms slung over each others' shoulders, her brother dancing with her aunt, and her mother holding a dish of ice cream in one hand and a beer in the other. Eventually Claudia slid the photos back into the inside pocket of her notebook and asked me to read her first test question: "Where do you live?" Claudia paused, then opened her backpack, pulled out an Addison High sweatshirt, and laid it on her lap. Slowly, with a pencil that long ago had had its eraser end rubbed flat, Claudia copied the letters from the sweatshirt to the blank space on her paper.

I leaned across the aisle to check on Felipe, Claudia's brother, who was remembering most of his vocabulary words but, as usual, was having trouble spelling them. I agreed with him that English words are "weird" and arranged to meet him in study hall to help him write an essay for his Introduction to Literature class.

Within fifteen minutes, Juan sat quietly drawing a picture of his girl-friend back in Texas. "You finished?" I asked. He nodded. I wasn't sur-prised; Juan is very bright. He had completed his test despite having missed the last two weeks of school after having been suspended for skipping school in order to help his family harvest pumpkins. "Hey, how do you say 'pumpkin' in Spanish?" I asked.

"*Calabaza*," he said.

Angela, a sixteen-year-old *Mexicana* whom Martinez had been help-ing since the beginning of the period, was the last to finish her test. School-work was, to risk understatement, difficult for Angela, for despite the fact that she spoke almost no English and that her education back home in Matamoros ended in the sixth grade, she had been mainstreamed into regular sophomore-level English-language content area classes and left to fend for herself. The predictable result was that in her three se-mesters since arriving in Addison, Angela had failed almost all of her courses, with the exceptions of ESL, typing, and gym. She often told me that she didn't like Michigan, that she wanted to return to Mexico to be with the friends and relatives to whom she wrote several long letters each week.

Waiting out the last few minutes of the period, I glanced at the clock and moved my desk back into its proper row, then walked over to the bulletin board and studied a poster published by *Newsweek* magazine. Over a world map, the caption read as follows: "The whole world is watching fifty countries guilty of persistent human rights violations." The guilty countries—among them China, Peru, and Mexico—were shaded red. The United States was a light and pleasant shade of tan—flesh color. The history teacher's printer advanced to another page.

As the goings-on in and around Addison's second-period ESL class suggest, rather than including the languages and experiences of stu-dents classified as "Hispanic" in the culture that the school legitimates and values as worth knowing, administrators and teachers too often ignore these students and their particular needs. In Addison, this ne-glect, this message that Latinos are not really among the public that the community's public school allegedly serves, contributes to a Latino stu-dent dropout rate of nearly 50 percent. Nationally, though dropout rates among whites and African Americans have declined in the last two de-cades, these numbers have continued to rise among Latino students, who now leave school at rates three to four times higher than the rest of the student population.[4] Speaking of the correlation between low edu-cational attainment and poverty, Walter Secada, the head of a national committee to investigate and recommend action concerning the high dropout rate among Latinos, has asserted that "for the social ills associated with dropping out to fall disproportionately on any one group is a recipe for social and economic disaster that will make the Watts riots look like Disney World" ("Educational Gap" 2).

Given the alienation of Latino students in many of our schools, the high rate at which these students drop out, and the likely socioeconomic consequences of their leaving school, it wasn't long before I had developed a sense of urgency, a keenly felt desire that the result of my work might be useful to people like Angela and Claudia. What was unclear to me, though, is what that usefulness should look like—how my work as an ethnographer might be helpful in addressing problems like these. I wondered, in other words, what role I might play in a *praxis* that would actually change the circumstances in which these students lived. In what I view as a partial answer to this question (a question I will later attempt to answer more completely), several writers have suggested that the benefit of ethnographic research in education is that it enriches our understandings of the contexts and complexities of teaching and learning.

As John Ogbu has documented, the history of anthropology as it relates to education dates back to the final decades of the nineteenth century. During this time, researchers worked toward making available to educators and policymakers knowledge about culture and its transmission that would refute false and prejudicial ideas concerning the intellectual and learning capabilities of non-Western peoples and of minorities, immigrants, and lower-class peoples in Western societies (276). Ogbu goes on to note that in the 1960s and '70s, the researcher's role was honed to refute the notion of "cultural deprivation" and to revise what was then conventional education research by encouraging investigation that does not divorce educational processes from their sociocultural contexts. Ogbu concludes that, complemented by a refinement of methods and the increasing popularity of ethnographic fieldwork, the purpose of anthropological description of educational settings is to provide a "database for analysis aimed at the understanding of specific problems, including those pertaining to cognition, language and communication, roles and identities, school-community relations, and the like" (282).

More recently, Shirley Brice Heath and Steven Z. Athanases have written of the contributions ethnography has made to research in the teaching and learning of English. Heath and Athanases argue that ethnographers have provided valuable descriptions of readers and writers as embedded within specifics of time and place. Such descriptions, the authors continue, help account for the role that language plays in cultural representation and, hence, contribute to our understandings of how "individuals become cultural carriers, transmitting and transforming ways of behaving, believing, and valuing within their social group" (267).

In sum, educational ethnographers are often seen as useful in that they contextualize language use: they help us think of speaking, listening, reading, and writing as aspects of and situated within broader cultural forces, thereby affording enriched understandings of the causes and consequences of different ways with words.

Working from this kind of analytical framework, in Addison I have depicted the school's officially sanctioned literacy practices as just one part of the larger symbolic discourse the school uses to reinforce the marginal status of its Latino students. I have, for instance, described Angela's unsuccessful attempts to answer questions in response to a chapter in a science textbook she cannot read; I have shown some of the ways in which events like Addison's homecoming football game reflect and help perpetuate hierarchical social identity within the school community; I have documented and critiqued teachers' beliefs in the importance of Latino students' acclimating to an allegedly unifying United States "national culture." I hope that these findings may be useful in that they may eventually lead teachers to view their pedagogy as a cultural practice that they can revise to be more responsive to the unique abilities and needs of their Latino students.[5] However, despite the potential of such research done well, at least two problems lead me to question whether ethnography as we now understand it will be useful in leading to positive social and political change on a scale that extends beyond classroom walls. The first problem, by now familiar, is epistemological. The second, closely related to the first but often left out of our professional conversations, is ethical.

By now the argument is common that researchers in the human sciences should be at least as concerned with *how* they are going about their work as with the results and content of cultural description and analysis itself. Researchers have, for the most part, rejected the notion that they can describe social phenomena as though there existed an empirical reality that is authoritatively "knowable" within a stable epistemological paradigm.

By acknowledging that culture is not only something researchers study but also something *from* which they study—that is, a medium which is going to influence what they see, how they see it, and how they talk about what they see—they have highlighted the role of hermeneutics, the process of reality-constructing interpretation, and have thereby introduced what many have referred to as the postmodern "crisis of representation." Essentially, this "crisis" has resulted from what Jean-Francois Lyotard called the contemporary "incredulity towards metanarratives" and the ensuing "uncertainty about adequate means of describing social reality" (xxv). But if our ways of knowing have been complicated by postmodern thought, this "crisis" is especially acute among those who attempt cross-cultural representation of the type I am pursuing in Addison. Indeed, people like me must confront the notion that if the ways we make sense of our worlds are so different from those of "the other," any efforts to represent one culture in terms of another are at best problematic, perhaps futile.

As the anthropologists George Marcus and Michael Fischer have argued, one of the greatest promises of ethnography is that it enables more productive and culturally sensitive representations than can be achieved from alleged "totalizing visions of reality" (8), for it is a method which demands that researchers—to use the words of Clifford Geertz—"hover closely" over the sites they are studying and employ "thick description" to represent other people's words and actions within the cultural contexts that give them meaning.[6] But even if we do our best to situate what we observe, even if we strive for what Geertz calls "local knowledge," the basic theoretical problem, our "crisis," persists. James Clifford puts it this way:

> If ethnography produces cultural interpretations through intense research experiences, how is unruly experience transformed into an authoritative written account? How, precisely, is a garrulous, over-determined cross-cultural encounter shot through with power relations and personal cross purposes circumscribed as an adequate version of a more or less discrete "other world" composed by an individual author? (25)

By posing this question as he does, Clifford, too, suggests what I have mentioned above—that the "crisis of representation" involves at least two issues: first, that critiques of dominant paradigms have raised questions concerning whether we can "know" and represent others; and second, the ethical implications of attempting to do so. If Geertz is right when he talks about ethnography as "putting words down onto paper" (*Works* 1), any research complicated by a social conscience will inevitably involve questions of rhetoric concerning how we will interpret and then "compose" ourselves and "the other" honestly and responsibly. Further, if, as Jay Robinson suggests, we understand rhetoric as an interpretive *act*, we must take seriously the notion that the way we represent our subjects and our selves is not politically or ethically benign, neither to them nor to us.

Especially in the past several years, writers have suggested that such representations too often amount to forms of imperialism and erasure. Edward Said, for instance, has argued in *Orientalism* that the genres of writing developed in the West to represent non-Western societies have included rhetorical devices which make Western authors active, while leaving their subjects passive. Eva Hoffman, in *Lost in Translation*, gives us this warning: "For all our sophisticated deftness at cross-cultural encounters, fundamental difference, when it's staring at you across the table from within the close-up face of a fellow human being, always contains an element of violation" (94). Thus, any cross-cultural "translation"—and I include my own in Addison—includes potentially oppressive self-representation: that is, usurping the ownership of another person's experience and putting it into our own terms. We, in effect, "hang" the other on our own rhetorical frameworks, and, even though we may have the noblest of intentions, our efforts to do right by our "subjects" may thus be thwarted by the possibility that what we think is best for them and what they themselves desire are very different things.

Given his insightful and ongoing articulation of ethnography as fiction, it is ironic that the tendency to separate the epistemological from the ethical is illustrated in Geertz's own discussion of the posthumous publication of Bronislaw Malinowski's *A Diary in the Strict Sense of the Term*, in which Malinowski writes candidly and disparagingly about the "natives" with whom he lived and worked. Geertz claims that the outcry and hand-wringing this publication prompted among anthropologists was made "to come down to Malinowski's moral character or lack of it" (*Local* 56). That is, people were upset that Malinowski turned out not to be as kind or gracious a person as everyone had assumed him to be. In Geertz's view, however, this focus on Malinowski's morality obscured the real question raised by the *Diary*: whether or not "anthropological knowledge of the way natives think, feel, and perceive" is even possible. Thus, the issue, Geertz summarizes, is not moral, but strictly epistemological. However, as Geertz himself elsewhere acknowledges, because ethnography is, in fact, writing (the act of representing another person with our words), the point that Geertz downplays in his discussion of Malinowski is precisely the one I believe needs to be underscored in our professional conversations: namely, that ethnography (especially what I have been calling the "useful" kind) is not just about epistemology. It is about ethics—if by "ethics" we mean something like a system of ideas guiding our conduct toward others. In short, I think there exists an intimate and dialectical relationship between how we *know* "the other" and how we *are with* "the other."

This is not to say that we should disregard the epistemological issues that so concern Geertz. As I have suggested, there are serious consequences of failing to see things from, to use Geertz's parlance, "the native's point of view" (*Local* 56). Indeed, Heath and Athanases have done well to remind us that in recent years, "educational research labeled ethnography has shown little evidence of being guided by what scholars in cultural anthropology and the ethnography of communication have articulated as sound principles to guide the conduct of ethnographic research" (263). To encourage ethnographers to adhere more closely to these "sound principles," Heath and Athanases rightly call for increased attention to the methodological features of anthropological research models and then provide a guide for negotiating the dilemmas an ethnographer is likely to encounter—dilemmas such as selecting research sites and informants, identifying which data to analyze, and ensuring the credibility of what an ethnographer claims to know by enhancing a study's validity and reliability.

To repeat, I share these writers' concern with the epistemological legitimacy of our work: ethnographers have an obligation to employ sound investigative methods such as "triangulating" data sources, checking for consistency between informant descriptions and our field notes, and clarifying the theoretical frameworks we use to make sense of what we see and hear. We owe it to our audience and our subjects to make our accounts—however imperfect and subject to our inevitable cultural filtering—as valid as possible in terms of the contexts that give them meaning.

My hope, however, is that these important conversations regarding methodological rigor take place within a broader context that includes scrutiny of the relationships we ethnographers initiate when we go beyond studying our subjects and begin acting with them. For if we strive to be useful, that is, if we use our research to inform a praxis characterized by direct and overt intervention in others' lives in order to effect positive change, we are engaged in activities that give the ethical issues surrounding ethnography new urgency. In Addison, I began my work by observing classroom activities, recording conversations, and writing descriptions and analyses of what I saw and heard. Eventually, though, I found that what I was learning enabled (even compelled) me to involve myself in the lives of Claudia, Felipe, and the other ESL students more assertively than I had before. I began tutoring these students, acting as their advocate in their interactions with teachers, lobbying counselors and administrators to make changes in school policies that I thought would help language minority students succeed. From my earlier attempts to understand and represent Addison's LEP students, I knew that one cannot divorce the epistemological from the ethical. As my role as an ethnographer began to change, however, I grew more aware that acting for, or in the interest of, others has its own, and different, ethical dimensions.

Most acutely, my concern with treating ethnography as a form of social activism is that the sociocultural privilege most ethnographers possess may lead us to import notions from our own cultural perspectives about which actions constitute positive change and then to impose these notions on our subjects. Given this danger, ethnographers must be circumspect concerning the ways in which the changes we help bring about will influence (and be influenced by) the relationships we establish with the people to whom we are trying to be useful. Indeed, if we presume to act with our subjects to change their worlds, it seems to me that we are obligated to ask hard questions about who determines what those changes will be, whose cultural values they represent, and—ultimately— whom such changes will benefit. Ethnographers who ignore these questions risk obscuring the colonialist potential of their work. If, however, we acknowledge that what we do in our research sites is a complex process that requires reflection and negotiation with our subjects regarding how we should understand them and act with them, we move toward making our research sites spaces where people encounter each other in relationships of mutual influence. The kind of ethnography I'm advocating, then, is one guided by a theoretical framework which includes an ethical sensibility that keeps us from making our work essentially a one-way transfer of values and ways of thinking and living.

This way of understanding the research I am committed to in Addison is, in some ways, threatening, for it implies that *I* may need to change, to remove the blinders that allow me to see the world only from my own privileged position, to rethink the assumption that Angela, Claudia, and Juan want more than anything else to be like me. But even though a mutually influential exchange between ethnographers and their subjects introduces yet another dimension of complexity and uncertainty to our work, Giles Gunn reminds us that this uncertainty brings with it new possibilities: "Unless there is reciprocal modification of each category by the opposite, of self by other and other by self, there can be no increase in self-knowledge, no challenge to prior conceptions, no risk of personal confusion or disruption" (11). To be open to such disruption is, I have found, more difficult than we often realize, for we live and work immersed in a history of imperialism that spans from the conquistadors to the marketing department at Nike and that constantly reminds us that what is worthwhile is imported from *el norte*: As the ubiquitous slogan says, *"siempre Coca Cola."*

This colonial spirit—which encourages us to assume that we know what is in our subjects' interest and that affords us the ability to act upon this assumption—is certainly a banner I admit to having carried with me to Addison. Sometimes I marvel at the mobility I enjoy there, the opportunities I have to accomplish what I am tempted to see uncritically as so many constructive things. On a fairly typical day last spring I sat

through fourth-period science class with Angela. At the end of the period, as the students filed out of the room, Angela's teacher, the next
day's substitute, and the special education teacher who worked as an
aide in the class all gathered around me as I stashed my notebook and
tape recorder into my backpack. They talked to me for almost half an
hour of their lunch period: "It's so hard to teach the Latino students,"
they said. "What can we do? We don't speak Spanish." What interested
me most about that conversation is not so much what was said, but the
teachers' admission that, despite Angela's having attended Addison High
for over a year, it took place only when I, the Anglo from the university,
came to call.

But I had to tear myself away, had to make a phone call to Steve, the
Prentice-Hall sales representative, to see about getting Angela a copy of
the Life Science textbook in Spanish. "Sure, Todd," he said, "it should
arrive within a week." Next, on to the principal's office, where I pulled
him out of a meeting to explain why Angela shouldn't take a scheduled
test to determine whether she has a learning disability, the results of
which could land her in a special education class where I am convinced
she doesn't belong. "But, sir," I argued quietly in the hallway, "Of *course*
she'll test LD; she's missed four years of school, and she barely speaks
the language." I learned later that day that the test had been postponed
indefinitely. (By now, I felt Kipling's burden resting comfortably on my
shoulders.) But no time to gloat; I had to run to the middle school for a
meeting with Martinez about a plan I had to form writing groups among
Latino students. After that, back to the high school to translate Angela's
computer test. You know, sometimes I get on a roll; I dash around
Addison High doing so many good deeds that I surprise even myself,
and at the end of the day when I climb into my white Honda and drive
off toward the horizon, I can imagine those Latinos to whose aid I have
rushed looking after me in astonishment and gratitude and wondering
out loud: "Who was that blue-eyed man?"

And then I drive home, reflecting on what a splendid adventure the
day has been, recalling the words of Melville's Ishmael: "I love to sail
forbidden seas, and land on barbarous coasts" (8). Still, my day is not
over, for I now must write, and as the voices of the choir of King's College in Cambridge, England, rise from a compact disc and fill my apartment like perfume, I feed my field notes into a Macintosh, translating
my and Angela's experiences into a form that fits rather handsomely
into a dissertation chapter or conference paper. By and by, though, I
can't help thinking that those good deeds, all the attention I enjoyed,
this act of writing, represent—more than anything—power. And even
though I'm pleased that Angela won't be forced to attend special ed.

classes and that she was able to pass her computer test, I can't help wondering whether that power has done to me what it tends to do to everyone else.

Perhaps I'm overly concerned; after all, we're only talking about ethnographic research—research that carries the possibility of so many fruitful connections. Indeed, as Stephen North has written, "[ethnography's] power as a mode of inquiry . . . derives from its ability to keep one imaginative universe bumping into another" (284). Still, what concerns me is that if, in Addison, one imaginative universe bumps into another, I have a pretty good idea which one will be pushed to the margins, and chances are it's not going to be mine. bell hooks, caricaturing a privileged voice, has described the potential consequences of such "bumping" in this way:

> No need to hear your voice when I can talk about you better than you can speak about yourself. No need to hear your voice. Only tell me about your pain. I want to know your story. And then I will tell it back to you in a new way. Tell it back to you in such a way that it has become mine, my own. Re-writing you I write myself anew. I am still author, authority. I am still colonizer, the speaking subject, and you are now at the center of my talk. (151)

As hooks reminds us, there is great power in the language of our research. For insofar as the ethnographies we write influence the institutions we construct and our agency within those institutions, the ways we compose ourselves, the "other," and the relationship between us do have consequences that are very real. In March 1995, I had a conversation in the Addison High staff lounge with María, a Chicana and twenty-year veteran of the school's counseling staff. As I ate my sandwich, I mentioned that Claudia, who had become notorious for her truancy, was not in school that day. María grew strangely pensive and said in a quiet voice, "I worry about that girl." Thinking of the likelihood of Claudia's again failing most of her classes, I nodded as I chewed. But María continued: "Todd, I'm afraid she won't live very long. I've seen it before; girls like Claudia just get lost. Their families are poor; they drop out of school; and they wind up on the streets of Detroit or Toledo. I'm afraid that she'll die of AIDS or a drug overdose, or that someone, a pimp or a drug dealer, will kill her."

My lunch went heavy in my hand. For it had suddenly become clear to me that if we interpret what we see in our research sites inadvertently, and if we write impoverished stories leading only to cosmetic changes in the ways we teach while failing to critique the structures of domination in which we are comfortably situated, we are implicated in policies that are, quite literally, deadly serious. At that moment, questions of Claudia's schooling and of what she and I could do to improve it were granted new urgency as my mind fixed on the image of a full body bag lying in a Detroit morgue.

Usefulness Revisited: Contingency, Locality, and Critical Empathy

By now I hope it is clear that among my concerns regarding ethnography is that the epistemological and the ethical inevitably converge— that there is no legitimate way to dismiss the difficulties and consequences of negotiating the kinds of cultural and socioeconomic boundaries we often cross when we enter our research sites. In Addison, because of factors like my age, ethnicity, and education, I was undoubtedly "other" to Angela, Claudia, Juan, and Felipe. And ours was a relationship fraught with the danger that our interactions would be in no significant way "reciprocal," that I would be "useful" only in terms of my own understandings and aspirations.

At no time did I feel these dangers more acutely than late one night when I received a call from a Chicana friend of mine. This was a close friend; we had taken several classes together and spoke on the phone at least a couple of times a week. On this particular night, we began our conversation by chatting for a while about things I don't remember. I'll never forget, though, what happened next. She apologized in advance, then said she was no longer going to be my friend because of the work I was presuming to do with Latino students. She explained, using words like "colonialism" and "imperialistic." When I hung up the phone, I remained sitting on the floor between my living room and kitchen, my back leaning against the frame of the doorway. I thought hard about Juan, Claudia, Felipe, and Angela. I wondered whether my inability to understand completely these students' experience might cause me to impose upon them my own values, whether by my research and tutoring I was encouraging them to act and think in ways that are legitimated by my own sociocultural perspective rather than theirs, whether my desire to finish my graduate degree was leading me to exploit them despite my good intentions. I wondered whether it would be better if I just stayed away.

I decided to keep driving to Addison, for I am convinced that to stay away is itself a form of action. To ignore is to neglect, and while George Bernard Shaw was right when he cautioned us against the objectifying arrogance displayed by Henry Higgins, he was equally astute to remind us that "The worst sin towards our fellow creatures is not to hate them, but to be indifferent to them; that is the essence of inhumanity." It is good that we hesitate at *fronteras* of ethnicity, gender, language, or social class. We have ample reason to pause and wonder whether we should take that next step and presume to participate in the lives of others, as I was participating in the education of Addison's ESL students. But eventually, I think, we must ask ourselves this: what kind of world do we want to live in? Is it one where, because of the potentially exploitative complexities of encountering "the other," we despair altogether of attempting such connections? Is it one where we resolve to live and work only in enclaves with our "own kind" (whoever that may be)? In my view, such isolationism is not only undesirable but also impossible, for the real question is not *whether* we will interact with those who are "different" from us, but *how* we will do so. Thus, despite—or, perhaps, because of—the high stakes, I have dared to hope that my education, my native language, and the color of my skin do not necessarily disqualify me from the work I am attempting to do. The fact that I am Anglo does not, in my mind, afford me the comfort of a hermeneutic and ethical paralysis that would absolve me from what I see as a responsibility to address some very pressing needs.

What my position of privilege *does* require is that I make that privilege a central part of the framework from which I view my work, that I constantly ask what that power means and how my own culturally embedded assumptions may influence what I see (or don't see), what I do (or don't do). We must try, in other words, to understand what Maxine Greene calls the "layers of determinateness"—those "effects of class membership, economic status, physical limitations, as well as the impacts of exclusion and ideology" (8–9)—that lead us to assume that we know what is best for others and that allow us mistakenly to define "success" in our terms rather than theirs.[7]

I should admit here that my own priorities and those of the students with whom I have worked are not always at odds. Usually, for instance, we agree that education is valuable. However, what keeps me from being completely sure that my own conclusions are consistent with the plans and desires of Addison High's Latinos is my memory of people situated in authoritative positions—teachers, administrators, tutors from the university—who confidently (and incorrectly) tell Latino students what they need. I have heard, for instance, Latino students being informed that they would benefit from being submerged in all-English content area classes, from canceling plans for an all-Latino student club in order to promote Addison's ethnic unity, and from attending after-school tutoring sessions rather than hurrying off to what one tutor called "a dead-end job." The fact that Latino students saw these suggestions as contrary to their interests suggests, I think, that once we base our understandings of what we should do in our research sites not solely on our own social and cultural perspectives but on those with whom we work, we open the possibility that we may contribute to our subjects' acquiring increased social and political freedom in the form of greater power to chose how they live their lives. This freedom, as Greene argues, should not be understood as the "negative freedom" of deregulation, self-dependence, and unreflective consumerism (7). Rather, it is a freedom that must be "an achievement within the concreteness of lived social situations," a purposeful activity in which people are able to name the causes of their oppression, "imagine a better state of things," and "share with others a project of change" (9).

To think of our work as an attempt not just to understand others but also to strive with them to rectify real problems is to conceive of the role of the social scientist as going beyond (though, again, including), for instance, my documenting what Angela does in class or conducting interviews with her. Rather, such a revision challenges the prescriptive nature of anthropology rooted in colonialism and places a new emphasis on how I am to *be together* with her in a relationship that encourages the type of freedom Greene describes.

Just what this relationship entails and, specifically, what the role of the social scientist should be within it is a subject John Dewey takes up in the final pages of *The Public and Its Problems*. In *Public*, Dewey is primarily concerned with describing the "conditions which must be fulfilled if the Great Society is to become a great Community; a society in which the ever-expanding and intricately ramifying consequences of associated activities shall be known in the full sense of the word, so that an organized, articulate Public comes into being" (350). Because the "articulate Public" depends upon bringing people together to participate in democratized communities, Dewey's explanation of the role of the social sciences in this process provides several useful guidelines to those who seek what I have called an "ethically attentive" ethnographic method.

First, Dewey contends that social scientists serving the interests of democracy must deny absolutist notions of desirable social action. To Dewey, whatever recommendations researchers offer (if we offer them at all) as a result of our investigations must be appropriate to the particular contexts of our inquiry; that is, we must acknowledge the *contingency* of possible courses of action: "A solution, or distributive adjustment, needed at one time is totally unfitted to another situation" (356). Once these possible solutions are implemented, Dewey argues for flexibility and adaptability—or policies and proposals to be treated "as working hypotheses, not as programs to be rigidly adhered to and exhausted." These programs, he contends "will be experimental in the sense that they will be entertained subject to constant and well-equipped observation of the consequences they entail when acted upon, and subject to ready and flexible revision in the light of observed consequences" (361–62).

When I first arrived in Addison, I had what I thought was a wonderful plan. I hoped to work with teachers to form writing and tutorial groups among Latino students—those who were fully bilingual and those who were considered "limited English proficient." These groups, I reasoned, would enable the non-English speakers to learn the language of Addison High more efficiently; to receive assistance in math, geography, and science while they learned English; and eventually to pass their classes, graduate, and move on to college or a comfortable career. What I discovered by and by, however, was that my best-laid plans were based on my own assumptions about what those students needed—assumptions based on some ideologically foundationalist notions of what was worth learning and what type of life was worth living. I was planning for their "success" as it is defined within a cultural/educational system that legitimates who *I* am, the maintenance of which is certainly in *my* best interests.

It's not that my original plan was terribly misguided. Like almost all ESL teachers I know, I still think that, in most cases, it's a good idea for Latino students to learn English and to further their education—especially if they plan to remain in the United States. Nonetheless, what I learned from observing and listening to Addison High's Latino students was that any project designed to work in their interests must respond to a wide range of academic and sociocultural issues that may have been left unattended by my initial plan. For instance, because students like Angela and Claudia had an immediate need to pass their classes, I spent much of my time relearning and tutoring basic math and science. One afternoon I found Felipe, an all-state wrestler, crying in a corner of the library because he was unable to read "The Cask of Amontillado," which was printed in English. He was especially upset because he had to pass sophomore English in order to remain eligible to wrestle. We spent the next several weeks working together during his study hall, reading his assignments, writing his essays—first in Spanish, then in English.

But the particular "solutions" in which I participated, those contingent responses, were not limited strictly to schoolwork. With Felipe, my being useful included helping him write a letter to his new girlfriend, who lived in Chicago. With Juan, I worked on filling out his application to work at the local Red Lobster restaurant. With Angela, I learned that I could be most useful by not bothering her, but by sitting across the room and waiting—simply being available. I don't wish to suggest here that these somewhat eclectic efforts are all that is required of those who wish to work toward Dewey's Great Community. Indeed, the type of collective action Dewey advocates is more reflective, deliberate, and broader in scope than these examples imply. Still, the point here is that what I initially thought would be useful and what Felipe, Juan, and Angela found useful were often very different things.

Dewey's argument that social action should be a response that is contingent upon specific circumstances suggests a second guideline for social scientists: namely, that because decisions regarding social action should be determined locally within communities characterized by democratic participation, the social scientist must assume no special prominence in planning and implementing social policy. As James Gouinlock has noted, Dewey is emphatic that social scientists in a democratic society would have no authority to prescribe solutions to social problems. "Instead, they would devote themselves to determining how the complex and powerful forces in society actually function. . . . In this way the knowledge needed by the public would be provided" (xxxii). Indeed, Dewey's crucial innovation regarding the "knowledge" generated by the social sciences comes in the way this knowledge is used and by whom, for while he concedes that the processes of inquiry and the dissemination of their conclusions "is a work which devolves upon experts," the framing and executing of policies is the business of communities operating in "face-to-face intercourse" (367).

This call for the social scientist to inform rather than to persuade (or coerce) an articulate Public suggests that, here in these local spaces, the role of the social scientist is to enter into relationships with others in which all participants share information and decision-making power. If I as an ethnographer am able to view my work as this process of forming equitable (even intimate) relationships with "the other," my time in Addison becomes not just a means to an end, but is itself a form of social activism—an ongoing enterprise of working with others on terms and toward goals that are mutually determined. Thus, my "real work," my genuine opportunity to be useful, does not begin when I write a journal article or deliver a conference paper. Rather, it is already occurring when I recommend to Felipe's study hall monitor that he be allowed to work with a bilingual friend, when Juan calls me over to help him summarize a story for English homework, when I ask Claudia for advice on how I might help my daughter resolve a conflict with a friend, or even when I sit in the back row of science class and wait for Angela to ask me a question. Ethnography, according to this understanding, becomes not a preparatory act, but is itself—as Dewey describes the Great Community he envisions—"a distinctive way of behaving in conjunction and connection with other distinctive ways of acting" (352–53).

In order to head off any possible misunderstanding of my present emphasis on relationships, I should emphasize that Dewey is arguing not for something as limited (or potentially trivializing) as isolated, individual "friendships." As Richard Sennett has argued, a society's emphasis on intimacy can be immobilizing if the "open expression of feeling" supplants individuals' desire and ability to act together as a public (11). Rather, Dewey's goal is a broad, systematized, society-wide transformation—a collective establishment and nurturing of a Great Community. Nonetheless, when we consider how this process must begin at the local level, definitions of "usefulness" previously thought of strictly in terms of sociopolitical policy tend to be recast to include questions of personal disposition. In other words, the question asked by, say, an ethnographer desiring to be useful becomes not so much "What can I do to/for others?" but "What is the nature of my relationship with this person? How can/should we *be together?*"

It seems to me that in order to ask these questions and to use them to help ourselves understand the role of the social scientist in democratic communities, we must strive toward exercising what Jay Robinson in classroom conversations has called "critical empathy": the process of establishing informed connections with other human beings, of thinking and feeling with them at some emotionally, intellectually, and socially significant level, while always remembering that such connections are complicated by sociohistorical forces that hinder the equitable, just relationships that Dewey (and, presumably, we) desire. Critical empathy is a hopeful but cautious concept—at once a unifying condition and a constantly mutable process that is possible only while looking inward, outward, around, backward, and forward. It is a disposition which urges us to understand the powerful structures and ideologies that seek to constrain us to think and act in prescribed (often exploitative) ways, while at the same time challenging us to break free from those constraints, to find room to maneuver with the other toward positive social change.

Critical empathy demands that I admit that I don't understand what it's like to be uprooted from my home and forced by poverty to relocate in an area where many people—politicians in their campaign speeches, administrators and teachers in the schools, other young people who live on my street—view my family and me as part of an alien "invasion," a threat to the moral and economic health of this country. Critical empathy enables me to feel the affection Felipe describes for his grandmother, whose picture he takes from his wallet and shows me in study hall; it suggests the possibility that the second-period ESL students and I might work together toward making Addison Public High more responsive to the public it allegedly serves. At the same time, critical empathy makes me keenly aware that when I delivered my last conference paper in a hotel ballroom filled with Anglo academics and graced by the light of chandeliers—a paper that discussed how literacy might serve the interests of democracy and justice—almost all of the people busily refilling water pitchers and making the beds upstairs were Latino.

Turning the Glass on Ourselves

I have said that being useful in Addison was difficult, that in my privileged situation lies the potential for making my work there yet another chapter in the long history of oppression. I have argued, too, that Dewey offers a productive way of understanding the role of social scientists who care about the interests of democracy, and that a crucial aspect of this role is to understand it as a relationship, a way of "being together" that is characterized by "critical empathy." In this final section, I will reflect on what I see as some of the additional consequences such an approach to our work will have for us as researchers.

As I have suggested, working toward the kind of community-building empathy Dewey and Robinson encourage requires that we scrutinize ourselves as a part of the process of understanding our relationships with others. We must peel back the "layers of determinateness," not expecting to find a "real self" underneath, but to understand more clearly how those layers themselves constitute who we are in that they influence our interactions (i.e., *how* we are) with others. Cornel West points out the need for this type of self-reflection in his definition of "prophetic criticism," which I see as closely aligned with notions of the Great Community and critical empathy. "Prophetic criticism," West writes, "is first and foremost an intellectual inquiry constitutive of existential democracy—*a self-critical and self-corrective enterprise* of human 'sense-making' for the preserving and expanding of human empathy and compassion" (xi, my italics).

Indeed, for West, "sense-making" that fosters "human empathy and compassion" relies not on a general criticism of society in a depersonalized, generic sense; rather, prophetic criticism demands a self-criticism which must be exactly that—a critique of the self, of me, and of the nature of my connections with others. To exact this kind of scrutiny is a difficult step to take, for to ask these questions is, for many of us, to critique our own positions as researchers whose privilege is grounded in our sociocultural status and in the assumption of our expertise. It follows, I believe, that to engage in such self-criticism honestly requires that we stop clutching our degrees and our supposedly detached methodologies to ourselves like fig leaves and to confront the frailties—and even the pain—that our privilege conceals. James Baldwin in *The Fire Next Time* articulates what our research and, in particular, the self-reflection that I believe must be a part of that research, demand:

> [A] vast amount of the white anguish is rooted in the white man's
> . . . profound need to be seen as he is, to be released from the tyranny of his mirror. All of us know, whether or not we are able to admit it, that mirrors can only lie, that death by drowning is all that awaits one there. It is for this reason that love is so desperately sought and so cunningly avoided. Love takes off the masks that we fear we cannot live without and know we cannot live within. I use the word 'love' here . . . in the tough and universal sense of quest and daring and growth. (95)

To be sure, Baldwin understands that "what we do not know about the other reveals, precisely and inexorably, what we do not know about ourselves." He sees the connection between our own well-being and a "tough," "daring," transforming love for others. Such a "quest" is uncertain; it demands a breaking free from the familiar, the comfortable. But there is hope, for as we wander, afraid to remove our masks and to heal, bell hooks steps into our path, holds up her hand, and speaks as a voice of the "other" who must—for all our sakes—be heard: "Stop. We greet you as liberators. This 'we' is that 'us' in the margins, that 'we' who inhabit marginal space that is not a site of domination but a place of resistance. This is an intervention. I am writing to you" (152).

Me, bell? Me, Angela? Liberation from what? hooks is talking, I think, about liberation in terms of a fundamental change in the way we teachers and researchers see our role in the world. She is talking about encountering others within a space of "recognition and understanding, where we know one another so well, our histories, that we can take the bits and pieces, the fragments of who we are, and put them back together, re-member them" (214). In sites where this type of re-membering can occur, ethnography becomes not a prescriptive, potentially colonialistic enterprise, but a chance for us to grow through our connections with others—interactions that keep us challenging ourselves and seeing ourselves in new ways. She urges the transformation of what was once our offering our hand in a gesture of assumed generosity into a grasping for emotional and spiritual freedom—a self-knowledge enabling us to understand more completely the parameters that restrict our acting in ways that help us realize our potential as human beings.

Though this type of "re-membering" may be accomplished only through struggle, through an unsettling disclosure of assumptions and power matrices that shape potentially exploitative relationships, I believe hooks's and Baldwin's (and Dewey's) words articulate an opportunity to be more than I am now, for as the Peruvian theologian Gustavo Gutierrez has argued, an awareness of the need for self-liberation is essential to a correct understanding of the liberation that is part of Dewey's transformation from society to community:

> [Liberation] is not a matter of "struggling for others," which suggests paternalism and reformist objectives, but rather of becoming aware of oneself as not completely fulfilled and as living in an alienated society. And thus one can identify radically and militantly with those—the people and the social class—who bear the brunt of oppression. (146)

I am convinced that the possibility of such liberation—for "the other" and for ourselves—depends upon the type of reciprocal modification called for by Baldwin and hooks, which is to say that the "fundamental, structural overhaul" of oppressive institutions Dewey advocates needs to begin, and end, in some very private spaces. But if a commitment to changing society requires a commitment to changing our selves, it seems to me that we must ask additional questions: how far are we willing to go in this crusade for democratization? What is the extent of the sacrifices we are truly willing to make in our efforts to establish a Great Community? I continue to ask these questions because even after three years, I struggle with whether I can (or even want to) "identify radically and militantly" with Addison's ESL students and whether I need to do so in order to engage in collective action with them.

And so I continue to assess the ethical validity of my work, especially since the personal investment I have made is so tentative, so dependent upon my own schedule and priorities. I can get behind the wheel of my car and be back to the comfortable books and scholarly conversations of Ann Arbor in an hour. One summer I was thinking about giving up my apartment near the University and moving to Addison, where rents are lower and where I could involve myself more completely in the world of Addison High's LEP students. A professor, however, cautioned me: "Be careful; you may need to get away sometimes." I thought of my friends nearby, the swimming pool at my apartment complex, the schedule of interesting films coming through town. I renewed my lease.

After my experiences in Addison, I honestly don't know whether my pursuing a terminal degree and tenure is a socially sanctioned form of hypocrisy—whether I should feel guilty that I can drop Felipe off at his house in the *barrio*, watch him walk up the warped steps of his sagging front porch, and then rush home in order to catch *La Traviata* at the University's performing arts center; whether, in order to be able to think of myself as "truly committed" to students like Claudia, I would need to sell everything I have and follow a selfless life not often modeled or rewarded in academia.

For now, I can only repeat what I have already said: that in order to be "useful," I must rely on a disposition, a way of participating in a dialogical relationship with "the other" in which we are somehow able to struggle together to identify and overcome forces of oppression—though these forces are very different for Angela than they are for me. Again, I don't wish to suggest that the expertise we gain from consistent and rigorous methodology has no value. My way of understanding what goes on at Addison High is something useful that I can bring to my relationships with the teachers and students there, and if I don't have anything more substantial to offer to people like Claudia and Felipe than my own good will, then I shouldn't think about traveling to Addison to encourage mutual action with them. Nonetheless, even though students may benefit from our advocacy, I believe we should be cautious about assuming what we know about these students and how we can be useful to them. Such caution is like the chafing seams of an ill-fitting shirt, keeping us uncomfortable, keeping us aware of our every move.

Thus, my view of what constitutes "good deeds" has changed since I began driving to Addison several years ago. I find that I am now more patient, more humble in the sense of being unsure of what might be "the right thing to do." In our interactions with those whom we study, I argue, then, for a provisional and restless peace. My hope is that teachers and researchers, invigorated by a desire to be useful, may learn to live with this paradox, may seek to establish relationships characterized by an ethical attentiveness which forsakes self-serving, isolating ideologies in favor of those that strive to effect justice through connections with others. I am convinced, finally, that the impetus to effect these changes, to revise what we desire, must take place in the hearts and minds of people living and working face-to-face, *cara-a-cara* with each other.

Notes

1. "Addison" and all names of students and teachers in this essay are pseudonyms.

2. LEP refers to students whose lack of facility in the English language may have negative consequences for their academic achievement in monolingual classes (Nieto 155).

3. Michigan is home to approximately forty-five thousand migrant workers and is the nation's fourth largest user of transient migrant workers (*Michigan's Hispanic Community: A Profile* 3).

4. Source: Marilyn McMillen, *Dropout Rates in the United States, 1992.*

5. See Todd DeStigter, *Los Olvidados: Literacy, Ethnography, and the Forgotten Students of Addison High, Dissertation Abstracts International,* Vol. 57, 1996.

6. See Geertz, "Thick Description."

7. Greene's emphasis on being able to imagine possibilities beyond those that are readily apparent is echoed in Gunn's notion of "thinking across" culture: "If we cannot think against culture, we can at least think across it. To think across culture rather than against it is to suppose that even if we can think in no other terms than those our culture provides, we do not have to accept the valuations that culture currently places on them" (1).

Works Cited

Addams, Jane. 1990. *Twenty Years at Hull-House.* Urbana: University of Illinois Press.

Athanases, Steven Z., and Shirley Brice Heath. 1995. "Ethnography in the Study of the Teaching and Learning of English." *Research in the Teaching of English* 29: 263–87.

Baldwin, James. 1993. *The Fire Next Time.* New York: Vintage Books.

Clifford, James. 1986. Introduction, "Impartial Truths." *Writing Culture: The Poetics and Politics of Ethnography.* Eds. James Clifford and George E. Marcus. Berkeley: University of California Press. 1–26.

Dewey, John. 1988. *The Public and Its Problems. John Dewey, The Later Works, 1925–1953. Vol. 2: 1925–1927.* Ed. Jo Ann Boydston. Carbondale and Edwardsville: Southern Illinois University Press. 235–372.

"Experts Call Educational Gap a Threat." 1995. *USA Today.* 6 September, 1–2.

Geertz, Clifford. 1983. *Local Knowledge: Further Essays in Interpretive Anthropology.* New York: Basic Books.

———. 1973. "Thick Description: Toward an Interpretive Theory of Culture." *The Interpretation of Cultures.* New York: Basic Books. 3–30.

———. 1988. *Works and Lives: The Anthropologist As Author.* Stanford: Stanford University Press.

Gouinlock, James. 1988. Introduction to *John Dewey, The Later Works, 1925–1953.* ix–xxxvi.

Greene, Maxine. 1988. *The Dialectic of Freedom.* New York: Teachers College Press.

Gunn, Giles. 1992. *Thinking Across the American Grain: Ideology, Intellect, and the New Pragmatism.* Chicago: University of Chicago Press.

Gutierrez, Gustavo. 1988. *A Theology of Liberation: History, Politics, and Salvation.* Maryknoll, New York: Orbis Books.

Hoffman, Eva. 1989. *Lost in Translation: A Life in a New Language.* New York: Dutton.

hooks, bell. 1990. *Yearning: Race, Gender, and Cultural Politics.* Boston: South End Press.

Lyotard, Jean-Francois. 1984. *The Postmodern Condition: A Report on Knowledge.* Minneapolis: University of Minnesota Press.

Marcus, George E., and Michael M. J. Fisher. 1986. *Anthropology As Cultural Critique: An Experimental Moment in the Human Sciences.* Chicago: University of Chicago Press.

McMillen, Marilyn. 1992. *Dropout Rates in the United States, 1992.* Berkeley: MRP Associates, sponsored by the National Center for Educational Statistics, Washington D.C. September.

Melville, Herman. 1976. *Moby-Dick.* New York: Norton.

Michigan's Hispanic Community: A Profile. 1990. Michigan Commission on Spanish Speaking Affairs. Department of Civil Rights. Lansing, Michigan.

Nieto, Sonia. 1992. "Linguistic Diversity in Multicultural Classrooms." *Affirming Diversity: The Sociopolitical Context of Multicultural Education.* New York: Longman. 153–88.

North, Stephen. 1987. *The Making of Knowledge in Composition: Portrait of an Emerging Field.* Portsmouth, NH: Heinemann.

Ogbu, John. 1986. "Anthropology of Education." *International Encyclopedia of Education.* Eds. T. Husen and N. Postlethwaite. Oxford: Pergamon Press. 276–98.

Sennett, Richard. 1977. *The Fall of Public Man.* New York: Knopf.

Shaw, George Bernard. 1952. *The Devil's Disciple.* Act II. *Three Plays for Puritans.* London: Constable and Co. 1–82.

West, Cornel. 1993. *Keeping Faith: Philosophy and Race in America.* New York: Routledge.

3 Three Codifications of Critical Literacy

Thomas Philion
University of Illinois at Chicago

Reading the world always precedes reading the word, and reading the word implies continually reading the world. As I suggested earlier, this movement from the word to the world is always present; even the spoken word flows from our reading of the world. In a way, however, we can go further and say that reading the word is not preceded merely by reading the world, but by a certain form of writing it or rewriting it, that is, of transforming it by means of conscious, practical work. For me, this dynamic movement is central to the literacy process.

For this reason, I have always insisted that the words used in organizing a literacy program come from what I call the "word universe" of people who are learning, expressing their actual language, their anxieties, their fears, demands, and dreams. Words should be laden with the meaning of the people's existential experience, and not of the teacher's experience. Surveying the word universe gives us the people's words, pregnant with the world, words from the people's reading of the world. We then give the words back to the people inserted in what I call "codifications," pictures representing real situations. The word brick, for example, might be inserted in a pictorial representation of a group of bricklayers constructing a house.

—Paulo Freire

Internally persuasive discourse—as opposed to one that is externally authoritative—is, as it is affirmed through assimilation, tightly interwoven with "one's own word." In the everyday rounds of our consciousness, the internally persuasive word is half-ours and half-someone else's. Its creativity and productiveness consist precisely in the fact that such a word awakens new and independent words, that it organizes masses of our words from within, and does not remain in an isolated and static condition. It is not so much interpreted by us as it is further, that is, freely, developed, applied to new material, new conditions; it enters into interanimating relationships with new contexts. More than that, it enters into an intense interaction, a struggle with other internally persuasive discourses. Our ideological development is just such an intense struggle within

53

us for hegemony among various available verbal and ideological points of view, approaches, directions and values. The semantic structure of an internally persuasive discourse is not finite, it is open; in each of the new contexts that dialogize it, this discourse is able to reveal ever newer ways to mean.

—M. M. Bakhtin

I have been invited by the editors of this collection to pose questions and to raise problems with regard to the notion of critical literacy. The particular questions that most preoccupy me at the present time are ones that I have formulated in the context of my engagement with passages such as the one above by M. M. Bakhtin. What happens when assumptions such as those articulated by Paulo Freire are applied by teachers to materials and conditions that Freire does not specifically describe in his work? In other words, what happens when the discourse of critical literacy enters into an interanimating relationship with more conventional but equally persuasive pedagogical discourses and points of view? How do teachers committed to critical literacy negotiate such dialogic interactions, and what new assumptions and practices do they develop as a consequence of their negotiations?

I pose these questions because, in my experience, educators committed to critical literacy rarely undertake their conscious, practical work in environments that unequivocally welcome or support their pedagogical goals and methods. In fact, as several ethnographies of contemporary education suggest, the prevailing environment of literacy education might be described as largely hostile to the assumptions outlined by Paulo Freire in my epigraph (Everhart 1983; Willis 1977; Heath 1983; and Fine 1991). Given the oppositional nature of the discourse of critical literacy, it seems to me incumbent upon us as educators committed to critical literacy not only to create cogent arguments for and descriptions of a pedagogy informed by Freire's notion of reading words and the world, but also to study and to reflect upon the verbal and ideological struggle that almost always accompanies the process of attempting to foster critical literacy. Detailed accounts of such struggles might re-assure literacy educators who seek to follow in Freire's footsteps that they are not alone in their efforts to negotiate a complicated educational environment that offers only limited support to them and their teaching. Correspondingly, such detailed accounts might prepare educators just beginning to explore the words and ideas of Paulo Freire for the struggles that they themselves undoubtedly will face if they commit themselves to his ideas. Most important—and here again I draw upon the insights of Bakhtin—detailed accounts of ideological and verbal struggle might reveal new and provocative ways *to mean* with regard to the theory and practice of critical literacy itself.

In the pages that follow, I present three codifications of actual contexts in which I have attempted to practice and/or to nurture critical literacy for the purpose of inscribing just such a Bakhtinian account of verbal and ideological struggle in the context of critical literacy education. Each of my codifications consists of a picture and a detailed "account" of my experience in the context represented in or by the picture.[1] Following each of these codifications, I highlight the assumptions and practices that I associated with the notion of critical literacy at that particular moment in time, and I reflect upon the way in which I negotiated the ideological and verbal conflicts that circumscribed my efforts to apply the discourse of critical literacy to new materials and new situations. In my conclusion, I evaluate the nature of my pedagogical evolution as represented by these codifications, and I propose a modest revision in the prevailing discourse with regard to critical literacy.

My goals in undertaking this self-reflexive project are three-fold: First, I hope to advance a notion that I myself did not appreciate enough when I first began to conceive of critical literacy as an important goal of my teaching; that is, that each person needs to create his or her own approach to critical literacy, and that there are no fixed or certain formulas for nurturing it. Second, I wish to highlight the way in which "mainstream" or "traditional" pedagogical practices and/or assumptions can interact with assumptions and/or practices associated with critical literacy for the purpose of creating a classroom environment in which students feel empowered to read and write critically and to change the world.[2] Finally, I hope to teach myself through my writing; that is, by describing and reflecting upon my diverse efforts to foster critical literacy, I hope to obtain a better understanding of who I have been and who I may yet become as a literacy educator. In doing so, I model a powerful means of educational change and reform, what Ann Berthoff terms REsearch, or "looking—and looking again" (33).

Codification One: English 319, "Theater and Social Change"

In September of 1984, I enroll in a graduate program in English Language and Literature at the University of Michigan. Before I move to Ann Arbor from New York City, I receive a letter from Buzz Alexander, a professor in the Department of English, inviting me to work as a graduate assistant in his upper-division English course "Vietnam and the Artist." I accept Buzz's invitation and, upon my arrival in Ann Arbor, I am introduced to an inspiring critical pedagogy. On Tuesdays, Buzz lectures to his one hundred or so students about various films that he has selected as the content of his course. In his lectures, Buzz presents a sophisticated Marxist critique of art and culture, and he weaves into his critique stories about his own and others' responses to the Vietnam War. On Thursdays, after we have viewed the assigned film, Buzz invites discussion and commentary upon his lectures, the film, and related issues. I participate in these discussions, and I observe the way in which Buzz's lectures and the films themselves provoke lively political and aesthetic debate. More important, I observe a vivid connection between our classroom discussion and actions in the larger world. For example, as I learn about why many people protested the Vietnam War, I also learn about current protests at the University of Michigan against the CIA and academic research sponsored by the United States Department of Defense.

My participation in "Vietnam and the Artist" is inspiring, but it also poses for me an unanticipated dilemma. Rarely—if ever—do professors in my other graduate classes create the clear connection between textual study and social action that Buzz fosters in "Vietnam and the Artist." I begin to feel that graduate education constitutes an avoidance of the world rather than an engagement with it, and I question my decision to pursue a career in higher education. Influenced by the way in which Buzz calls into question his own and others' values and actions, I begin to reflect upon my own beliefs and my intentions with regard to my future work. I ask myself: what sort of English teacher do I want to become? What kind of students do I wish to teach? What sort of political commitments do I wish to articulate, and what sort of community do I wish to serve and to help create?

During my second semester at Michigan, I explore questions such as these in the context of "Theater and Social Change," a new undergraduate course that Buzz teaches and in which I enroll as a student. I read Paulo Freire's Pedagogy of the Oppressed, *Jonathan Kozol's* The Night Is Dark and I Am Far From Home *and* On Being a Teacher, *and Augusto Boal's* Theater of the Oppressed, *and I participate in discussions about these texts. I also read and discuss various plays that raise political issues and that purposefully seek to shape audiences' responses to those issues. Toward the end of this experience, I help to create a guerrilla theater group called "The Pinkertons." In our first "action," Buzz, myself, and several other University of Michigan students infiltrate the line of a movie theater in downtown Ann Arbor in order to inform moviegoers about the recent firing of two experienced union projectionists (see Figure 1). Thereafter, our actions become more visible and dramatic, and we initiate with others in our community a boycott of the theater chain responsible for the firings. In my final paper for "Theater and Social Change," I share with Buzz my decision to return to New York City upon the completion of my Masters degree in order to become a high school English teacher. Citing Buzz's critical pedagogy as a model for my own, I explain that I hope to engage my future students in reading, writing, and thinking that forwards the creation of community and systematic social change.*

Figure 1. The author performing in a guerilla theater action.

I begin with this pictorial and written codification of my experience in classes taught by Buzz Alexander because it represents what I still consider an exemplary model of critical literacy. In "Vietnam and the Artist" and "Theater and Social Change," I felt myself invited to read words and the world, and to re-write the same. I also observed and practiced useful techniques with regard to surveying and situating teaching within the word universe of learners. Perhaps most important, I felt myself powerfully changed by Buzz's teaching such that I began to conceive of critical literacy as an important goal of my own teaching.

The assumptions that I developed as a result of this experience parallel the assumptions that Freire outlines in my epigraph. First and foremost, I learned that critical literacy entails involvement in the multidimensional activity of reading, writing, speaking, and listening. In "Vietnam and the Artist" and "Theater and Social Change," I observed the way in which Buzz engaged his students in these different but related activities; Buzz moved his students dynamically among lectures, films, journal writing, literature, and participation in large and small group conversations. Additionally, Buzz invited his students to develop final projects that integrated these different activities and that drew upon other forms of expression such as art, music, video, and drama. Critical literacy, as I came to understand it in this context, was an enterprise broad enough to include a wide range of social and aesthetic practices. Nurturing critical literacy, I learned, requires that teachers create opportunities for learners to engage in and to develop fluency in a dynamic mode of expression of their own choosing.

A second assumption I developed was the idea that critical literacy consists of dynamic movement between reading words and reading the world. In particular, two methods of nurturing this dynamic movement were conveyed to me: one was to create a curriculum both provocative and explicitly political, and the other was to create contexts for classroom conversation in which learners could reflect upon the relation between the words that they had read and the world from which these words were drawn or to which they might be applied. Curricula such as the ones that Buzz developed invited discussion of political issues and reflection upon one's stance in relation to such issues: open-ended conversations in which students were invited to identify issues and to explore relations between texts and personal or public experiences served the same purpose. In my mind, the notion of critical literacy became linked with the organization of an overtly political or issue-oriented curriculum and with the implementation of student- or response-centered techniques of classroom discussion.

As I watched Buzz enact this approach to critical literacy, I couldn't help but notice the way in which he attempted to develop his students' commitment to the creation of radical or systematic social change. In the context of his lectures and his classroom conversations, Buzz invited his students to intervene in the world for the purpose of subverting traditional hierarchies and attitudes and creating reciprocal relations amongst people. Consequently, I acquired the notion that intervention in the world did not merely entail writing about it; rather, intervention in the world meant taking political, personal, aesthetic, and material risks for the purpose of challenging dominant political norms and expectations. The street dramas of the Pinkertons are one useful model of this sort of inter-vention, I believe. By writing, speaking, and—most important—acting in the world beyond the classroom, the Pinkertons engaged in the sort of conscious, practical work of which Freire speaks. To nurture critical literacy, I came to believe, teachers have to create classroom conditions whereby students can engage actively in re-writing and re-envisioning the world beyond the classroom.

Two other important assumptions emerged in my consciousness as a result of my interactions with and observation of Buzz's teaching. One was that critical literacy could only be nurtured in the context of attend-ing carefully to the word universe of learners. Through his teaching, Buzz modeled for me how to engage in this activity; in the first few weeks of "Theater and Social Change," Buzz invited me and other stu-dents over to his house for a potluck dinner and an in-depth introduc-tion. Throughout the semester, Buzz built upon this event by asking his students to share with one another not only their readings of texts, but also their responses to his teaching and to various other activities taking place on campus or in the world beyond. In parallel fashion, before we Pinkertons developed our street dramas, we researched carefully the lives of the union projectionists who had been fired from their jobs, and we examined with equal care the rationale and events that led up to the firing. Through my participation in these activities, and my observation of Buzz's teaching, I became aware of the importance of surveying stu-dents and their word universes, and of then helping students to engage in this same practice in relation to the subjects of their own writing and teaching.

Not only did I learn to attend to the word universes of others, but I also became aware of the importance of situating literacy programs within the word universes of learners. One practice I associated with this assumption, in addition to those described above, was Buzz's use of student vernacular for the purpose of developing insight with regard to radical concepts and practices. By subverting the traditional rhetori-cal distance between teachers and students, and by articulating an emo-tional but intellectually provocative discourse, Buzz presented the ideas and practices of radical intellectuals such that they came to be under-stood, for many of his students, within the context of a personally mean-ingful word and world universe. Again, my experience with the Pinkertons provided me with additional insight into that lesson. Typi-cally, our street dramas drew upon language and rhetorical devices fa-miliar to our audience. For example, in the performance that is repre-sented in Figure 1, an overly confident corporate owner (whom I repre-sent in the center of the picture) sweeps into town and buys a movie theater; thereafter, he expresses, to the tune of "Oklahoma," the joy he feels as a result of his decision to replace union projectionists with unskilled minimum-wage workers. This articulation of words and sound familiar to our audience helped to create a dialogic context such that many moviegoers considered (and some even acted upon) the challenging appeal articulated later in our performance that they step out of line for the purpose of indicating solidarity with fired union workers.

The assumptions and practices, then, that I learned to associate with critical literacy were fluid classroom conversations, experienced in both small and large groups; the creation of a curriculum that provokes reflection upon political issues and that provides a motivation for conscious, practical work in the world; creative final projects and classroom activities in which students engage in dynamic movement between reading, writing, listening, speaking, and other modes of expression; attention to the words and worlds of learners; and conscious, practical work aimed at the creation of progressive or radical social change. This last assumption is one that I understood to be most important: the need to create connections between classrooms and other contexts such that students begin not only to re-write words in the classroom, but words and worlds beyond.

Although I cannot say that I experienced any significant verbal or ideological conflict with regard to Buzz's critical pedagogy, I did choose to ignore two additional assumptions that informed Buzz's approach to his teaching. In designing "Theater and Social Change," Buzz limited his enrollment to those students who expressed a commitment to changing the world in ways that Freire implies; that is, from a Marxist political perspective, or from a perspective informed by a radical awareness of power issues. In his final written comments to me in the context of "Theater and Social Change," Buzz emphasized the importance of identifying and working with learners who possess or who indicate an interest in this commitment. However, as I went into my teaching, I didn't subscribe myself to this assumption; instead, I believed that a commitment to critical literacy might be inculcated in all students, regardless of political or ideological orientation, and it was toward this goal that I aimed my future teaching.

The other assumption that I now read in Buzz's approach to critical literacy, but that I largely disregarded at the time, was the notion of articulating a clear text to students with regard to one's teacherly assumptions and beliefs. In his classes, Buzz articulated his assumptions and expectations through lectures and other direct statements. However, because what most impressed me about Buzz's teaching was his subversion of traditional pedagogical roles and discourse, I failed to appreciate the complexity of Buzz's stance as a critical pedagogue. For me, nurturing critical literacy came to mean listening and responding to the needs and interests of students; lecturing and other teacher-centered activities, I assumed, would interfere with and prevent student engagement in dynamic reading, writing, and thinking.

Codification Two: An Action Research Project in Inner-City Detroit

In September 1990, after teaching reading for two years in a parochial middle school in New York City, and after completing all of the course work for a doctoral program in English and Education at the University of Michigan, I begin an action research project in an upper elementary school classroom on the fringe of downtown Detroit. My primary goal in undertaking this project is to help Mrs. A., an experienced upper elementary school teacher, to incorporate whole language methods of instruction into her teaching.

During the first few weeks of this project, I suddenly find myself unable to communicate with Mrs. A. about our classroom activities. My difficulty stems from my emerging awareness of the complexity involved with Mrs. A.'s articulated desire to change her literacy teaching; although she says that she desires to move from what she terms a "traditional" approach to teaching to something more like a "whole language" approach, I see conflicted evidence of movement in this direction. Adding to the complexity of the situation are the different ways we envision my role in our collaboration: Mrs. A. conceives me as her pedagogical assistant, while I wish to share equally in the role of classroom teacher. This conflict surprises me because I had worked with Mrs. A. for a number of months in advance of my project, and she had expressed an enthusiasm for collaborative teaching. Although I am uncertain as to how to read my inability to speak to Mrs. A. about my uneasiness, I sense that my difficulty is related to other cultural and contextual issues. I am a white male doctoral student who needs to complete a dissertation; Mrs. A. is an African American woman who has been teaching for many years in the Detroit Public School system.

It takes about a month for Mrs. A. and me to break through the tension that circumscribes our collaboration. After a particularly heated, but ultimately useful, conversation in which Mrs. A. shares with me her feeling that I am trying to control and to take over her classroom, we fashion a mutually agreeable arrangement whereby I spend the majority of my time helping students to compose and to revise their writing. I obtain a Macintosh computer from the University of Michigan, and I set it up in the back of Mrs. A.'s classroom. At specified periods during the school day, Mrs. A.'s students come to me to write on the computer and to confer about their writing. When I am not talking with kids about their writing, or showing them how to operate the computer, I ob-

serve the dynamics of the classroom around me, and I keep my eyes peeled for "collaboration," the ostensible subject of my research project.

Near the end of November, my attention is drawn to a group of five boys who sit around a table near me in the back of Mrs. A.'s room. Almost daily, these boys read, write, and discuss comic books that they either have acquired or are in the process of themselves creating. Whenever Mrs. A.'s attention is drawn elsewhere, or whenever the boys' attention to Mrs. A. or their assignments diminishes, they pull out their comic books and work clandestinely on them. Because I can identify with the boys' interest in comic books as well as their apparent desire to revise the nature of their classroom activities, I initiate exploratory conversations with them. These conversations occur before and after activities that Mrs. A. organizes, and sometimes even during them (like the boys, I whisper in order to hide my words from Mrs. A.). From these interactions, I learn that these boys have organized their very own comic book club, complete with a secretary and a list of comic book heroes that they hope to draw someday.

Although I am pleased to have made some meaningful connections to students who seem to have an intrinsic and authentic commitment to collaboration, I fear that my underground interactions with these boys will result in a new conflict between myself and Mrs. A. Anxious to avoid this conflict, I ask Mrs. A. if I can meet with the members of the comic book club once a week for the purpose of reading and writing comic books, and developing insights with regard to the notion of collaboration. Because I am aware that Mrs. A. does not share my assumptions about the value of comic book reading and writing, I tell Mrs. A. that I will attempt to foster a conversation about comic books that will contribute to the boys' classroom learning. Although Mrs. A. is skeptical about all of this, she agrees. We decide that I can work with these boys for one hour on Friday afternoons in a newly created "publishing center" that is just down the hall from our classroom.[3]

In meetings that occur over the duration of the second part of the school year, the comic book club composes texts like the one shown in Figure 2. These texts are often quite sophisticated; unfortunately, because they are so complex, the boys take a long time to develop them. As the boys work slowly and meticulously on their comic books, they talk excitedly about topics such as sports, family, comic books, television, school, and girls. As I listen to the boys and observe their writing and drawing, I discover that I am unwilling to force upon these students any fixed structure or series of lessons. Our open-ended conversations are lively and entertaining, and they seem an important part of the boys' effort to write and draw comic books. Even though I often want to bring some critical perspective to our conversations, especially for the purpose of analyzing the form and content of the comic books that these boys are reading and drawing, I resist the urge to impose upon my students. Instead, I just observe, draw, and talk with these kids, almost as their friend.

Figure 2. Detail from a story by a member of the comic book club.

Over time, I begin to develop a rationale for both my interest in this literacy practice and my resistance to the notion of situating myself as a teacher within it. As I interact with these boys, I learn that their interest in comic books has been nurtured by parents who make the time and effort to take their kids to comic book stores and conventions. I begin to read the boys' interest in reading, writing, and drawing comic books as an expression of their commitment to literacy practices nurtured outside of school, and as a legitimate response to the lack of challenge and intrinsic motivation in their classroom learning. I also begin to see how this particular literacy practice enables the boys to grapple with some of the issues that they face in their own life, like responding to violence or authority figures. Most provocative, at least for me, I begin to see how the boys' energetic and fluid conversation about issues or topics of intrinsic interest enables conversational roles that they almost never play in Mrs. A.'s classroom. One boy, Troy, especially captures my attention in this regard. He is a small boy who never speaks and who rarely even raises his eyes to meet Mrs. A. in the context of her classroom; however, in the context of this comic book club, he is an active speaker and participant, and he frequently comes to me for advice and encouragement. I don't have any great insights into why this is, but I do know that I appreciate the way in which our fluid and unstructured conversations enhance Troy's confidence and his articulation of words, both spoken and written. I appreciate, too, the way in which these same fluid and unstructured conversations create community amongst the boys and between them and myself; as the boys learn, I learn, and it is this development of community through engagement in literacy that I feel is the most significant consequence of our work together.

Toward the end of the school year, I enact a more conventional teacherly stance in relation to these boys. I set some deadlines for the completion of writing and drawing, and I call a comic book artist to speak to the boys about the process of creating comic books. Unfortunately, this comic book artist works during the school day. As a substitute, I invite the boys out to Ann Arbor during their spring vacation, and we spend the morning exploring a friend's collection of Japanese comic books; the boys, my friend, and I discuss, among other things, the different attitude of the Japanese toward the representation of violence (Japanese comic books are much more graphic than our own), and the possible reasons for this. Just before the end of the school year, I arrange for the boys to present some of their work at an educational conference that takes place at our school. The boys show their art and explain the stories that they are trying to tell, and I explain the rationale for my collaboration with these boys. I argue that reading and writing comic books allows these boys to develop fluency within a particular art form, and that as they develop this fluency they learn many lessons that educators routinely attempt to teach in their classes (i.e., the importance of appropriate spelling, revision, dialogue, and the development of coherent narrative structure). Literacy educators, I suggest, ought to create multidimensional classroom spaces in which students can engage in activities such as comic book reading, writing, and drawing at the same time that they engage in more conventional literacy activities. Even though the boys' comic books are, for the most part, unfinished, the educators who attend this conference respond enthusiastically to the boys' work and to my presentation. When my project ends, it is these boys to whom I am closest, for they have taught me to listen and to observe my students, to learn more about the activities that my students enjoy, and to reflect carefully upon the relation between these activities and my own teaching.

In the years immediately following my experiences in "Vietnam and the Artist" and "Theater and Social Change," I had many opportunities to nurture critical literacy, first in the context of my teaching of reading in a parochial middle school in New York City, and later in my teaching of courses in composition and secondary English education at the University of Michigan. In each of these contexts, but especially in the one that I have represented above, I struggled to develop my commitment to critical literacy given a social and discursive context that posed numerous challenges to my assumptions. The lessons that I learned as a result of my struggles were paradoxical: on the one hand, I developed a deeper commitment to and appreciation of many of the assumptions and practices that I had learned in the context of my own education. On the other hand, I came to question many of these same assumptions and practices, and I began to conceive of new practices and goals for my teaching.

Foremost amongst the assumptions that I developed a deeper commitment to was the notion that teachers ought to provide learners with opportunities to engage in and to develop fluency in a dynamic mode of expression of their own choosing. In the context of my action research project, I observed an enhanced motivation with regard to the comic book club's learning; even though I sometimes had to remind the boys of deadlines that we had negotiated, they almost always entered the publishing center ready to write, talk, and draw, and to ask me questions about this enterprise and my own experiences writing, teaching, and working. As I noticed this enhanced desire to learn, I also observed the way in which the reading, writing, and drawing of comic books challenged members of the comic book club and nurtured abilities in reading, writing, listening, speaking, and drawing. Writing and drawing comic books demanded of the boys with whom I worked not only time, but also commitment, perseverance, and a knowledge of narrative conventions such as dialogue and plot development (see Scott McCloud's *Understanding Comics* for more insight into the challenge inherent in reading and writing comics). By the end of my project with the comic book club, I conceived comic book writing and drawing not as "childish" activity, but instead as serious and difficult literacy practice.

As my understanding of the value of multidimensional literacy activities grew, so too did my appreciation of the notion of attending carefully to the word universes of learners. Within the context of my action research project, I devoted the majority of my attention to trying to understand why Mrs. A.'s students behaved, wrote, read, spoke, and listened as they did. Strategies of action research such as individual and small group conferences with students, journal writing, reading and writing surveys, and tape recording of large and small group conversations became a part of my pedagogical repertoire, and helped me to locate—though not easily nor with absolute precision—the perspectives and assumptions of learners. As in my experience with the comic book club, I drew upon the knowledge and insight that I obtained as a result of these action research strategies to revise and develop curriculum and classroom space such that engagement in critical literacy might take place.

More often than not, however, my struggles to foster critical literacy led me to question and to revise my pedagogical assumptions and practices. Foremost amongst the assumptions and practices that I interrogated was the notion of how to involve students in the dynamic activity of reading words and the world. As a learner of literacy, I had developed the assumption that dynamic movement between words and the world could best be achieved through the organization of a provocative and explicitly political curriculum of literary and theoretical texts. However, in the context represented above, and in the other classroom contexts in which I taught immediately after my experience in "Vietnam and the Artist" and "Theater and Social Change," I discovered that my authority to organize such a curriculum was extremely limited. I rarely was invited to choose texts to teach, and I could not mandate the purchase of alternative texts.[4] Confronted with this challenge to my assumptions and practices, I began to develop what Patti Stock terms a "dialogic" conception of curriculum. What I take Stock to mean by this term is the notion of students and teachers talking with one another about goals, interests, and assumptions, and creating together activities and contexts that enable the achievement of mutual or reciprocal aims and interests. Having observed some students reading and writing comic books, this is exactly the sort of critical practice that I sought to enact in the context of Mrs. A.'s classroom. I sought, in other words, to talk meaningfully with both Mrs. A. and her students, and to create a revised curriculum that would allow for different approaches to shared educational goals. This alternative approach to curriculum enabled me to circumvent the constraints that I faced in terms of organizing a coherent curriculum committed to critical literacy, and it provided me with a new means of situating my teaching within the word universes of my students.

As I moved in this dialogic direction, I quite naturally re-examined the goals of my critical pedagogy. As a learner in classrooms organized by Buzz Alexander, I had developed the assumption that systematic social change, or a commitment to it, ought to emerge from my teaching. However, what I soon realized upon my immersion in actual classrooms was that my ability to orchestrate dynamic movement between the classroom and the world—at least in the radical ways represented by the

Pinkertons—was severely limited by the structure of schools and by the maturity of my students. While I retained a commitment to the idea of making dynamic connections between classrooms and the larger world, I began to conceive the need to subordinate this goal to the less ambitious but equally vital aim of involving students actively in reading, writing, listening, and speaking. In other words, I became more sensitive to the needs and interests of individual students, and to the importance of developing student abilities in reading and writing—regardless of whether or not my classroom activities or my students' literacy practices clearly advanced the cause of systematic social change. Social change, I began to think, might begin with helping individuals to become more alert and motivated readers and writers, and in creating classroom contexts in which comfortable yet challenging engagements with literacy occur.[5]

My experience with the comic book boys suggests how this focus on individual engagements with reading and writing might sometimes result in the production of texts and contexts where there exists a dynamic and perhaps even radical re-shaping of words and the world. In Figure 2, taken from a comic book written and drawn by one of the members of the comic book club, an aspiring motorcycle racer must make a decision with regard to the sort of person he wishes to become. Late to an important motorcycle race because he was dealing with a gang issue in his neighborhood, he tries to figure out what to tell his coach. In making this decision, the racer is torn between competing commitments: on the one hand, he feels responsible to his coach, and desires to achieve success in the realm of motorcycle racing; on the other hand, this racer feels that it is important to address problems that people face in neighborhoods beset with crime, gangs, and violence. The world and conflict depicted here in words and pictures parallels the world and conflict that I perceived the creator of this comic book himself positioned within. In the neighborhood surrounding the classroom in which I enacted my action research project, there existed a real fear of gangs and a concern about violence; in school, however, students rarely had opportunities to explore meaningfully these issues. Writing this comic book, I believe, enabled this boy to articulate the contradiction at the core of his learning experience, and in this sense to grapple with it.[6] Although this boy's reading of words and the world never grew into a more visible or coherent radical political stance, it indicates, I believe, the beginnings of a commitment to exploring difficult social and political issues that circumscribe the teaching and learning of literacy in inner-city environments.

My emerging sensitivity to students and to the way in which discursive practices of intrinsic interest to them might facilitate engagement in critical literacy led me to question my own deeply embedded assumptions about what sort of discourse most contributes to an empowering learning environment. In the context of my work with Buzz Alexander, I had developed the belief that open-ended conversations and the creative use of a personal vernacular might facilitate collaboration. However, in the context of my action research project, I noticed that practices such as these often impeded my ability to establish collaborative relations with Mrs. A. and her students. To work well with Mrs. A., I had to accept her position as the "head" of her classroom, and I needed to enact the role of her subordinate. Similarly, in the context of the comic book club, I eventually discovered that situating myself in the more traditional roles associated with the term "teacher" enabled me to help the boys to bring their comic book writing and drawing to a satisfying conclusion. In light of these discoveries, I began to value the notion of providing direction to students and of shaping clear understandings of goals and responsibilities—qualities that I had earlier deemed as unimportant to the fostering of critical literacy. Surprisingly, I began to see the value—depending upon the situation—of what Andrea Lunsford and Lisa Ede term "hierarchical collaboration," or interactions between learners and teachers that are unambiguous in terms of authority and responsibilities (153).

Ultimately, my appreciation of the important role that hierarchies and traditional roles associated with the term teacher can play in learning and in collaboration led me to question my prior assumptions about the illegitimacy of what Freire terms the "banking" concept of education (1970, 58). Talking with Mrs. A. and the comic book boys, and especially their parents, I began to understand why many people attach so much importance to the notion of teachers conveying directly and unambiguously to students skills and knowledge deemed necessary to economic and social success within mainstream society—even when those skills and knowledge clearly are narrowly conceived. For Mrs. A. and many other adults in the community in which I worked, rote learning and isolated practice in reading and writing skills were essential prerequisites for success in a wider mainstream culture unsympathetic to the intrinsic goals and language practices of African Americans (see Delpit 1986 for a similar perspective). Not wanting to impose my own assumptions upon these subjects, I developed the multidimensional perspective in relation to traditional schooling that I highlighted in my codification. Instead of using my involvement with the comic book boys as the basis for a call to revolution in literacy education, I drew upon my involvement to argue that "traditional" schooling could live side by side with activities such as the comic book club. In fact, from my new perspective, I had trouble distinguishing between the two, for I had observed that the writing and drawing of the comic book club had been enhanced by "traditional" lessons undertaken in Mrs. A.'s classroom, and that the lessons that the boys had learned through their engagement in comic book reading and writing about narrative form and structure had flowed into their response to traditional school assignments. In light of observations such as these, I began to argue for an approach to literacy that meets the intrinsic needs and interests of learners at the same time that it aims to achieve other important goals within a community.

Perhaps the most important new assumption and practice that I came to value as a result of my experience with the comic book club was the notion of re-educating myself—of not only surveying learners and situating my teaching within the word universe that I discovered, but of consciously questioning my assumptions and revising my pedagogical stance in collaboration with learners. In the context of my work with the comic book club, I found myself engaged in an activity that I really had no idea how to teach. Before I could work well with these boys, I had to reflect upon my own conflicted relation to the activity of comic book writing and drawing, and I had to educate myself with regard to the practices that might nurture success in it. A part of critical literacy, then, a part of nurturing it, I came to believe, is being prepared to revise and to re-educate oneself, to engage dynamically in critical literacy even though one is teaching it. And it is this lesson that I took with me into my subsequent teaching.

Codification Three: English 481, "The Teaching of English"

Today, I am a secondary English teacher educator at the University of Illinois at Chicago, a large public research university located just west of the downtown "Loop." Since 1992, I have taught a variety of courses in the UIC Secondary English Teacher Education Program. The course that I have taught most consistently (every semester since my arrival at UIC) is English 481, "The Teaching of English." Students in the UIC Secondary English Teacher Education Program take English 481 the semester before they student teach, and in conjunction with a course in the College of Education that places students in area high schools for sixty hours of observation and practice teaching.

My approach to English 481 has changed many times over the past five years, usually in response to changes in my reading of the needs of the students in it and the larger context in which the course is situated. One of the more

Figure 3. Members of an Electronic Book Club.

obvious and significant ways in which my teaching has changed is that I now use computers to prepare my students for future teaching. Initially, I integrated computers into the English 481 curriculum in order to show students how to access information related to the teaching of English available in the library and on the Internet, and in order to enhance my students' marketability as prospective English teachers. Later, I used computers to help students to draft and revise unit plans and other assigned writing. While I continue to use computers for these reasons, I now also use computers to model the notion of a reading workshop and, more importantly, to pose questions about what is involved in reading texts and the world. The primary means by which I pose such questions is the Electronic Book Clubs, a five–week unit in which students in English 481 select books and discuss them using the Interchange component of the Daedalus Integrated Writing Environment (DIWE).

Basically, the Electronic Book Clubs work like this: on the first day of the unit, I introduce my students to the core assumptions that I now have about how to involve adolescent learners actively in reading, writing, listening, and speaking. Engagement in literacy, I argue, requires intrinsic motivation, self-awareness, collaboration, and commitment.[7] Following this presentation, I organize my students into small groups of three or four people each, and I invite each of these "book clubs" to select four texts to read and to discuss over the next four weeks of class. Book clubs choose their texts from a collection of twenty-nine sets of five young adult novels that I place on a table in the center of our classroom, and from a list of commonly taught high school novels.[8] *Additionally, each book club determines a schedule for reading and the completion of assigned roles and responsibilities. Near the end of this process of organizing and situating the electronic book clubs, I read selections from my students' own descriptions of classroom environments in which they have been actively engaged in learning. These selections provide me with yet another way of explaining and situating the electronic book club activity in which they are about to engage.*

Prior to these activities, I share with my students written descriptions of the roles and responsibilities that I ask them to play before, during, and after their electronic book club discussions. The roles and responsibilities that I assign are similar to those suggested by Harvey Daniels in his book Literature Circles, *but they are designed specifically for an audience of prospective high school English educators. The* Language Lover *is to read his or her text with the goal of identifying language that might be unfamiliar to high school students;* Language Lovers *must locate two different types of language: "historical and cultural language," and "important" words potentially unfamiliar to adolescents. Thereafter, they are to create two separate lists of words, and to explain in a couple of paragraphs how they would go about introducing these words to students and developing knowledge of them beyond the use of a dictionary. The* Form Focuser *is to pay attention to the genre and structure of the selected text, and to specific stylistic features of the text; thereafter, he or she is to write a brief reflection sharing his or her insights and exploring concrete ways of helping adolescents to become aware of and to appreciate these features. The* Booktalker, *as the name implies, is to prepare a presentation about the relevant young adult novel as if she or he were attempting to inform adolescents of a potentially good book to read. The* Reflective Practitioner *has the most difficult of responsibilities: he or she is to prepare questions for peer discussion that focus on the characters in the text and readers' responses to these characters; additionally, the* Reflective Practitioner *facilitates the written discussion within DIWE, and reflects afterwards in writing upon the discussion. After each meeting of the Electronic Book Clubs,* Reflective Practitioners *create a three- to five-day sequence of classroom activities focused upon a twenty- to thirty-page section of text. As the* Reflective Practitioner *develops these activities, I ask him or her to highlight the interpretive question that structures classroom activities, to indicate the rationale for the lessons, and to identify state and teacherly objectives that the lessons potentially fulfill.*

Once the book clubs are organized and questions have been clarified with regard to the roles and responsibilities associated with this activity, my students and I begin to meet once a week in Scailab, the computer facility for the UIC English department (see Figure 3). *Over the duration of the Electronic Book Club unit, students present their booktalks and discuss their books using*

Interchange. Interchange enables users to exchange written communications with other readers and writers almost immediately; messages that others have sent can be seen at the top of the computer screen, and a place to compose messages is located at the bottom. By scrolling up and down, users can read the messages of peers in a fluid electronic conference that is similar to asynchronous exchanges of e-mail. Whenever book club members read words that they want to respond to, they can write in the bottom half of the screen, and then send their message, which is distributed immediately to all participants in the conference. While this activity is taking place, I monitor the reading and writing of the various book clubs, and I provide written feedback to the booktalk presenters. After the meeting of the book clubs is over, I use the transcripts to learn more about how my students read texts, and to understand better their various abilities with regard to collaboration, question formation, and response to texts.

Perhaps the best way for me to explain what I am trying to do in the electronic book clubs is to repeat words that I share with my students the first time that I take them to Scailab. Before my students begin to explore DIWE in preparation for their book club discussions, I tell them that reading this lab requires the same sort of attention that I am asking them to give to their selected young adult novels. As they go out into area schools for the purpose of observation and practice teaching, they should keep in mind the importance of reading. In situations that will be as strange and unfamiliar as our computer lab, I tell them, they will need to investigate the history of the context that they are in, and to explore the strange and unfamiliar words, customs, and habits that can be found therein. They also will have to be attentive to the form and structure of their classroom environments, and they will need to pay special attention to characters, or people, located in their classroom texts. That said, I begin to orient my students to the lab itself. I provide some historical information about its creation, and I highlight various important words and icons on the board and on the computer screen in front of them. I draw their attention to the arrangement of the room, and to the rationale behind the arrangement. My hope is that they will remember to read in this way in the future, and in doing so create a situation where they can re-write their teaching, and their world, in light of the practice in which they are engaged in this laboratory.

If what I learned in the context of my action research project in Detroit was the importance of re-educating myself for the purpose of better educating literacy learners, then this is exactly the lesson that I have tried to build on in the context of my teaching of English 481, "The Teaching of English." In this secondary English education context, I experiment and revise almost every semester in an effort to engage my students in meaningful learning about teaching and literacy. Probably no better example of my own engagement in this process of re-education and critical literacy is my work with the Electronic Book Clubs.

The assumptions and practices that shape this activity are similar to the assumptions and practices that I highlighted in my previous section. My interest in and use of computers stems not only from a commitment to helping my students to enhance their marketability as secondary English educators, but also from my commitment to learning environments in which learners are invited to move dynamically among activities such as reading, writing, listening, and speaking. Of particular interest to me is the way in which reading words in the context of Interchange highlights the visual dimension of reading practice. As with the reading and writing of comic books, this visual component is provocative and, typically, stimulating. Usually, students express joy and enthusiasm with regard to this activity—especially once they become comfortable with the way in which Interchange operates. At the same time, using DIWE makes participation in a discussion about texts more of a challenge; students have to figure out the new "rules" for conducting a conversation, and they have to become more expert improvisers in the sense that they can not carefully plan their responses to texts, as they typically do in large group discussions and in their writing. The additional challenges of logging into Interchange and finding the appropriate sub-conference for discussion make the Electronic Book Club experience a highly dynamic and demanding endeavor.

Correspondingly, this activity represents well my commitment to locating and surveying the word universes of my students, and in the case of the Reflective Practitioner, my commitment to engaging learners in this same activity. Through the electronic transcripts, I am able to read the words exchanged by my students about texts; in doing so, I am able to obtain additional insight into their responses to texts and their assumptions about what sorts of questions are important to ask of texts. Especially when my students play the role of Reflective Practitioner, they engage in a similar activity of locating the "word universes" of learners and situating a literacy program within a meaningful learner context. Furthermore, I ask Reflective Practitioners to re-read the written transcripts of their conversations for the purpose of locating key questions that might be useful for high school students. Typically, the observations that my students and I make during the course of this activity flow into our conventional large group conversations. Because their experiences in Interchange highlight the contingent nature of talk about texts, students become hyper-aware of the constructed nature of classroom conversations. Often, we explore the question as to how conventional classroom conversations are different from electronic discussions, and this exploration results in greater attention to assumptions about classroom discourse and to the way in which conventional classroom discussions move and develop—who responds to whom, when, and why. For me, this is the most powerful dimension of the Electronic Book Clubs— the way in which they invite reading and writing of textual words, but also re-reading and re-writing of classroom words and worlds.

In this sense, then, the Electronic Book Clubs unit develops appreciation of the dynamic relationship between words and the world, and the possibility of re-writing the same. Over the duration of the semester in which students enroll in English 481, this notion is made even clearer through student participation in classes in the UIC College of Education; in these classes, students observe and practice teach for sixty hours in area high schools. Students move dynamically amongst engagements in high school classrooms, activities in university classes, and words that they are reading and writing in the context of the Electronic Book Clubs. My hope is that my students will see the connections between these differently situated activities, as well as the tensions, and use the Electronic Book Clubs as a reference point for re-working the school environments in which they are beginning to situate themselves.

Although my ability to ensure that my students see the Electronic Book Clubs as a reference point for social change is limited by their prior experiences and assumptions, as well as by my ability to articulate the same clear rationale for the Electronic Book Club unit that I have developed here, I still conceive the work that my students and I undertake in the context of the Electronic Book Clubs as having an explicitly political, and perhaps even radical, dimension. By directing my students' attention to books written for and marketed to a young adult audience, I mean to raise questions about conventional notions of literature and multiculturalism. What I hope to draw my students' attention to is the way in which prevailing notions of literature and multiculturalism often fail to take into account the reading interests and habits of a particular age group (adolescents) and a particular culture (popular culture). By asking my students to read and to write in response to a diversity of texts—many of which are not a part of the conventional high school literature canon and many of which address provocative social and political issues—I am asking my students to broaden their assumptions about what the term literature means and what is involved in teaching multiculturally. Additionally, by inviting my students to choose books, to discuss them in small groups, and to engage in open-ended but structured conversations about texts, I mean to suggest the value of creating classroom environments in which there exist options for reading, writing, speaking, and listening. While there is no clear political orientation here, I do believe that there exists an opportunity for important and even radical shifts in both pedagogical content and methodology to occur if a useful intersection of aims, assumptions, and methodologies occurs with respect to myself and my students.

That said, I do conceive some important differences between my above approach to critical literacy and my prior approaches, and I believe that those differences largely are the result of my engagement with the new discourses, materials, and ideologies that circumscribe my current work as a secondary English teacher educator. One significant difference lies in the way in which I conceive the act of reading. In prior contexts, I conceived this act in broad terms, as Freire does in the passage that I cite at the start of this essay. However, as a result of my experiences working with prospective English teachers, and especially student teachers, I have been challenged to conceive the act of reading in more specific terms. Through the Electronic Book Club activity, I try to provide my students with a framework in which to conceive the act of reading itself; in particular, the roles of the Electronic Book Clubs are drawn from the notion of textual study that Robert Scholes proposes in his book *Textual Power: Literary Theory and the Teaching of English*. Here, Scholes suggests that textual study entails attention to cultural and historical language, literary devices, issues of interpretation, and criticism. As students advance through English 481, I attempt to complicate Scholes's view of the act of reading by introducing students to the reciprocal teaching method, which suggests that reading involves predicting, summarizing, questioning, and clarifying (Brown and Palincsar). Additionally, I try to talk about reading in such a way that my students notice that I appreciate the active role of the reader in constructing texts (Rosenblatt) and the way in which reading entails drafting and revision, much like writing (Jensen). By articulating these assumptions about the act of reading, I aim to help my students to think more clearly about the process of reading, and to nurture their awareness of how they read texts such that they can begin to help adolescents to engage in commensurate practices.

Another important difference is that I have become more assertive about my own pedagogical assumptions and methods, and about the curriculum that I believe is important for learners to experience. From my current perspective, it is important not only to create literacy programs that draw upon the existential experiences of learners, as Freire suggests, but also ones that draw upon my own existential experiences. Again, my interactions with students in English 481 have been important in this regard; as with my experience in the comic book club, students in English 481 have indicated to me their desire for direction and structure, and their hope that I will convey to them as much knowledge as I possibly can muster with regard to their future roles and responsibilities. I continue to believe in the importance of dialogue and negotiation; however, I now find that I am more comfortable with the notion of talking directly to my students about my own assumptions with respect to mutually relevant questions. I have found that when I do so I satisfy the desires and expectations of many of my students, and consequently create a more dynamic and collaborative context for learning.

Even though I perceive myself as more assertive in my teaching, as more willing and able to share with my students direct statements about my pedagogical assumptions and goals, I continue to entertain questions with respect to my teaching. Ironically, the questions that I currently find myself considering grow out of my new confidence with regard to curriculum and instructional methods and assumptions. Have I sacrificed too much in terms of dialogue with the students who enroll in English 481 as a result of my commitment to the pre-planned units of activity that I present to them? Am I overloading my students with too much activity such that I diminish my students' potential to do their best work? Are my assumptions about what and how my students ought to learn now outdated or too distant from my students' assumptions and those of their prospective employers? More importantly, are they too removed from the needs and assumptions of the adolescents that my current students will teach in the future? As yet, these are questions to which I have not developed firm answers. They are problems that I am thinking about, and that I anticipate I will address in my next semesters of teaching. It is this commitment to and awareness of the need for pedagogical revision, for continued teacherly reading and re-shaping of words, work, and the world, that I continue to perceive as central to the development of critical literacy.

Conclusion: A Final (Provisional) Self-Evaluation

As I look back over the words that I have written here, I am aware of the way in which my teaching has shifted over the years, in response to a variety of social and ideological contexts and discourses. These shifts, I believe, are positive signs of growth and development; they are signs of vitality in my teaching, and of my immersion in a diversity of compelling pedagogical points of view. However, I also value a point that Bakhtin makes in my epigraph; that is, that there exists an element of competition among the diversity of discourses that circumscribe any given teacher or context of teaching, and that there are social and political implications to the ways in which these discourses get negotiated. In these last few paragraphs, then, I assess the political implications of the pedagogical evolution that I have represented through this essay, and I offer yet another reading of that evolution.

The most obvious conflict or contradiction that I read in my narrative is the one related to the notion of linking critical literacy to systematic or radical social change. Because of my positive experience in courses taught by Buzz Alexander, I think I forever will assume the importance of making this connection. As I look back over my narrative, I read a movement away from this radical political commitment; while I like to think that my current work follows in the footsteps of my work with Buzz Alexander and the Pinkertons, I'm also aware that the current context in which I work, and the content of the classes that I teach, deviates significantly from the path that Buzz charted through his teaching. This is perhaps a roundabout way of saying that I see a difference between nurturing awareness of what is involved in the act of reading and performing guerrilla theater for the purpose of helping fired union projectionists to regain their jobs.

How do I account for this movement? For the most part, my rationale is drawn from my own experience, and from my commitment to the words written by Paulo Freire that I cite at the start of this essay. In attempting to change the world, I have become more and more aware of the importance of the act of reading. I think I acquired this awareness especially in the context of the action research project that I described earlier. Before I could change that world, before I could contribute meaningfully to student learning or to Mrs. A.'s development as a teacher, I had to understand and appreciate better the context that I was in, the perspectives of the people involved, and their many different ways of working and thinking in the world. Correspondingly, I had to reflect upon the relation between my assumptions and other assumptions, experiences, and cultures that I observed and interacted with every day in that project. The lesson that I learned as a result of this project is that it is important to discipline or to subordinate the desire to change the world; it is important to read the world, to write it, and to use that reading and writing experience to create social change in collaboration with others. This notion of the importance of the act of reading does not preclude the possibility of creating classroom contexts in which activities like the ones that I engaged in with the Pinkertons occur; however, it does produce what I believe is a healthy skepticism with regard to how to change the world and what sort of new worlds to create. If there is one thing that I want my students to leave my secondary English education classroom with, it is this idea of the importance of the act of reading, of examining assumptions in the world and in one's self before launching any ambitious effort to make the world a better place.

Another tension or conflict that I read in my narrative is related to the notion of being assertive and direct about one's pedagogical goals and assumptions. Even as I write this, I suspect that some readers are saying, "Yes, I can see that tension—you argue above for the importance of the act of reading, but before you talked about the importance of directing students, of teaching them directly, and sometimes even narrowly." My current response to this problem is to say that it is important to remember that both teachers and learners are involved in the act of reading. Teacher talk is only a problem, is only a negative in classrooms if we feel that learners should learn to read independently and without help and guidance. To the contrary, learners depend on teachers to provide a structured classroom text, and to assist them in the reading of that text. As we invite learners to read words and the world, we need to invite them to read us, too. One of the best ways to do this is to be clear and assertive about assumptions and expectations—or at least as clear and assertive as we can be at any given time. Students learn from their engagement with a variety of texts, and we shouldn't shy away from the knowledge that we, too, are one of those important texts that learners read.

A final tension that I read in my narrative is my endorsement here of the notion of creating "multidimensional" educational contexts. For many people, this endorsement undoubtedly will be problematic: how can teachers endorse the idea of teaching "traditionally," of taking seriously the notion of valuing forms of instruction and uses of discourse (such as standardized tests) that are narrow in their goals and conception? Alternatively, others will ask how we can balance attention to narrow forms of instruction and isolated uses of discourse with attention to students' intrinsic aims and interests—isn't this "watering down" our educational environments? From my current perspective, however, learning is a matter of integrating—not separating—these diverse ideologies and discourses. As Haki Madhubuti recently put it, "We all have professional languages, but we should be comfortable to leave them at work. When I go to the bank, I don't say, 'Yo bro, I need a loan.' But we do not have to bring the language of commerce home" (359). What I take Madhubuti to mean is that there exists a dynamic relationship between different sorts of language use, and that it is important for teachers and learners to read the context of language use (as I have been attempting to model here) and to make informed decisions about the language use best suited to particular needs and purposes.

The more I reflect upon my teaching, the more I re-read and re-write my pedagogy, the more committed I become to the notion that I am suggesting here of embracing conflicts, or contradictions. More positively, my current belief is that the various conflicts and contradictions embedded in the act of teaching are paradoxes; they are puzzles or dilemmas that are instructive and provocative. It seems to me important to understand that critical literacy consists of a series of paradoxes: reading words, but also the world; working and re-shaping, but also surveying and situating; identifying and working within the word universes of learners, but gathering together and presenting teacherly word universes. In this essay, I have attempted to mix together these paradoxical elements in a useful way, just as I strive to mix them together in a useful way in my everyday teaching. It's a tough thing to do, I admit. Perhaps all that we teachers of critical literacy can do is to keep trying to mix these elements creatively, to keep evaluating the nature of our efforts to mix, and to keep challenging ourselves to think better and more clearly— more provocatively—about our work and how to nurture environments committed to learning and to the creation of community.

Notes

1. In her essay "Exploring Academic Literacy: An Experiment in Composing," Cheryl Geisler explains that accounts are "stories we tell each other about who we are, where we've been, and how things appear from our perspective" (40–41). Accounts, Geisler suggests, are necessary "when something in the normal run of conversation is disrupted, when an exigency makes manifest a lack of common ground for understanding"(40). Because I anticipate that my pictures will provoke a "disruption" in my readers' reading practice, I inscribe accounts consistent with Geisler's assumptions for the purpose of creating the common ground necessary for useful conversation.

2. In undertaking to make this point, I am drawing upon assumptions articulated by critical theorists such as Michel Foucault and Ross Chambers, who both suggest the dynamic relationship between "dominant" cultures and "oppositional" or "alternative" ones. See the interview with Foucault entitled "Truth and Power" in *The Foucault Reader* and especially the Introduction to Ross Chambers's *Room For Maneuver: Reading (The) Oppositional (In) Narrative.*

3. This "publishing center" was actually an old faculty room that had been converted into a site for student publication of writing. It had three or four tables in it, and some minimal supplies such as a paper cutter, paper, pencils, markers, and various binding devices.

4. An interesting exception occurred in the context of my teaching in a New York City parochial school. Here, I organized my students for the purpose of buying paperback copies of Richard Wright's *Native Son*. With my principal's permission, my class made popcorn and sold it during one of our monthly school movies. This was the first and only novel that I was able to incorporate into my students' curriculum during my work as a Catholic school teacher.

5. Here, again, my views have been shaped by the words and work of Ross Chambers. In *Room For Maneuver*, Chambers explores the potential of nonrevolutionary individual or group "survival tactics" to produce important transformations in human thinking and behavior (1). Chamber argues—and I

have come to agree with him—that revolutionary or systematic approaches to social changes repeat the methods of power in overcoming it (xv). Alternatively, Chambers suggests that individual and nonsystematic approaches to social change—such as reading and writing comic books—sometimes produce meaningful shifts in the workings of prevailing power systems, even though they do not overcome them. I believe that my account of my work with the comic book club represents well some of the important "shifts" that can occur in prevailing power systems through what Chambers terms "the oppositional."

6. My interpretation here draws upon the important work of Robert Brooke, who argues in his book *Writing and Sense of Self* the important role that stories and writing in general play in the activity of identity creation and negotiation.

7. For more information and insight into my assumptions about fostering engagement in literacy, as well as the Electronic Book Clubs, visit my home page on the Internet at http://www.uic.edu/~philion.

8. These twenty–nine sets of young adult novels were purchased with the assistance of a grant from UIC's Center for Urban Educational Research and Development.

Works Cited

Bakhtin, M. M. 1981. *The Dialogic Imagination.* Ed. Michael Holquist. Trans. Caryl Emerson and Michael Holquist. Austin: University of Texas Press.

Berthoff, Ann. 1987. "The Teacher as REsearcher." *Reclaiming the Classroom: Teacher Research as an Agency for Change.* Eds. Dixie Goswami and Peter R. Stillman. Upper Montclair, NJ: Boynton/Cook.

Brooke, Robert E. 1991. *Writing and Sense of Self: Identity Negotiation in Writing Workshops.* Urbana, IL: NCTE.

Brown, Ann L., and Annemarie Sullivan Palincsar. 1984. "Reciprocal Teaching of Comprehension-Fostering and Comprehension-Monitoring Activities." *Cognition and Instruction.* Ed. David Klahr. Hillsdale, NJ: Erlbaum. 117–75.

Chambers, Ross. 1991. *Room for Maneuver: Reading (The) Oppositional (In) Narrative.* Chicago: University of Chicago Press.

Delpit, Lisa D. 1986. "Skills and Other Dilemmas of a Progressive Black Educator." *Harvard Educational Review* 56: 379–85.

Everhart, Robert. 1983. *Reading, Writing and Resistance: Adolescence and Labor in a Junior High School.* Boston: Routledge and Kegan Paul.

Fine, Michelle. 1991. *Framing Dropouts: Notes on the Politics of an Urban Public High School.* Albany, NY: State University of New York Press.

Foucault, Michel. 1984. "Truth and Power." *The Foucault Reader.* Ed. Paul Rabinow. New York: Pantheon.

Freire, Paulo. 1987. "The Importance of the Act of Reading." *Literacy: Reading the Word and the World.* Eds. Paulo Freire and Donald Macedo. Boston: Bergin and Garvey. 29–36.

Freire, Paulo. 1970. *Pedagogy of the Oppressed.* Trans. Myra Bergman Ramos. New York: Continuum.

Geisler, Cheryl. 1992. "Exploring Academic Literacy: An Experiment in Composing." *College Composition and Communication* 43.1: 39–54.

Heath, Shirley Brice. 1983. *Ways with Words: Language, Life, and Work in Communities and Classrooms.* New York: Cambridge University Press.

Jensen, Julie, ed. 1984. *Composing and Comprehending.* Urbana, IL: National Conference on Research in English: ERIC Clearinghouse on Reading and Communication Skills.

Lunsford, Andrea, and Lisa Ede. 1990. *Singular Texts/Plural Authors: Perspectives on Collaborative Writing.* Carbondale: Southern Illinois Press.

Madhubuti, Haki. 1997. "NCTE to You." *College English* 59.3: 358–59.

McCloud, Scott. 1993. *Understanding Comics: The Invisible Art.* Northampton, MA: Kitchen Sink Press.

Rosenblatt, Louise. 1995. *Literature as Exploration.* New York: MLA.

Scholes, Robert. 1985. *Textual Power: Literary Theory and the Teaching of English.* New Haven, CT: Yale University Press.

Stock, Patricia Lambert. 1995. *The Dialogic Curriculum: Teaching and Learning in a Multicultural Society.* Portsmouth, NH: Boynton/Cook.

Willis, Paul. 1977. *Learning to Labor: How Working Class Kids Get Working Class Jobs.* Westmead, England: Saxon House.

4 Not a Luxury: Poetry and a Pedagogy of Possibility

Laura Roop
The Literacy Consortium

> The quality of light by which we scrutinize our lives has direct bearing on the product which we live, and upon the changes which we hope to bring about through those lives.
>
> For women, then, poetry is not a luxury. It is a vital necessity of our existence. It forms the quality of light within which we predicate our hopes and dreams toward survival and change, first made into language, then into idea, then into more tangible action.
>
> —Audre Lorde

In this passage, Audre Lorde, an African American feminist poet, argues that poetry—a genre sometimes associated with elitism and unbridled individualism, or rendered trivial through school exercises—should not be viewed as a frill for those who are marginalized in society. In Lorde's view, poetry writing and reading permits one to know and name the world, to reimagine it, and finally, to act upon that vision. When Lorde speaks of poetry as forming "the quality of light by which we scrutinize our lives," she creates a metaphor of poetry as sunlight or spotlight, searching out, seeing and reseeing, making the unconscious or subconscious visible through imagistic language that resonates for writers and for their readers. Lorde's experience as a poetry maker teaches her of its potential freeing power.

Like Lorde, I have experienced the power of poetry in my life. Poetry writing has permitted me to "give name to the nameless so it can be thought" (Lorde 283) as I recovered from rape; it allowed me to speak "a true word" calling back beloved friends edging toward self-destruction. Reading powerful, moving poems by writers across the ages, I have felt my spirit awaken and deepen. Because of these experiences, I have become a teacher and teacher educator who advocates for the genre's potential in the lives of the learners with whom I work.

Poetry and Other Imaginative/Aesthetic Genres

In *Poetic Diction*, English critic and language philosopher Owen Barfield, a contemporary of C. S. Lewis, describes poetry as language that evokes aesthetic imagination, which he defines as "a felt change of consciousness" (48). Barfield says that

> ... the poetic conducts an immediate synthesis of percepts. Brought into contact with these by its partial attachment to some individual human brain and body, it meets—through the senses—the *disjecta membra* of a real world, and weaves them again into the one real whole.... (191)

Barfield's remarks about poetry's effects on the subjectivities of readers and writers are useful to me as I reflect upon the genre's relation to critical literacy. In this essay, when using the terms "poetry" or "poetic," I have in mind Barfield's definition. Of course, experienced poets consciously use the visual impact, the sounds, and the patterns of language to create something that readers regard as poetry. Indeed, it is that to which Barfield alludes when he says that the "poetic conducts an immediate synthesis of percepts." Mind and body, spirit and matter meet. However, the student and teachers about whom I am writing are relative newcomers to the genre; thus, I am most intrigued by their intentions and their lived experiences as they engage in writing *toward* poetry. I regard a writer's text to be "poetic" when the intent of composing is to evoke a felt change of consciousness for the writer and/or her readers, when the writer is attempting to "transform" a personally meaningful narrative into a work of art through deep imaginative play.

A Pedagogy of Possibility and Its Relation to Poetry

North American educators Henry Giroux and Roger Simon, building upon John Dewey's pragmatic philosophy and Paulo Freire's more overtly political stance, argue for transformative education, which they name "a pedagogy of possibility." A pedagogy of possibility begins from a cultural politics which

> is centrally committed to the task of creating specific social forms (such as schooling) that encourage and make possible the realization of a variety of differentiated human capacities; rather than denying, diluting or distorting those capacities. It is a cultural politics concerned with enabling ways of representing and understanding our social and material world that encourage, through the develop-

ment of competencies and capabilities, the expansion of the range
of possible social identities people may become. (Simon 141)

Giroux clarifies the term further:

> Such a pedagogy transcends the dichotomy of elite and popular
> culture by defining itself through a project of educating students to
> feel compassion for the suffering of others, to engage in a continual
> analysis of their own conditions of existence, to construct loyalties
> that engage the meaning and importance of public life, and to be-
> lieve they can make a difference, that they can act from a position of
> relative strength to alter existing configurations of power. This no-
> tion of pedagogy is predicated on a notion of learned hope, forged
> amidst the realization of risks, and steeped in a commitment to trans-
> forming public culture and life. (99)

How can we teach children to hope? How can we teach them they can
study the world and transform it? How can we show them the value of
empathy? How can public educators, who often see themselves as relatively powerless, learn the same basic lessons? These questions, seemingly rhetorical, are critical ones.

While I do not want to exaggerate my claims for poetry, I believe that,
at its essence, poetry has the potential to lead writers and readers to
"feel compassion for the suffering of others," to "engage in a continual
analysis of . . . conditions of existence," and to "believe that they can
make a difference." In her article "Metaphors and Possibility," educational philosopher Maxine Greene argues that "to use imagination is to
summon up an 'as/if', to look at things as if they could be otherwise"
(5). She notes that "it often takes metaphorical thinking to break with
old certainties in this way," and that "poetry still is the source of the best
examples" (20).

Greene claims that metaphor is akin to empathy, quoting Cynthia
Ozick, a contemporary poet, who writes, in *Metaphor and Memory*,

> Through metaphor, the past has the capacity to imagine us and we
> it. Through metaphorical concentration, doctors can imagine what
> it is to be their patients. Those who have no pain can imagine those
> who suffer. Illuminated lives can imagine the dark. Poets in their
> twilight can imagine the borders of stellar fire. We strangers can
> imagine the familiar hearts of strangers. (qtd. in Greene 20)

Many, including Henry David Thoreau, have argued that the poet has
chosen to live "an examined life," a life of wide-awakeness. I have come
to believe that as teachers of young people, we, too, must wake up to
our own stories, as human beings and as learners. We must "engage in a
continual analysis of our conditions of existence," just as Giroux says
our students must. Unless we are alive to our own stories, we probably

will find it difficult to help others wake up to theirs. Unless we carefully and thoroughly interrogate the experiences and moments that have made us who we are—the moments of deep learning, confusion, anguish, blindness, and elation—we risk unconsciously sabotaging our stated aims as educators. For instance, many practitioners say that they want their students to find literate activity pleasurable and to use literacy for a variety of purposes. However, if they themselves do not enjoy reading or writing, if they have little confidence in their own abilities to use literacy to accomplish various goals, and if they leave their personal feelings and experiences unexamined, their actions may strongly contradict their words. Learners may witness their teachers' unwitting demonstrations of literacy's irrelevance.

In *The Peaceable Classroom*, reflecting on her own evolution toward a pedagogy of nonviolence, teacher and poet Mary Rose O'Reilley quotes Parker Palmer, dean of studies at Pendle Hill, a Quaker center for study and contemplation:

> We prepare for a meeting for learning by trying to become vulnerable to both hurt and healing in others and in ourselves. . . . Whatever the subject of study in the classroom, the shadow subject is ourselves, our limits, our potentials. As long as that remains in the shadows, it will block both individual and group from full illumination. But if both hurt and self-doubt can be brought into the light . . . then learning will flower. (qtd. in O'Reilley 118)

In order to write and read poetry insightfully, in order to guide others toward wide-awakeness as teachers of critical literacy attempt to do, we poets and teachers must consciously take up the "shadow subject," becoming reflective about our lives. Such reflection is a form of inventory-taking—what's here, what's not? Why? How do memories or imaginings echo through our lives to these moments we are living?

To compose an aesthetically satisfying text from such reflection requires what I call "transformations"—purposeful recreating and even reimagining of stories—for dramatic, evocative effect. Once we realize our stories can be transformed, first very literally in concrete acts of revision, it becomes possible, over time, to move toward the metaphoric realization that our lives can be changed as well. Additionally, the act of writing artfully from deep-seated commitments and passions teaches writers about the power of words. When poets and teachers tap into deep feeling and explore through language, they cannot help but care, if only about the scraps of language on the page or in the air. When poets and teachers tell stories, causing others to laugh or weep or frown, they cannot deny their own power, at least temporarily, to affect the world.

Life into Art: Lessons from Aesthetic/Imaginative Writing

In the following sections, I intend to ground my argument about poetry's role in the education of young learners and their teachers in concrete instances drawn from my experience as a writer, as a teacher, and as a teacher of teachers. I'll begin with a classroom episode from several years ago while I worked as a visiting poet/teacher in a fifth-grade classroom. The episode focuses on the responses of a fifth-grade boy, Adam, as I led the class through a series of textual "experiments." Adam's notes and drafts have been included to illustrate a child's possible response to the proposed experiments (see Figures 1 through 7). The sequence of activities described in the fifth-grade classroom mirrors sequences of poetry-related activities I have designed for high school students, including the young woman discussed in the section "The Shadow Subject—Myself," and for teacher-learners, including Sharon Galley and Laura Schiller, whose writing and teaching practices are discussed in subsequent sections.

Fifth Graders Experiment with "As/If"

The fifth-grade classroom was orderly. The twenty-four desks were in neat rows. Textbooks were stacked neatly in cupboards; walls were covered with posters of insects labeled by their entomological categories. The children were polite and entirely too quiet. After being introduced as the guest poet, I nervously read a poem I had written, deemed appropriate for an audience of fifth graders, then launched into an explanation of its source.

"Poems come from stories we care deeply about. As writers, we have to discover what really matters to us." I told them that in their brief ten or eleven years, they had lived enough to have something important to write about, maybe even enough for a lifetime of writing. Over the next several days, I led the children to launch a number of beginnings. We also read and discussed poems by other writers, both children and adults. We were fishing, but my own experience as a writer has taught me that some waters are more plentifully stocked than others. We explored memories of moments that were somehow important, either because they caused great joy or pain, or because we learned something. I encouraged the children to ask and answer "what if"—what if something else had happened, something funnier, more dramatic, more painful, more joyous. We looked at photographs that "interested" us, then tried to imagine what was going on, the names and places and stories. We practiced observing closely, using all of our senses. Most importantly, we tried to figure out *why* we had chosen to tell the stories we did. Answering why helped us begin to identify our commitments, fears, and obsessions, our own motivations.

Adam, for example, decided to write about a photograph of a man who appeared to be skydiving near a tropical waterfall. The image apparently caught Adam's eye because he had dreamed of skydiving someday (see Figure 1).

Because I am a writer of poetry, essays, and articles, I refer to my own experiences as a writer and as a learner in order to understand what and how to teach. For instance, my memories of being a young writer in school tell me that inexperienced writers often believe they haven't lived enough to write well. In school settings, teachers often "give" them ideas and topics to write about; students (and teachers) inadvertently learn to put aside their own interests, memories, and passions when engaging in school activities. Many young learners have never seen an experienced writer at work; often they have no idea that writers struggle to make meaning, that texts are usually drafted and redrafted repeatedly, and that few beginnings lead to publishable texts. The fact that so much of their rough, preliminary work is graded leads young writers to conclude that writing should be directed to that one-person audience, the

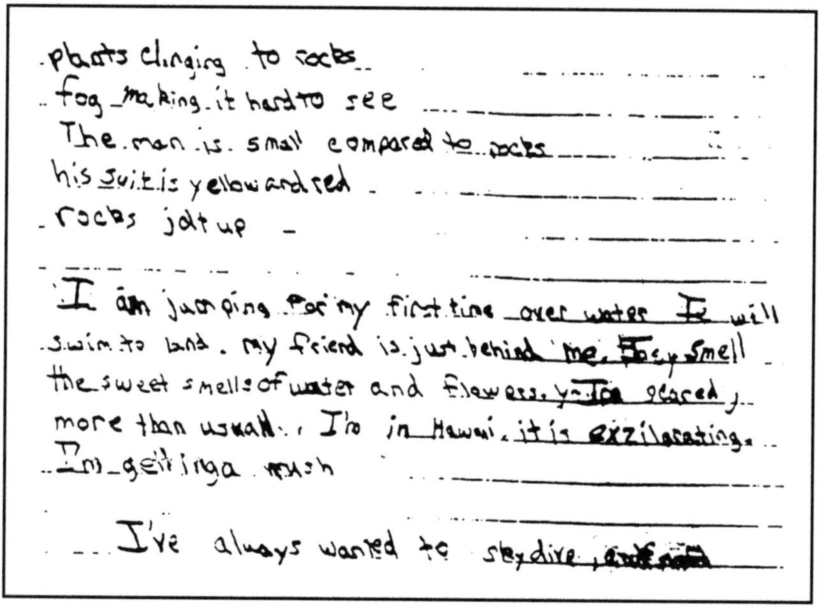

> .plants clinging to rocks
> .fog making it hard to see
> The man is small compared to rocks
> his suit is yellow and red
> .rocks jut up
>
> I am jumping for my first time over water I will
> swim to land. my friend is just behind me. They smell
> the sweet smells of water and flowers. y-I'm scared,
> more than usual. I'm in Hawai. it is exzilarating.
> I'm getting a rush
>
> I've always wanted to skydive, and now

Figure 1. Adam's notes on an "interesting" photograph.

teacher, and that clean copy is the aim, rather than interesting, risky thinking that may lead toward understanding.

The quiet, orderly classroom grew louder and began to bustle with activity. The neat rows of desks moved into ragged circles of talk as I consciously modeled "experiments" I hoped the children would try. I wrote with and for the children, we read many published texts out loud, and we discussed how those grown-up writers were struggling with similar problems. The children were insightful as they discussed poems they chose from an anthology. Throughout our sessions together, I moved from child to child, getting to know each one just a little bit from the stories they told in notes and drafts and discussions.

During the second week, I asked each child to select the beginning that he or she cared most deeply about, and to risk putting it on the page so it looked like a poem. I told the children that I found it always a little scary to do this—after all, what I wrote didn't necessarily sound like a poem yet, or have the polish of finished work—but if I didn't begin to see it as if it were a poem, I didn't know how it would ever become one.

Once children had rough drafts of "things-like-poems," I shared the notes and drafts of a poem I had written (see Figure 2). I explained how the seed of the poem came to me in an image that flashed through my mind while driving down a highway. I showed them the first squiggly lines, written so I wouldn't forget, then the brainstorming notes, where I searched for images, memories, and connections with the initial thought. I pointed out that my notes weren't complete sentences, that I now see I could have chosen other directions and trains of thought than I did. I read the places in my notes that had surprised and interested me when I first reread them, and showed how I let those surprises surface in the drafts. I pointed out an instance where I let go of a fact (I had been with my parents, walking across the frozen lake) to go with a wish (I wished it had been a more romantic occasion) because the moment seemed so isolated and romantic in my memory. I talked about revision as reimagining, and about the way experienced writers learned to trust their best lines and to follow those lines beyond the actual "facts" to "what could be." The children were called on to experiment with revision. First they read their poems very softly out loud so they could "feel" the poem in their mouths. They marked places that sounded or felt funny or awkward. Second, they looked for places where a reader might need more help getting the "picture" of what was described or felt. To see how Adam responded to this invitation, see Figure 3.

Next, the fifth graders copied favorite lines on a separate sheet of paper, ignoring the original temporarily, then trying to follow the good language to other good language. I noted that writers launched many experiments, some of which "failed" in that they wouldn't necessarily

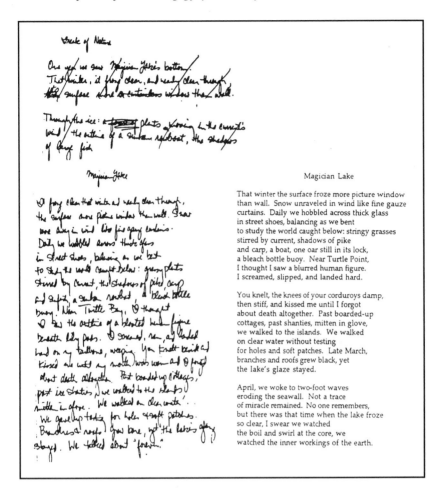

Magician Lake

That winter the surface froze more picture window
than wall. Snow unraveled in wind like fine gauze
curtains. Daily we hobbled across thick glass
in street shoes, balancing as we bent
to study the world caught below: stringy grasses
stirred by current, shadows of pike
and carp, a boat, one oar still in its lock,
a bleach bottle buoy. Near Turtle Point,
I thought I saw a blurred human figure.
I screamed, slipped, and landed hard.

You knelt, the knees of your corduroys damp,
then stiff, and kissed me until I forgot
about death altogether. Past boarded-up
cottages, past shanties, mitten in glove,
we walked to the islands. We walked
on clear water without testing
for holes and soft patches. Late March,
branches and roofs grew black, yet
the lake's glaze stayed.

April, we woke to two-foot waves
eroding the seawall. Not a trace
of miracle remained. No one remembers,
but there was that time when the lake froze
so clear, I swear we watched
the boil and swirl at the core, we
watched the inner workings of the earth.

Figure 2. Excerpts from the author's notes and drafts.

improve the text. Students told each other which experiments were working for their particular texts. See Figure 4 for Adam's response.

Finally, I asked that each child try a "radical" revision experiment. If the poem was a fat paragraph, what would happen if it were broken into stanzas and made skinny? If the speaker of the poem was a young boy, what would happen if the poem was spoken by an elderly woman? If the poem rhymed, what would happen if the writer went back to early notes and made it an unrhymed poem? Children were asked to jot down what they were trying on the corner of their papers. I offered suggestions to those who were stuck (Adam's next draft is shown in Figure 5; Figure 6 depicts another of his attempts at the "follow your best lines" experiment).

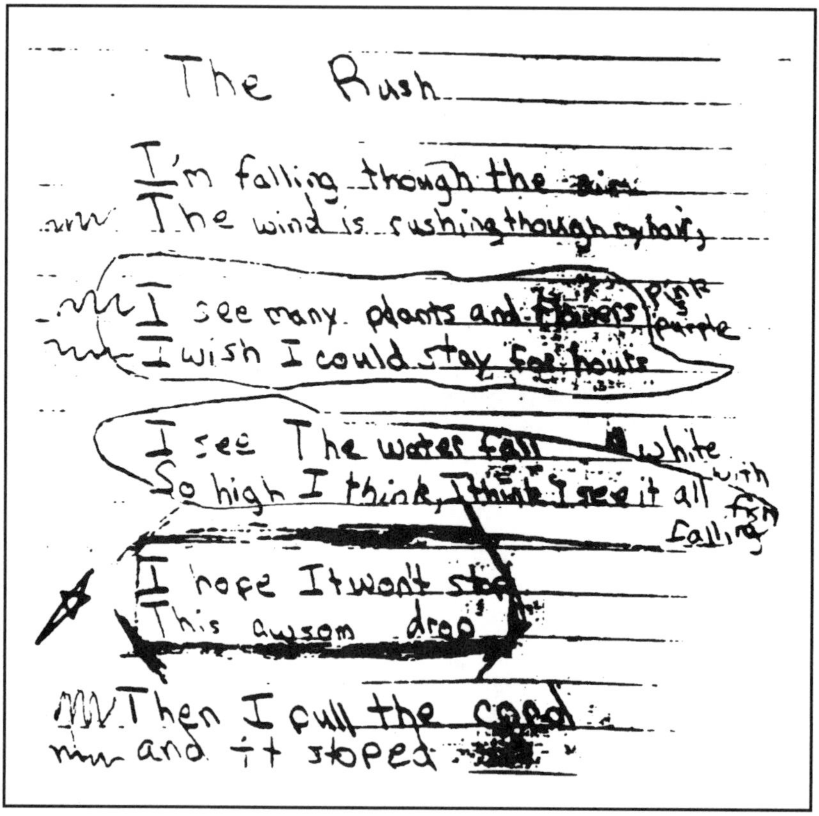
The Rush

I'm falling through the air
The wind is rushing though my hair,

I see many plants and flowers pink purple
I wish I could stay for houts

I see The water fall white with foam
So high I think, I think I see it all falling

I hope It won't stop
This awsom drop

Then I pull the cord
and it stoped

Figure 3. Adam's draft and correcting marks.

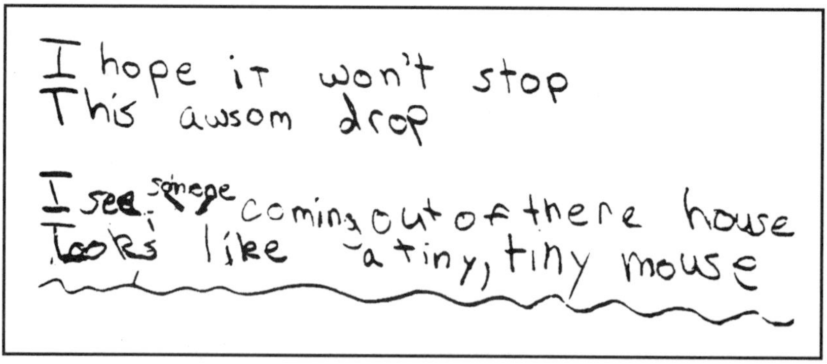
I hope it won't stop
This awsom drop

I see someone coming out of there house
Looks like a tiny, tiny mouse

Figure 4. Adam's favorite lines and his extension.

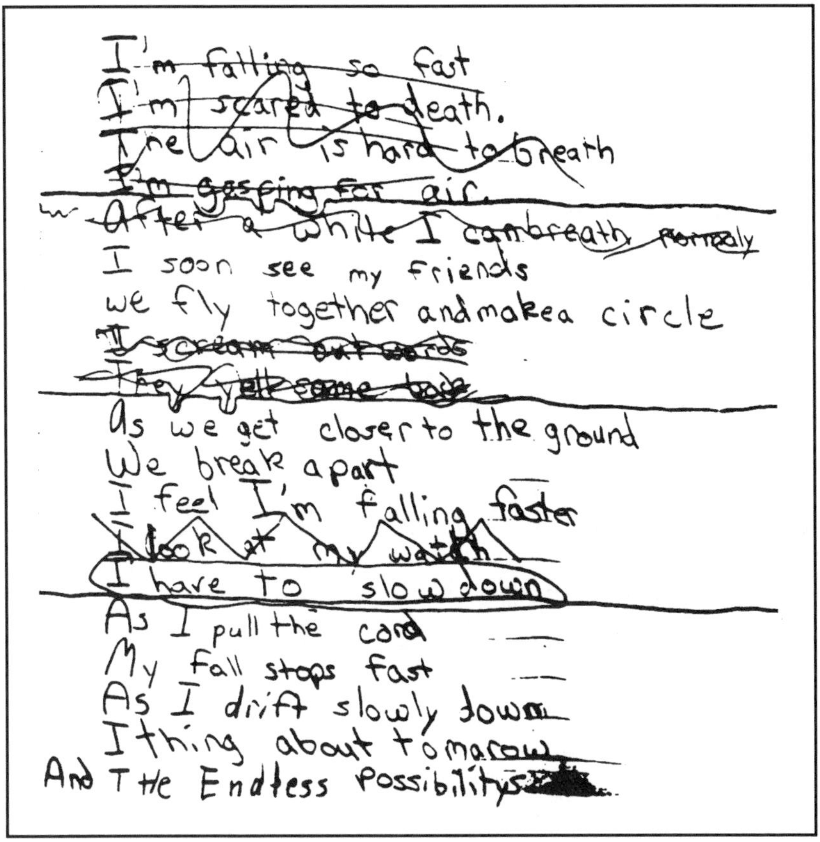
I'm falling so fast
I'm scared to death.
The air is hard to breath
I'm gasping for air.
After a while I can breath normally
I soon see my friends
we fly together and make a circle
I scream out words
They yell some back
As we get closer to the ground
We break apart
I feel I'm falling faster
I look at my watch
I have to slow down
As I pull the cord
My fall stops fast
As I drift slowly down
I thing about tomarow
And The Endless Possibilitys

Figure 5. Adam's next draft.

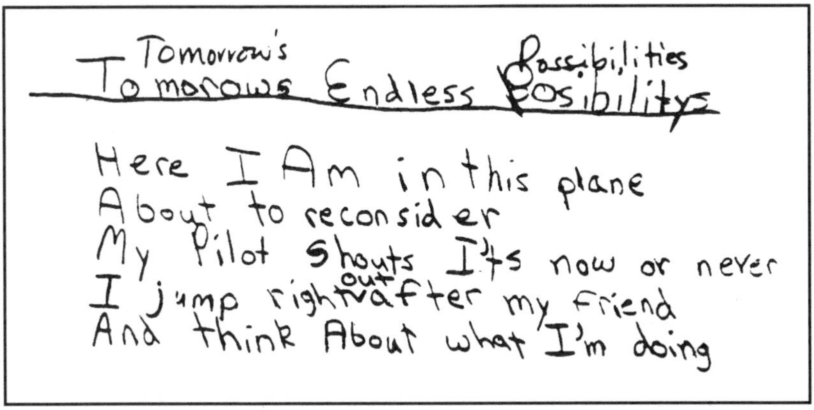
Tomorrow's Possibilities
Tomarows Endless Posibilitys

Here I Am in this plane
About to reconsider
My Pilot Shouts It's now or never
I jump right out after my friend
And think About what I'm doing

Figure 6. Adam trying the "follow your best lines" experiment again.

Tomorrow's Endless Possibilities

Here I am in this plane
About to reconsider
My pilot shouts it's now or never
I jump right out after my friend
And think about what I'm doing

It's like swimming, but harder
I get to my friends
We all hold hands
We're yelling and screaming
And all feeling great

This is a feeling I can't describe
Like jumping off of someplace high
But higher
You feel the air, you feel the wind
You feel the tightness of his hand

As the ground creeps closer
We very slowly let go
Of unreality and the hands
That joined us
For what seemed an eternity

Figure 7. "Tomorrow's Endless Possibilities"—final draft.

What Adam Learned

Adam's final draft of "Tomorrow's Endless Possibilities" (Figure 7), when juxtaposed against his first draft (Figure 3), shows that he has returned to and extended earlier meanings. In his notes, he indicates that he wanted to imagine his way into the perspective of an adult skydiver, because he "always wanted to skydive and surf" (Figure 1). In "The Rush," he does try to speak from the perspective of a skydiver, but he is kept from a very satisfying attempt by his sense that a school poem must rhyme (Figure 3). He probably has no model for the revision process, and does not seem to conceive of the multiple drafts and changes that may be needed before the poem succeeds. He marks favorite lines and adds several descriptive phrases: "pink and purple" to describe flowers, and "white with fish falling" to describe the waterfall. His first real experiment, copying favorite lines on a separate piece of paper and seeing where they lead, "fails." He is forced into gratuitous rhyme by his previous lines (Figure 4). When he is given "permission" to experiment by my example, permission even to abandon his draft and begin again, he tries another version of that adult voice. He allows himself to imagine his way into the situation again, to "image" the experience until it begins to come alive for him. He returns to and elaborates upon the mention of "friend," creating a new picture, a circle of skydiving friends (Figure 5). Crossed-out lines and other revision marks tell us that Adam is increasingly engaged with the text. He is trying a number of experiments that I have mentioned in class, breaking the poem into stanzas and eliminating lines that aren't satisfying for reasons of sound and meaning. He transfers a strategy that has "failed" him previously—abandon the original draft temporarily and follow your best lines to new text—to another context and modifies it slightly when he takes the last lines of the radical revision experiment, "I thin(k) about tomarow/And It's Endless Possibilitys," and shapes them into a title (Figure 6). He lets that line lead to an entirely new series of lines. Surprisingly, Adam does not use many words or phrases of the extensively marked draft in this new version of the poem. He does include the image of friends holding hands before the parachutes open, but begins the action of the poem inside the plane, with the speaker balking at the jump.

The final draft of "Tomorrow's Endless Possibilities" has many of the qualities of a crafted, heartfelt poem written by an experienced writer. Adam creates a text that has resonance; the poem is about a sky dive at the same time it is about future possibilities. His speaker is an adult, judging from the diction—"reconsider," "creeps," "unreality" and "eternity." The speaker has a range of complicated feelings throughout the jump—fear, exhilaration, timelessness, camaraderie, connection to the spiritual world, and loss. The speaker tries to describe an indescribable feeling through similes which are then qualified—"like swimming, but harder" and "like jumping off of someplace high/but higher." The poem's ending, "As the ground creeps closer/We very slowly let go/Of unreality and the hands/That joined us/For what seemed an eternity," moves into abstract, philosophical territory while maintaining the concrete image just as many professionally written poems do.

Adam's decision to omit end stop punctuation causes the reader to free fall through the stanzas until the end, where the reader drops into the white space of the page. Adam has shaped his poem into four five-line stanzas. He does not use end rhyme, but chooses (perhaps subcon-

sciously) to unify the poem with subtle patterns of repeated sound—
"reconsid<u>er</u>," "nev<u>er</u>," "hard<u>er</u>"; "frie<u>nd</u>," "ha<u>nd</u>," "wi<u>nd</u>," all one-syl-
lable words; and "slow<u>ly</u>," "unreali<u>ty</u>," and "eterni<u>ty</u>."

The growth of Adam's text, from "The Rush," a typical fifth-grade
attempt at poetry, to "Tomorrow's Endless Possibilities," a resonant poem
with levels of diction, craft, and commitment that usually mark a far
more experienced writer, over the course of a single week, calls for several angles of discussion. Adam's poem was sparked and partially drafted
in fairly typical fifth-grade classroom workshop conditions. Adam did
not receive special coaching, although I did comment on some of each
child's work in writing and in brief, one-on-one conferences. However,
I suspect that Adam had a notion that the professionally written poems,
stories, novels, and articles that fifth graders read were different, or perhaps were *supposed to be* different from the things fifth graders wrote.
From my experiences talking with other young writers, I expect Adam
had little conception of the work that writers do to create texts that move
readers. In our sessions together, I concretely demonstrated the ways
writers searched for personally meaningful topics and modeled the sorts
of imaginative transformations experienced writers knew to try. Along
the way, I tried to create an atmosphere where risk-taking experimentation was possible and necessary.

Adam's drafts were among the handful from this fifth-grade class
that showed profound growth over the span of a week. Some children
tried revision experiments that were less successful; some children were
less enamored of their subjects. Two points should be made from this
fact: First, I would have no way to know about the growth of children's
drafts if I hadn't encouraged them to save all of their work. Notes, drafts,
and final versions tell me something about the seeds of engagement and
the strategies attempted. More important, young writers need to learn
to trace their own commitment and growth; experienced writers usually know to save notes, plans, and drafts for reference, difficult as that
may be in a computer age.

Second, it would be unlikely that all learners in a class at any level
would catch on immediately to concepts such as the writerly search for
one's passions and revision as "reimagining." Some students will need
different examples, different topics, different conversations, and more
practice. The fact that Adam and some of his classmates successfully
transformed rough notes and failed textual experiments into substantive
poems could easily serve as a model for other children. Potentially, Adam
and several others could become peer coaches.

As a teacher, I know that if Adam is aware of growth in himself over
a short period of time after a risk was taken, a seed has been planted

which may very well sprout. In this particular writing episode, Adam wrote *as if* he were an experienced, committed writer. He held on to his desire to say something from a skydiver's point of view, but treated his early words and textual experiments as though they were temporary, aiming to create something important and aesthetically satisfying. If I had had the opportunity to work with Adam as his classroom teacher, I would have known to refer to the experience of "Tomorrow's Endless Possibilities" when he worked on other projects and written pieces. I would have had chances to know him personally, and could have further encouraged him to delve into topics and issues of personal significance. The experience of experimentation, engagement, and success could have become a metaphor for what we hoped Adam would encounter in future learning situations—real possibilities for tomorrow.

The sequence of activities I led Adam and his classmates through was very similar to those I have constructed for high school students and prospective teachers. I've also created similar sequences for practicing teachers in the context of a National Writing Project Summer Institute, a five-week workshop where teachers become writers and teach one another about their learning. Although I adjusted my pace and examples to the levels of comprehension and response they displayed as I listened to their classroom conversation and observed them reading and writing, these fifth graders were clearly able to grasp difficult, writerly concepts when provided with accessible examples and models, including that of my own process.

While I couldn't follow up with this class of fifth graders beyond this brief visit, I have used Adam's drafts, along with those of other students, as examples for Writing Project teachers attempting to revise their practice. The drafts epitomize the growth that is possible if a writer is willing to risk experimenting. The teachers tend to understand the examples in several ways: They are a model for what teacher/poets should be willing to attempt as they work on their own writing; they are an argument for the capabilities of children and teenagers; they are evidence of the profound growth that is possible in a classroom where a teacher models writing strategies. Also, they exemplify the sort of evidence a teacher should be watching for in a reading/writing workshop.

The Shadow Subject—Myself

While the previous section may give glimpses of my approach to teaching and the ways I use my own drafts and experiences of poetry to coach both children and adult learners, it does not illuminate the depths or potential dangers of self-reflection I and other poet/teachers must engage in as we bring "hurt and self-doubt into the light" so that "learning will flower," as Parker Palmer eloquently argues. Perhaps the following experience better illustrates this point.

About ten years ago, while working as a high school teacher, I became deeply concerned about one of my students. This young woman had been sexually assaulted as a small child and was in agony emotionally; she was institutionalized for several weeks during one semester, as images of abuse flooded her memory. While I tried to coach her literacy and to connect with her personally, I felt almost helpless in the face of her anguish. In fact, her pain pushed me to relive my own trauma: I had been raped five or six years earlier, and had long been struggling to regain my own sense of balance. Eventually, I wrote a poem, explaining to myself and to her, the ways I was learning to survive:

Let Me Tell You How

How is habit, Elizabeth:
pruning roses. I let last year's
bramble prick until my ungloved hands
bead with blood. I cut back to where
the green streaks up the shoot,
picturing myself cupping blossoms
full and lush as magnolias.

After nightmares, I leave a bulb
lit in the closet. I move my red sweater
to the back so the light won't have a
frightening cast. Damn the electric bill,
it burns a full week, until I forget
once again there was ever a man.

To drink, I block the apartment
entrance with an umbrella chair
so I'll stumble on the way out. I
pour a coffee mug of bourbon, turn
on the blues and pull, aiming to reach
dead drunk before crazy.

I have rules for my lover. We talk
for at least an hour before he holds
my hand, he looks until I see him, then
speaks our names if he's to love me.
He can never lunge or grab me, or even
pretend. This I'm sure you understand.

To sleep, I say the names of roses: dark
Carousel, Aztec, Crimson Glory, Dortmund,
Gypsy, the red Peace, Karl Herbst, then
pink Bewitched, Duet, Picadilly, Sunbonnet,
Pascali, Elizabeth of Glamis, words
calling up the bloom and the armor.

> None of this may work for you, or
> for me tomorrow. There will always be
> another woman learning her way
> down a thistled hillside. Why,
> Elizabeth, we can't answer, but if
> you find a path to the valley,
> call to her. Tell her how.

The poem was a risky, deeply personal statement written as I tried to say to myself what was in my heart as I reached out to this troubled young woman. My efforts on her behalf went well beyond the boundaries of traditional English teaching, and probably some educators would find it inappropriate that I eventually gave her a copy of the poem. I was trying to say, *You aren't alone. I, too, have been devastated, and I understand that we are changed utterly by such experiences. Survival is day-to-day coping, writing, and reaching out to others so they can learn they are not alone, either, as I am reaching out to you.* In my work with this student, I talked about the power I felt when I took an episode from my experience where I had felt especially powerless, and shaped it into a work of "art," that others—my private audience and the larger public audience—could appreciate. My student took these words and actions very seriously. When I met her initially, she was a successful writer of school-assigned essays, but did not do much writing for her own reasons outside of school. She had little experience reading and writing poems at that time. Over the next year, she became quite a skilled writer and reader of poetry, winning a first prize for a collection of poems in a *Detroit Free Press* student writing competition, one of a handful out of approximately six hundred entries. Her interest continued when she went on to college, although she remained troubled and self-destructive all of the years we stayed in touch. At some point, I became aware that "Let Me Tell You How" was a form of teaching—I was attempting to teach my student that I cared about her, that she was not alone in her anguish, and that writing could be used in a powerful way.

Subsequently, I have used my own poetry writing on several other occasions explicitly to "teach." Like "Let Me Tell You How," these other poems were written for particular individuals, as well as for a larger audience. In those other instances, too, I was conscious that if I were to write "a true word," I might be able to use poetry to reach someone in crisis in ways that talk or prose could not. In my other "teaching" poems, however, I have tended to take stories or facts about the individual, to reimagine those stories, and retell them with compassion, so the individual could see himself/herself anew. For instance, a friend who had been physically and emotionally beaten as a small child, grew up to be a self-destructive adult, for whom fictionalizing had become problematic.

He lost a prestigious job when his half-truths and lies were discovered, and he felt guilty, humiliated, and despondent. In a poem entitled "The Changeling," I tried to remind him that, as a child, he had needed to pretend in order to survive, and if he could, he should try to love that vulnerable child. In this case and in others, I believe I was trying to communicate the strength, beauty, and hope I saw in individual lives, even as they were despairing. I think it is fair to say that the writing of poetry has served to develop empathy and compassion in me in certain instances; thus, I recognize the possibility for such development in other writers. Of course, acts of connection and communication are fraught with risk as well; one's aims can be more complicated or selfish than one realizes, or the intended recipient can be hostile or unresponsive to the writer's intended message.

Engaging in Continual Analysis—Sharon Galley Prays for Illumination

Just as I use poetry to teach myself and others, other teacher-writers with whom I have worked have come to regard poetic writing as a "vital necessity," and have shared that insight with their own students. One such teacher is Sharon Galley, a veteran fifth-grade teacher at Haviland Elementary School in Waterford, Michigan. Galley aspired to be a writer during her college years, and experimented with poetry and journal writing as an elementary classroom teacher, encouraged by a workshop experience at Martha's Vineyard. However, she says that writing took on a new function as she grieved after the death of her husband, David. Perhaps not coincidentally, Sharon Galley applied to a National Writing Project Summer Institute I was directing, the Oakland Writing Project Institute, in June 1993, a little more than a month after her husband died. She talks about the role writing played during that difficult passage:

> I didn't really understand this thing of working out or making meaning until I journaled after David died. So many times, I would just know I would have to write just because I couldn't figure out what the hell was going on. I would sit down at the computer and bang on the keyboard, typing as fast as I could, never really knowing where the words would lead me. This actually started happening during the Writing Project. . . .
>
> I started working out meaning that summer and I must have written just tons. . . . It was such a revelation to me, that I would sit down so confused and so upset, and I could come away, and I could feel so much better, because it started to make sense and clarify the muddle in my brain. I mean, David's death never will make sense, but at least I could get on to the next time I needed to journal.
>
> When I shared my journal entries with a church support group, explaining how I used writing, my minister said he saw journaling as a type of prayer. What a revelation that was! And how true.

Galley's minister's assessment resonates with the words of Owen Barfield, who wrote, "When the poet probes either his internal world or the external world he is involved in a spiritual process, a form of prayer for illumination, perfection."

An excerpt from her journal, which is a weave of poem drafts and prose entries, illustrates the kind of search she was engaged in:

> So this is one of the dragons (reference to Flannery O'Connor's es-
> says, "The King of the Birds" and "The Fiction Writer and His Coun-
> try") of my life. I guess I could say that brain tumors are the epitome
> of dragons. David said that. But dragons have some redeeming
> value: they're fascinating. I mean they're scraggly and sharp and
> pointed and breathe fire. Brain tumors do that too. They reach out
> with sharp scraggly cells and envelope whatever is close, closing
> off memory cells, walking orders, life's decisions. Reducing life to
> its basest existence.
>
> Just what gives a brain tumor the right to have such power? Just
> what gives a dragon the right to destroy beauty by fire? Why can a
> brain tumor destroy vibrancy, intellect, humor with absolutely no
> qualms about sapping life right out of someone? A brain tumor is
> much more evil than a dragon. It isn't even fascinating. It's just evil.
> But wait a moment—a brain tumor still does not have control over
> love. Aha! So we can keep that. We can keep looks with eyes, touches,
> a feeling of linkage, connection between us. We can keep that. I still
> have that.

In this entry, Sharon Galley rages at the tumor that killed her husband, comparing it unfavorably to a dragon. Yet, in the process of writing about what she has lost, she discovers, at least for the moment, what remains. In a poem written on the heels of the dragon entry, "Swans on the Bay," Galley's speaker notes the contrast of the swans' down against rocks, their dark almond eyes and the "nail-tough beak." Reflection on the swans leads the poem's speaker to embrace the contrasting forms of grief she is experiencing, both the "sharp prolonged grief that pierces my insides" and the "peaceful sorrow that hushes my sobs."

Sharon Galley says that the personal and aesthetic writing she has been doing has influenced her teaching. This influence is reflected in her teaching log; one entry describes a mini-lesson she gave on writing "from the heart," when she noticed a number of her students were writing fiction that seemed "silly . . . even shallow," and poems that were safely abstract. Galley now understands that poetry can be "a way of looking . . . examined life is what it is." After her mini-lesson, she records observable, concrete signs that some students begin to take on issues and moments of greater consequence. She claims that "the more poetry kids write, the more they start digging below it (the surface of life)." She says poets "get right to (depth), sooner," and she feels her own writing "now is on a different level." For Sharon Galley and now, for her students, poetic writing is essential, not a luxury or frill.

Toward a Pedagogy of Possibility—Laura Schiller Opens Pandora's Box

When Laura Schiller, a sixth-grade language arts and social studies teacher at Birney Middle School in Southfield, Michigan, reflects upon the role of imaginative/aesthetic writing in her revision of teaching practice, she mentions the drafting of a poem, "My Grandma's Arms," as a turning point. She had never written a poem before, but decided to experiment during the course of a Summer Institute that I led in 1992.

> You were talking about the way poems are like photographs, pictures. I was looking for a photograph of personal significance. I chose not to write about my husband—there could have been ramifications—I *could* write about my grandmother. She was dead; what harm could there be? I didn't have any idea what I was opening up. It was a Pandora's box. I was closed out of her death—she died when I was nine. This was something in my life that had been left unresolved.

The "photograph" she chose to write about was an image in her memory. Schiller describes the writing and rewriting of the poem as a cathartic experience. As she wrote, she cried. Laura Schiller says she didn't feel "bad"; she felt as though she was finally acknowledging her feelings. "To this day, I cannot read the poem without crying," she says. The act of reading (her own) words that moved her was a lesson in itself. "I was given permission to be affected when I am reading; I allowed myself to feel more deeply." Schiller notes that this was the first time she ever wrote a poem or something personally significant. Her previous experiences with writing had been largely informational and detached from her life. Yet, in this instance, she brought the shadow subject—herself and her unresolved feelings about her grandmother—into the light, permitting learning to flower, as Palmer suggested.

The experience of writing and revising "My Grandma's Arms" became emblematic for Schiller partly because it represented an episode of risk-taking and experimentation. She had written in a genre she had never before attempted, she had written her way into something deeply personal, she had willingly drafted and redrafted text (some twenty draft pages), and she had allowed the writing of the poem to spill out of the "school" into her life. The implications of the experience for her own teaching of writing were evident.

While it is fairly easy to sketch out the connection between this writing episode and Laura Schiller's evolving approach to teaching writing, I want to make a stickier sort of case: Schiller espouses a pedagogy of possibility that is now linked to her growing knowledge of aesthetic/ imaginative, or poetic, text and its creation. In her classroom, poetic writing has become an important path toward "compassion for the suffering of others," toward "continual analysis of conditions of existence," and toward personal voice. Schiller uses her own personal narratives-turned-poems, stories, or memoirs to model the power of literacy in her life for her sixth graders. In her classroom, poetic writing is used to realize "a variety of differentiated human capacities," as Roger Simon says a pedagogy of possibility aims to do, "rather than denying, diluting, or distorting those capacities."

In an article she wrote for the January 1996 issue of *Language Arts*, "Coming to America: Community from Diversity," Schiller describes how she "reimagine(d) her curriculum" in response to diverse student lives and languages in Southfield, a multiethnic, multiracial, Detroit suburb, by co-creating, with her students, a year-long thematic study of immigration.

> I would invite stories about our ancestors, our heritage, slavery, and immigration from both parents and students, written in whatever language the authors felt most comfortable. I wanted to model that literacy is valuable in all languages . . . and everyone . . . can participate.

Within the theme "Coming to America," students had opportunities to explore the relationships between factual narratives and personal stories, and aesthetically crafted and/or imaginative genres, including memoirs, biographies, drama, poetry, and historical fiction. Schiller's students also researched such emotionally charged issues as racism, ethnic scapegoating, and the current debate over immigration policy, and shared their learning with younger students and their own families through oral presentations and a class book, *Coming to America*, that included works in home languages and in translation by parents, grandparents, and students. While Schiller willingly tackled difficult concepts and issues with her sixth graders, she explained in the article that she has come to understand that "in the language arts classroom—whether conferencing, revising, or sharing—developing a nonjudgmental learning community is the first priority." Her emphasis on the development of a tolerant, caring classroom community with parents, students, and her colleagues set the stage for the recognition and development of her students' various talents.

Laura Schiller imagined a community where people could communicate with and care about one another, regardless of their cultural and linguistic differences. She imagined a classroom where the divide between student lives and school literacy is permanently bridged. By imagining and articulating her vision of *what could be*, she began to work toward the realization of her dream. As Maxine Greene paraphrases Freire, "Imagination and conjecture about a different world than the unjust one that exists for so many are as necessary to the transformation of reality as a design is for a craftsperson or an artisan" (21).

Conclusion

When I work with children and with teachers, I am aware that I am doing far more than teaching a genre when I talk about searching for the subjects, ideas, and moments that can cause one to write poetry. The search for one's strongly held commitments is part of a lifetime quest for self-knowledge. As a teacher, I know I am helping learners discover their own natural points of engagement in the learning process. A child who is fascinated by birds, a teenager who dreams of a world without war, an adult who is haunted by the death of a parent—each has a story to tell, and each has enduring questions. As points of engagement are discovered, it is the work of the teacher to show how literacy can be used to throughly explore the obsessions, tell and transcend the stories, and take purposeful action. When I talk about imagining "other" versions of a moment or life story, as certain poets have done, I am aware that this process is critical in many facets of life. Anyone who has ever made a difference—musicians, politicians, philosophers, inventors, parents—has had to create alternate possibilities, through words and action. The willingness and ability to imagine other possibilities are prerequisites to conscious learning and intentional change.

The creation of a community of learners is, first of all, an imaginative act. A teacher must envision a democratic space where diverse learners discover new meanings and care about each other and themselves. She must believe each one has important stories to tell, that each one is capable of growth and change. The classroom is a microcosmic society, a potential model for teachers and for students as they attempt to relate with others in the world outside of formal schooling. In my experience, teachers such as Sharon Galley and Laura Schiller, who are highly effective at transforming student understandings, are conscious that methods of inquiry and acts of creation in their disciplines can become metaphors for ways of living. Scientific questions can be posed and solutions explored; impossibly complex musical compositions can be learned and performed; new worlds can be imagined and created through poetic writing. If teachers have opportunities to see *themselves* as creators, if they *consciously* experience moments of growth, they probably will be able to foster such growth in other learners. In the democratic classrooms of teachers who understand that poetry is not a luxury, hope and compassion are taught, along with a powerful, enfranchising literacy that makes the extraordinary possible.

Works Cited

Barfield, Owen. 1973. (1928). *Poetic Diction: A Study in Meaning.* Middletown, CT: Wesleyan University Press.

Galley, Sharon. *Mourning Song.* Unpublished manuscript of journal entries and poetry.

Giroux, Henry. 1992. "Critical Literacy and Student Experience: Donald Graves' Approach to Literacy." *Becoming Political: Readings and Writings in the Politics of Literacy Education.* Ed. Patrick Shannon. Portsmouth, NH: Heinemann. 15–20.

Greene, Maxine. 1995. "Metaphors and Possibility." *On Common Ground: Strengthening Teaching through School-University Partnership* 5: 5, 20–21.

Lorde, Audre. 1982. "Poems Are Not Luxuries." *Claims for Poetry.* Ed. Donald Hall. Ann Arbor, MI: University of Michigan Press. 282–85.

O'Connor, Flannery. 1969. (1961). *Mystery and Manners: Occasional Prose.* Eds. Sally Fitzgerald and Robert Fitzgerald. New York: The Noonday Press (Farrar, Straus & Giroux).

O'Reilley, Mary Rose. 1993. *The Peaceable Classroom.* Portsmouth, NH: Heinemann.

Ozick, Cynthia. 1989. *Metaphor and Memory: Essays.* New York: Knopf.

Palmer, Parker. 1976. "Meeting for Learning: Education in a Quaker Context." *The Pendle Hill Bulletin* 284: 1–7.

Schiller, Laura. 1996. "Coming to America: Community from Diversity." *Language Arts* 73.1: 46–51.

Simon, Roger I. 1992. "Empowerment as a Pedagogy of Possibility." *Becoming Political: Readings and Writings in the Politics of Literacy Education.* Ed. Patrick Shannon. Portsmouth, NH: Heinemann. 139–51.

5 Unsheltered Lives: Battered Women Talk about School

Carol L. Winkelmann
Xavier University

To study literacy and its uses is to commit oneself to the study of contexts and relations. Literacy exists only as human activity in context, and our job as students of literacy is to decide which activity and which contexts are worth studying and what relations we must seek to establish between literacy, language, learning, schooling, and life before and after schooling.

—Jay Robinson, *Conversations on the Written Word*

If it was ever possible ideologically to characterize women's lives by the distinction of public and private domains—suggested by images of the division of working-class life into factory and home, of bourgeois life into market and home, and of gender existence into personal and political realms—it is now a totally misleading ideology, even to show how both terms of these dichotomies construct each other in practice and in theory. I prefer a network ideological image, suggesting the profusion of spaces and identities and the permeability of boundaries in the personal body and in the body politic.

—Donna J. Haraway, "A Manifesto for Cyborgs"

The bible says the meek shall inherit the earth and, ladies, we know this is not true.

—A woman in shelter

Introduction: An Ethnography of Violence Against Women

The Women's House is an urban shelter for battered women in a midwestern city in the United States.[1] In May 1992, I began volunteering there, one evening a week. In the beginning, I came to the house for two reasons: to serve as a general volunteer and to learn as an ethnolinguist about women and violence. For a while I performed a variety of shelter services: answering the hotline; conducting interviews with

104

women who were moving into the house; caring for children; and driving women to job interviews, social service agencies, and the courthouse. In the meantime, I read the various literatures on domestic violence—social work, sociological, and feminist literatures, and I attended local conferences and workshops designed for agencies, churches, and women. I began to keep an ethnographic journal and to study women's language and culture. My intention was praxis-oriented: to immerse in theory and action in the light of women's lived experience with violence.

For a long while I did this in the conventional way of my field: that is, very quietly.[2] In 1994, I came out. I began to share my credentials as an academic and a researcher directly with shelter women because the shelter invited me to establish a literacy or story-writing circle. I started to offer my time to shelter women as a literacy worker, so I began to create and, in fact, to proffer a public identity as a teacher-researcher. Despite the new claim to authority, however, the code of the literacy circle has always been consensual. In keeping with a non–obtrusive sensibility, I do nothing apart from the will of the women; I simply provide the occasion to get together to talk and to write.[3] I take it as a sign of success that, after one session, a participant did not even know we had had "group." She thought we were just "having a good time" with writing until the literacy person arrived.[4]

The name of the program, *VoicePlace,* was chosen by women living in the house at the time we began the sessions. One night a week, the women help me clear the dining room table of the remaining dinner plates, children's toys, ashtrays, highlighted want ads, and informational fliers. Paper and pencils are passed. We pick a topic by consensus—any topic, although they mostly write about their shattered lives—and we write, we read aloud what we've written, and we talk. The moods of the sessions shift drastically, often within a session itself, as the women explore their feelings about a variety of topics. The moods swing from jubilation at having escaped a knife-slinging spouse (to name just one all-too-frequent scenario), to anger about the second-class status of women, to desolation about leaving behind a marriage, a life, a dream.

Sometimes we decide not to write. I bring my laptop computer, we talk, and I record the conversations. This particular activity—*talking into the computer,* as we call it, or *telling stories to the computer*—is a favorite activity. I bring copies of the conversation the next week. The women take pleasure in seeing their voices captured by the computer. They love to see their words in print, their stories in writing. To shelter women, talking into the computer yields real results: they can see their words in print immediately. They have direct and immediate control over their language because I always offer them the opportunity to change their contributions in any way they wish, either during a conversation or after they have read the printout.[5] The printed conversations go into a book along with the stories they pen themselves. The book is meant to be passed from one woman to another as they come and go from the shelter. The women delight in knowing their words are reaching the wider community and, because their stories are captured in print and so seem to have staying power, they believe their words actually matter. They come to believe their personal lives are significant, even in the public forum. "It's my five minutes of glory. Everyone gets five minutes and this is my five," said one woman. Further, their personal pain has a positive outcome—educating others about violence against womankind. In short, I learned how to invite shelter women and workers into my research as reporters, participants, co-investigators, and collaborators (Mishler 123) and also as social co-activists.[6]

The shelter women teach me to listen more deeply to learn how women use language to negotiate their way in an unkind world. That is, even though I am the feminist, the linguist, and the ethnographer of literacy, the women have been the teachers. They teach me about the meaning of their lives as women and about the meaning of my own life as a critical educator. Now I am no longer blind to the people around me: I can see I have family, friends, and students who have been assaulted, violated, and abused. You do too. This is the reality of life for women in the late twentieth century. The oft-repeated maxim—domestic violence is the single greatest cause of injury to women—translates into these frightful numbers: Three out of every four women are assaulted in their lifetimes. Domestic violence occurs in one out of every three American households. One woman is physically abused every eight seconds in the United States, and one is raped every six minutes.[7]

Like many sheltered middle-class women and men, I sometimes wish to disbelieve the nature and extent of violence against women. The statistics are simply staggering. The unsheltered women—that is, those living in the shelters—do not have the luxury of suspending belief. They must reckon with bruises and bandages and broken limbs. Sheltered, unsheltered: the story-telling binds us. It is a way to make sense of the sheer awfulness of it. After the embarrassment of making public a private discourse of family shame, broken homes, and betrayed loves, women who have been assaulted often have a desire to *tell all*. In the shelter and sometimes even in the neighborhoods before they come to the shelter,[8] the women know why I am there and what I do. They call me the Story Lady, and they know I am a teacher-researcher-writer.

Over these several years, I have become increasingly conscientized by my work. As I learn more and more about violence against women from battered women and the staff women who worked with them, I have come to understand not only the rich possibilities of, but the real demand for, action research and overt border-crossing pedagogical interaction. I now teach a course on women and violence at my university. In it, my students and I explore the linguistics of violence against women in its historical, sociological, and literary contexts. The students engage in community service at the shelter. Sometimes, on donated computers, they help women write their stories. The shelter women also interact with my students through the Internet. Through these new ways of "being schooled," we have all learned the importance of being present to one another as we teach and learn for social change.

Between two very unlikely cultures—the cultures of the shelter and of the university—the borders have been crossed. This essay is the story of what I have learned by traversing these boundaries. There's too much to tell, of course. After a few words about what it means to be a battered woman and a brief look at some shelter statistics, I will limit my essay to what the women in the shelter think about school. There are good reasons to focus on this particular topic. If any part of the population has been forsaken by the institution of school—the place where students are ostensibly taught to think, to read, and to write critically—it is the girls and young women who attended them as elementary, junior high, and high school students. Clearly, most teachers have had nothing to say to girls about the ugly facts of the violence in their everyday lives. This is the *evaded curriculum*.[9] Yet, shortchanged and ill-prepared, shelter women have a lot to say to educators about schools.

The Women in Shelter

What does it mean to be a battered woman? The meaning alters as the vantage point to the bruises and broken bones shifts.[10] Cultural and social workers educate in the community by offering a composite portrait of the most vulnerable women affected by violence. Some of the traits frequently given are low self-esteem; feelings of self-blame and failure; economic dependency; and fearfulness, anxiety, and depression. Among the characteristics given for batterers are tendencies toward low self-esteem; isolation and insecurity; drug and alcohol dependency; feelings of guilt and failure; jealousy; denial; and an inability to express intimacy. It is recognized, on the other hand, that each perpetrator and victim has a particular style: a cluster of behaviors of their own. They engage in a series of isolated violent events that constitute an ongoing pattern or style of violent interaction.[11]

Whatever the particular pattern, the result is the same. In long-term relationships, abusive partners diminish the self-esteem of the women who live with them, devastating their lives, consuming their energy in matters of survival, and deadening their potential as contributing members of the local community and civic society. In other words, through degrading words and dangerous deeds, violent partners attempt to limit the human agency of their wives or lovers, often reducing them to fearful, dependent, and coerced beings. Simply, battered women are oppressed women, women struggling for full human agency.[12]

One question for the educator is this: What relationship, if any, exists between the school life of girls and the adult life of battered women? Educating children to assume their full potential as adults in community and civic society, to assume their full human agency, is the goal of our educational endeavors. From the vantage point of a critical educator, shelter women have been failed by the school system because schools—I will argue—all too often create obstacles for girls and women who are trying to assume their full human agency. About this failure, the women ought to be able to speak for themselves.[13]

First, however, a few shelter statistics. Like most urban shelters, the Women's House operates at full capacity. In 1994, the hotline staff fielded 12,498 telephone calls: a monthly average of 1,042 calls. Most hotline callers want basic information. Oftentimes, they simply want to know if they actually are victims of domestic violence. They are not sure if the particular constellation of abuses they experience—physical, sexual, and psychological—constitutes violence.[14] Frequently, they describe their personal situations, get affirmation, encouragement, and a list of options for breaking out of their volatile home situations, and then they hang up. Other women need immediate escape from dangerous partners. If there is room, they come to the shelter; if not, they are referred to other shelters or they put their names on a waiting list and try to cope until there is room. In 1994, the shelter accepted 230 women with their 286 children. This is an average of nineteen women and twenty-four children each month. The average length of stay was thirteen days: the shortest stay was one day and the longest stay was seventy-one days. Ethnically, the women reflect the lower- and working-class population of the local community. Of the 230 women who lived there in 1994, 143 women were African American, eighty-four were white women, and three were of other races. Many of the white women have Appalachian heritage. Nearly all are desperately poor. In 1994, 135 women reported incomes of $0 to $4,990.00 per year. This is well below the national poverty level which the federal government defines as $14,335 per year for a family of four.[15]

According to the psychiatrist on staff, who consulted with shelter residents once a week until federal funds were cut last year, nearly half of the women were treated for some form of "mental illness," mostly depression.[16] The shelter psychiatrist estimated that 25 percent of the women are chemically dependent. The drugs most commonly used by the women are alcohol, marijuana, and crack.

Although data concerning family, mental health, and medical history are gathered regularly by the staff for the purposes of funding the shelter, training personnel, or assisting women to find employment, educational data are not regularly compiled. If they were compiled, the results would be mixed. Most women I've encountered either have high school diplomas or have dropped out of school. Of the many women who dropped out, some have GEDs. A definite minority have some vocational, college, or university training. Several women I have encountered have had bachelor's degrees and one had a master's degree. Many women express interest in job training; yet, because they are preoccupied with family crisis and perhaps because there seems to be so little opportunity to do so, few women express serious, immediate interest in school. The torn flyer advertising GED training on the shelter bulletin board is one the shelter staff seldom replaces; contrarily, the fliers for various support groups for battered women are well circulated and well used.

The Shelter as Research Site

As if censure of the school system for not fulfilling its public charge is not cause enough for inquiry: What other reasons make the shelter a good place to learn about school? First of all, there is a dearth of research on adult literacy learners. As Wendy Luttrell points out, there have been few studies of how adult literacy learners "view their skills, knowledge, or competencies" (1993, 513). There is, she writes, "a curious gap given the conventional wisdom that says past schooling experiences are determining factors in current educational pursuits." In her research, Luttrell considers women who voluntarily seek adult education programs to improve their personal or economic situations. She explores their school memories, particularly memories about "teachers' pets," to learn how women view their own ways of knowing. The women in her study distinguish "schoolwise" and "streetwise" or "commonsense" knowledge, and they see themselves as in control of the latter as opposed to the former. Of course, schools do not reward streetwise sense. Luttrell also argues that schools, by privileging an ethics of work and public life over an ethics of care, alienate girls and render their gifts and talents invisible.[17]

In my research, I consider women who are not voluntarily seeking adult education programs to improve their personal or economic situation. They are seeking basic survival elements: food, housing, and jobs. They are in the midst of crisis and, while they come voluntarily to the literacy circle to talk and write about their lives, they are not primarily seeking educational improvement. Instead they are highly skeptical of their own capacity to take care of themselves and their children. This is precisely the point. Most women in the shelter are acutely aware that they are ill-prepared to take financial care of themselves or their children. They believe they do not have the skills, knowledge, or competencies to make it without federal or state funds for basic subsistence, funds which—in the current political climate—are ever-diminishing. In fact, most of them do not have the skills, knowledge, or competencies to take a place in the technology-driven, competitive world of work. Their futures are bleak and they are angry. I hear questions such as these: Why are we in this position? Why can't we get adequate jobs? Why haven't we learned marketable skills? Streetwise knowledge is essential for survival. Commonsense and an ethics of care are good. But commonsense and care are one matter; marketable jobs skills are another.[18] Many women blame their economic failure on a variety of reasons, including racism, classism, sexism; most of all, they blame it on themselves. Many women in the shelter feel they were detoured somehow from career goals by life issues, often issues of survival in inhospitable environments; consequently, they simply are not up to the challenges now looming large in their future.

In *Reviving Ophelia* Mary Pipher, a clinical psychologist, offers explanation. She attends to the development of adolescent girls, arguing that cultural conditions are creating unprecedented stresses on girls. Sexism, violence against girls and women, and different, lowered expectations for girls cause them to lose touch of their interests, their confidence, their personhood. Pipher argues that adolescence is a time of the betrayal of the self: girls betray their deepest selves in order to please others. In the context of schools, schoolgirls are dissuaded from traditionally male educational goals and from overall high achievement. Instead, they are socialized to less fulfilling, ultimately less lucrative careers—if any at all apart from ones geared around their biological functions as sexual beings. Sensing their lesser worth, girls are left confused, angry, and depressed. Their human potential at this stage of their lives is left unrealized.

The 1992 AAUW Report on *How Schools Shortchange Girls*, produced by the Wellesley College Center for Research on Women, provides the facts. Simply put, schools are bad for girls. They teach negative self-image through a variety of ways, including, sex-segregated courses, bias in testing, sexual harassment, inequitable teacher attention and encouragement, sexist stereotyping in schoolbooks, unequal distribution of resources,[19] fewer opportunities for extracurricular activities and sports, and sheer neglect. Not surprisingly, girls leave school with a diminished sense of worth. They have lower self-esteem and self-confidence; they have higher anxiety and depression. Together, the hidden curriculum (of sexism) and the evaded curriculum (of critical life issues) often leave girls with an education in learned helplessness and worthlessness. If there is not significant intervention, they will remain disadvantaged.

For girls in lower socioeconomic brackets and for girls of color, the picture is most dismal. What is the result of the negative messages, the lowered expectations? Among other critical life issues, diminished ability to take a secure place in society and the economy. Not particularly focusing on girls, but in an enlightening way nevertheless, Jay MacLeod tries to sort out the mechanisms through which schools perpetuate classism. In an ethnography of schoolchildren in a low-income neighborhood, MacLeod argues that, by sorting kids out according to ostensible meritocracy criteria, schools play a role in the legitimation of inequality. Kids believe they succeed or fail in school on the basis of merit (113). In fact, the reasons they fail may have little to do with merit; however, they leave school with "leveled aspirations," that is, negative assessments of their capabilities and a lack of opportunity structures to elevate their aspirations (112–13). Lower-class people with depressed aspirations, MacLeod argues, are unlikely to achieve middle-class status. Class relations are reproduced though a token few adolescents may escape. The argument is starkly simple,[20] and MacLeod does not focus on girls. But the simplicity yields well in explanatory power for the situation of girls. When girls are not offered equitable opportunity structures, models, and mentors, they also end up with deflated aspirations.

The works of Luttrell, MacLeod, Pipher, and the Wellesley College Center for Research on Women, alongside the works of many other theorists and researches who have begun to concern themselves particularly with the education of girls, are rich in suggestions for imagining the past and possible worlds of women.[21] We are beginning to understand the profundity and profusion of ways in which gender issues are webbed together with class and ethnicity/race issues to create obstacles to socioeconomic success and lead to inefficacious human agency. The scholars give us some insight to how schools may have functioned in the previous worlds of shelter women. But the shelter women can give us insight to how the worlds of schools, scholarship, and teachers continue to affect their lives today. The shelter is a good place to learn about schools because it is one place many women reckon with their ill-preparedness for economic independence. Invited to reflect, they can see clearly the failure of schools to prepare them for the struggles looming ahead. The web of life for battered women is, and has been, one of not-so-subtle cultural messages of inferiority and incompetence. As places ostensibly preparing girls for the future, schools are part of the problem. In the interests of social change and school reform, it behooves us to learn what battered women know about schools.

Battered Women and the Idea of School: The Themes

To learn what women know about schools, I listen to their stories. In addition to searching my field notes for my senses of women's attitudes about schools, knowledge, and ways of knowing, I conducted a series of literacy sessions in which women talked and wrote about schools and school memories. I interviewed select women (e.g., Harriet and Lydia) in private in-depth sessions. The women were asked to review my transcriptions of group and individual sessions and revise as they wished. Here I offer some distillations, some themes, some core concepts, that I believe run through the storytelling. The women offer school memories, experiences as mothers of school children, reflections on education, reports on adult education or college experiences, and the like.

This is an interpretative process, of course, for both myself and for the women who re-invent their lives in the act of storytelling. There are no validity checks apart from resonance, no scientific samples, no calculable evidence; yet Paulo Freire, like many other emancipatory researchers, reminds us that people have their own generative themes of significance available to those who will listen deeply (1987; 1986; 1973). This is an attempt to articulate some of those themes of significance. Here, I will present each theme, offer some of the voices that led me to distill the theme in the way I have,[22] and briefly comment on possible or available meanings. In the subsequent section of this essay, I will elaborate an argument about the implications of these themes for literacy workers and schools.

1. School Is Not Location: It's Relationship

For shelter women, school is not necessarily a place for studies: academic or vocational learning. Despite the best intentions of teachers, school is not centrally about book-learning. Instead, school is an encounter with others. It is a relationship or series of relationships. As school is now structured, the teacher is not the primary relationship; rather, peers form the primary relationships. As in all human encounters, relationships with peers can be problematic or positive. Power is gained or lost. Significantly, many shelter women have had their share of problematic relations; in consequence, the dropout rate is high.[23] The comments of the following women suggest to us that the academic or intellectual aspect of school life cannot be understood outside of its relational aspects:

> Ina: I went to school up to the tenth grade. I hated it. I don't think I really had no friends. I didn't like being there.

> Cora: He [her abusive partner] let me go to school to work on a degree in psychology. He wanted the credit cards I could get as a student. . . . I went for a year. He made me call when I got to school and call again when I got home. He thought I would be with someone else. [She subsequently quit the university.]

> Lydia: [I quit high school because] I didn't like the inner city kids. It wasn't race. They liked to fight. They had attitudes. I tried to get along with everybody. I don't like fights. [Before I moved to that school district] I partied too much in school. It was a social thing.

> Maria: My fifteen-year-old doesn't hang out with the crowd. He's a loner. Except in the classroom. . . . He's a loner. But when he is in school! It's like: Antonio, Antonio, Antonio! I think it's a blend-in thing. [My son] wanted to laugh and hang out with the boys. . . . The teachers are so upset with him. . . . He won't do it until he gets ready. His English teachers tell me Antonio is not a bad child, but he won't do it till he gets ready to do it.

> Myra: [The best types of classes] even in the elementary school would be music, art, sharing class. They could add one: a sharing class where they learn about sharing.

These shelter women view school as interaction, conversation, or dialogic activity rather than as a site of knowledge or information dispersion. School is relationship. This is not to say, of course, that book-learning doesn't happen in schools; it is only to say that these women primarily remember school as a social nexus, for good or ill.

2. Institutional Relationships Are Inequitable

One reason institutional teacher-student relationships are not primary is because the relationships are not equitable. The teachers, as part of the system, discriminate between students. The discrimination is based on "merit," and complicated by race, class, and gender. I will address each of these categories below.

Inequities of Merit

Merit is cause for school inequity. Resources in schools, including teacher attention, are supposedly (and sometimes unfairly) allocated on the basis of intellectual merit. Sometimes the women see merit as an absolute criteria for their institutional status, yet they believe there was something not quite right about how the criteria were applied to themselves as individuals. In other words, merit as a criteria is not wrong in and of itself; rather, merit is misapplied.

> Harriet: When I went to school, there were certain classes you couldn't take. They wouldn't let you because they thought you were not smart enough.
>
> Ina: My school was really hard. You could learn how to use the computer. The teacher told me I couldn't come because I wasn't smart. But my first job when I graduated was as an IBM computer operator! I went back and told him! I showed him!
>
> Angelique: Society is set up in a triangle and very few are up in the triangle. You know the triangle you learn about in sociology? Carol, you know that triangle I mean? They teach you about it in school!
>
> Maria: When I went to school, they had general classes and the academic classes. They discriminated against the lower kids. The zeeks. They called them zeeks. They were the slow kids. They were like queer animals. They labeled kids: academic, average, basic, and zeeks. The zeeks, they were the slow learners. They kept them in the basement. . . . Later they put them in separate buildings.

Maria, like the others, seems to have a problem with the way children get sorted out in school. Like Basil Bernstein, Jay MacLeod argues that school kids sort themselves out into course trajectories and then careers that reproduce class relations. In support of a dialectical view of class reproduction, Jane Gaskell argues that working-class females have a choice about course trajectories and they make choices most fitting to their lived experience. For example, if girls know secretarial skills are their best chance to land a job, they will sign up for typing courses. In my research, shelter women do not accept tracking, but they feel forced to accept their lot. If anything is amiss, then the criteria were misapplied or the attitude with which the criteria were applied by the agents of the school was morally deficit, thus invalid. Maria, Ina, and Harriet know they failed to live up to the standards of intellectual merit, but they suspect the evaluative process and its consequences. Angelique recognizes the hierarchical nature of the social organization of school life; she sarcastically notes that schools teach you what they reproduce or enact.

Inequities of Class

Other times the women are very analytical or articulate about the inequities. Rather than accept the possibility of a misapplied meritocracy,
they recognize how race, class, and gender affect the relations that affect
schooling. This recognition reflects a theorizing out of their own lived
experience. Lydia, a thirty-one-year-old white woman, has clear memories of how class discrimination interfered with her education. She moved
with her newly divorced mother and brother from a suburban middle
class to an urban working class school district, so she had first-hand
experience of class differences in school. After recalling the memory of
how the divorce impoverished the family, she tells how the expectations of others shifted along with the family's financial situation. Later,
she speculates about the role of educational researchers in school discrimination:

> I left [the suburban high school] midway through the year. . . . I
> thought they looked down on me. I mean the teachers. Just the big
> people. The teachers, the principals, the counselors. They looked
> down on us because we were poor. . . . My mom, she didn't have the
> money to dress us like everyone else. So when I wanted to quit and
> get a job and get my GED, she was in agreeance with me. I don't
> want to go on like this anymore, I said.
>
> I always thought I'd be the first of my girlfriends to get married
> and pregnant. . . . It was expected of me. The bad girls, the poor
> girls, get pregnant and married. They have five kids. You know, the
> bad girls always do that. I had a baby when I was twenty and I gave
> him up for adoption.
>
> [The researchers] have these studies and they found that the in-
> ner–city kids were lesser than the suburb kids. That's stereotyping.

Harriet, a forty-five-year-old African American woman, says:

> In the high school that I went to, there was a lot of well-to-do whites,
> the upper crust, they were nice kids. I'm not saying they weren't.
> But the teachers kind of like did a little more for them, said a little
> more, put in a little more, as opposed to John Doe who they felt like
> maybe he'll fade out into infinity. Yeah, they'll never hear from him
> again you know.
>
> When I think back, I think, yeah, well, anytime anything came
> up—the proms, the king and queen—it was always those [wealthy
> white] kids who got it. The boys also who were on the football team
> and there was those who were the presidents of clubs. There was a
> clique. They came from families, the families had the money, and
> they were well known. Their fathers were realtors and attorneys
> and on the board of the school. They were always the vice president
> of this organization and that one. They were elected for this or for
> that one. It was always the well-to-do kids.

Race Inequity

Harriet, an African American woman who views herself as not "fitting in automatically" with other people of color, initially resisted other women's view of racism as a recurrent factor in daily school life. Although Harriet has a good sense of class inequities, she has trouble thinking about school conflicts primarily as racial conflicts.[24] If pressed, she admits:

> When we first started—kindergarten, first, second, third grade, there were some minor problems with discipline. My mother went to school once for me and once for my sister to talk about discipline. They realized my mother was a really caring mother. She went to all the PTA meetings and school activities. That had something to do with it. They have an idea that a black family doesn't care. Sometimes you see it. Maybe that's because of the black kids they get, they don't think they care about schooling. Maybe that's what happened to us.

Myra, however, targets racial bias (and gender bias too) as a complication in her education.

> [Mrs. Pottinger] couldn't deal with the idea that a black girl was intelligent. She told my parents I was disrupting class! I would get done with my work early and look for something to do. I got my work done and she couldn't deal with the fact that she needed to give me more work and give me more things to do. . . . That was one teacher who didn't understand that some blacks are smarter than whites and some girls are smarter than boys. As little kids, we didn't think things like that back then.

Gender Inequity

Myra recognizes the layers of discrimination that girls of color must confront in the schools. She is not the only woman to have experienced gender inequity in the school.

> Kim: Why do men hate and mistreat women? It goes back to schooling. What do you get scholarships for? Boys get them. Men run the government, the law, the state for the man. . . . For the man, of the man, by the man.

> Maria: They [teachers] tell boys different from girls. Boys would go into certain fields. Girls weren't told to go into those fields. If you did, they thought you were queer.

> Lydia: In chemistry, there weren't any girls. One day these women and I were talking. I said: why don't you see any girls in physics? Why do you think that is? One said boys are smarter. I said wow! Give yourselves some credit! [She said] "Women are getting into nursing or women's careers. You don't need it." I was just amazed.

> God! What a horrible thing to say about women! Women aren't as smart as men!

> Betty: Sometimes they have really subtle messages. Maybe you weren't encouraged in math or science. They prefer boys for some classes or activities. . . . I think the encouragement is subtle. Boys get higher paying jobs in physics. They are encouraged. They get better jobs with better pay because of the classes they are encouraged to take.

Clearly, these women understand the complexity and the long-term impact of gender inequity. Interestingly, some women believe that even if a well-intentioned teacher tries to initiate better relations with a student, the system will not allow it. The structure of schools is such that hierarchy must obtain at any cost.

> Harriet: If a teacher tries, it can go wrong. I heard a teacher was accused for sexual harassment for giving a girl special attention. For holding her hand. She was trying to teach her.

Harriet's comment reveals some of the complexity of status in schools. As we've already seen in the case of Antonio, status in the peer subculture may definitely outweigh the status of intellectual merit. Yet, in her school memories, Harriet recalls the environment as one in which class, race, and gender inequities appeared regularly, if somewhat erratically. Shelter women generally see teachers attempting to dole out school status by intellectual merit and intellectual merit as a construct fraught with race, class, and gender ambiguities that frequently operates against the well-being of girls. Yet teachers did not necessarily have the last word. There is the possibility of intervention.

3. Mentors Offer Visions of Opportunity and Possibility

Recently researchers have considered the role of mentors in the education of girls.[25] Everyone needs the guidance of a sympathetic, knowledgeable adult or more experienced peer. Shelter women know it. The need spans their adolescent to adult lives.

Teachers, of course, are not necessarily mentors and, in many respects, the culture of the high school especially mitigates against the development of a mentoring relationship. Kids race from class to class, teacher to teacher. Classes are large and often impersonal. There are few adults in the school who have the time or opportunity to fill such a role.[26] Yet, if they don't have the intervention of a positive mentor inside or outside of school, girls may fall by the wayside. This is one theme I have heard over and over: the women now living in the shelter were often girls who had little positive leadership in the family, neighborhood, or schools.

The isolation crosses over to their adult lives. As adults, battered women are typically women isolated from family and friends. They have no network of support. The isolation cloaks the blows and guarantees the dependence of the victim who has no one else to whom to turn.

Many shelter women, of course, did look to mothers, aunts, older sisters, and friends for guidance (and I will address this shortly). On the basis of my ethnographic data, I cannot argue for a direct correlation between the lack of mentors and the vulnerability of women in later life; nevertheless, I believe the relationship exists. The evidence is coming to light: our culture does not take care of its girl-children.[27] There is a semiotic web of sexist cultural codes, rules, and regulations limiting the full and independent human development of girl-children and women. Negative images of what it means to be female abound. Simultaneously, there is a dearth of positive role models and mentors for girls and young women to show them how to advance in the world of school and work, thus leading them away from economic dependence on males: a primary cause for the perpetuation of domestic violence.[28] Here are some shelter voices:

> Ina: I feel like I need a one-on-one thing with someone. I can't do everything by myself. Like a mentor to say this is how you do things. To show me the way.

> Debra: I went to jail in January and I got my GED in March. I got in the top 10 percent of the state scores and won two scholarships. For the college of my choice! But then someone threw one of them pipes in my face. A crack pipe.

> Lydia: I don't have a hero. I don't have a mentor. Nobody. I don't know anybody who played a positive role in my life. My mom loves me, but I don't know anyone I really looked up to.

> Harriet: You need to work one-on-one with students. Not everyone learns the same. Not until my early 20s did I have a mentor. Not really before then. After my 20s, I got mentors.

Clearly, these women felt the lack of positive role models. When women recall mentors, the mentors are not part of the formal or institutional culture of schools. They are from the neighborhood or the family. They are most frequently slightly older friends acting generously and gratuitously. In fact, they are most often identified as "friends" first and "mentors" on reflection.[29] About these mentors, shelter women have something to teach to those of us who wish to mentor in the schools. This is what the shelter women say:

> Myra: She was a support in good and bad times. A good ear for listening. . . . She was always there no matter what . . . for the coming in of life and the coming home which death brings.

> Debra: She was dependable, respectful, caring of others, a great mother to her children and also others' children. She was always there for me day or night no matter what, honest about her feelings, has a great sense of humor. I could say things to her I couldn't say to my mother and she would give me motherly advice.

> Harriet: Two women I had as mentors. I called them like my mother figures. Both passed away. I need one now and I got to find one. Everyone needs older friends. You can't talk to your mom about everything. They are more objective. These women, they were general life mentors. One was closer to my mother's age than the other. I dated her son. We became very good friends. They were just there for me. Even before I married my husband, I was asking for their opinion you know and they gave it. They were African American women. My mother died in '90 and my father in '91. One [mentor] died in '91 and the other one died in '93. The women now [in the shelter], I think, I hope, they look up to me. I don't have any kids, no children, but still I think, I hope, they look up to me as a mentor.

Unlike superiors in hierarchical organizations, mentors are not designated to lead subordinates because of presumed or past merit. Instead, they are persons who, through dynamic relationship, earn and re-earn the respect freely given. There are no underlings in a mentoring relationship. As you will see in the next section, the mentor does not wield authority and power over her charge, and the protégé has the opportunity to become the mentor if, in the moment, a different kind of knowledge or expertise is required. In fact, the mentor is actively looking for opportunities to invite the mentee to leadership. This is the source of the respect between mentor and mentee. The mentee is not given anything; rather, the wisdom is generated in the dynamic between them as one offers and relinquishes and the other accepts and assumes. In waiting for the teaching moment, the mentor expands the moral imagination, the vision, of the mentee through honest talk. In waiting, the mentor lends clarity to difficult situations, shares experiences, encourages and supports.

4. The Self Is Re-created in Community as Opportunities and Relationships Shift

Mentors help others see the opportunities for growth and change. In articulating such or similar strategies for schooling, however, middle-class researchers may have a tendency to look at lower-class persons as material for improvement. After a discussion in which he notes the pervasive violence in the lives of lower- and working-class girls, Peter McLaren writes,

> When we embrace the derisory ideology that conceives of disadvantaged girls as under-socialized, as "unfinished products," on the

conveyor belt of social success, we place a veneer of the basic class
structure and gender bias of society and obscure the ways in which
the structure of the system determines to a great extent which class
and gender will be successful and which will fail. (220)

He argues teachers must "work unyieldingly" to empower students both
as individuals and as potential agents of social change (221). With this
argument, I agree. However, McLaren fails to see the utter resourceful-
ness of lower and working class women and their view of their own
subculture as a wellspring of hope for transformation. Myra, Harriet,
and Debra remind us: shelter women see women in their community as
their hope for change.

Other women, both shelter women and workers, speak of the willingness and capacity of women to conceive and reconceive of themselves in response to their life situations. As opportunity and relationship shifts, such women are able to become mentors to others and find a
renewed sense of self in community. They are not waiting for the schools
to address their situations. They re-create themselves, shifting their identity, forming and reforming alliances in sometimes functional, sometimes
gratuitous responses to other human beings.

> Sheila: Since I have been here my ideas about women have changed.
> I look at the world in a different way. Women are beautiful. I had
> these same images of women in my head—from the magazines and
> movies I see. I have always found beauty in women's faces. Now I
> see beauty in all of a woman. I feel happy about my own self. I
> admire big women. I see beautiful women all around me. I see the
> women here and am awed at their strength. To be strong enough to
> put themselves in this situation. Strong enough to want to try anew.
> Women are so unique in their womanhood. . . . Because I am a
> woman, I am special and different in my thoughts and reactions.
> It's easy to overlook the feminine way because we focus mostly on
> the masculine way. I begin to notice things in terms of women. I
> used to think masculine because I live in masculine conditions. Now
> I struggle to educate myself and other people about women's ways.

> Harriet: I know I would be like a tutor. I was the mentor to other
> people. Two in particular I had. One, his name was Johnson. He
> was a black boy. I tutored him in math or something. I always won-
> der what happened to him. He needed help in math. He was a year
> younger. In the class behind me. There was a young girl who lived
> on our street, she was three years younger than me. Now she is a
> [county] sheriff. We showed them [the assessors at school], didn't
> we? Her name was Sandie.

> Betty: Women together is the power, the only power we have: women
> together.

> Ina: We should have a Million Dollar Lady Walk.

There is a collective sense to the empowerment of these women. They assume new identity in relationship with one another, then outwards toward others. This is a critical feature of mentoring left out of accounts by academics and educators: the collective sense made available through mentoring. Yet, it is this feature—the sense of collective agency—which holds hope for social change. It is this strategy we need to emphasize in our pedagogies: the provision of mentors as co-learners and co-agents in a process of education for social change.[30]

Lest we romanticize much: sometimes women are less magnanimous in their responses to others. Lydia is impatient, but she clearly understands why it is important to seek out others and to develop a sense of an independent self-in-community.

> Lydia: All these years I thought I was so screwed up, but when I listen to these [shelter] women, I think how fortunate I was, to have the things I have, to come this far with school. Somewhere, something happened right. Somehow I haven't gone over the brink of sanity. I think of them: get a grip! Some of them drive me nuts. I'm not trying to run their lives, but when I give advice, for everything I say, there is a reason they can't do it. I said the same things. It's bullshit. The problem is because of their relationships, they think they can't do it. You need to go to groups, to talk to other people, to go to counseling, go to school. There's help, but you have to reach out for it. The counselors helped me tremendously. I still had my days, but when you talk, it helps you keep things focused. I didn't know things about myself. Patterns of behavior and what not. I just learned these things about myself by talking. If you have good self-esteem, you can do something with your life instead of thinking: okay, who's going to take care of me next?

There is nothing idealistic about Lydia's view of community. Yet, women like Lydia are survivors in a violent and inequitable culture not because the schools have prepared them for life and work in the late twentieth century: on the contrary. Women are survivors in a world blighted by gender, culture, and class inequities because often they intervene for another and re-create themselves in positive relationship with their sister-kin.[31] This is the message shelter women come bearing to literacy workers. The simple truth often keeps them alive.

What Do Shelter Women Say about School?

Many shelter women are just beginning to understand the nature and extent of their oppression, past and present. But they are not helpless victims and, once they understand oppression and the possibility of solidarity, their consciousness expands by leaps and bounds. It makes them wonder about their lives generally, how they got to where they are, who their allies and oppressors are, and what steps they need to take to make a life change. One of the purposes of shelter life is to encourage women to see that the problem of violence against women is first and foremost a cultural, socioeconomic issue. It is not a personal or private issue. Violence against women in its many manifestations—from physical abuse and rape to the neglect of the well-being of girls—is made possible by the collusion of countless aspects of culture, including our major institutions, such as school.

How issues of race, class, and gender biases bridge over from school settings to adult life is a complex topic indeed. And perhaps there are as many views about school as there are students. But, for shelter women, there are some commonalities. The women simply do not view the schools as places that prepared them to take their place in civil society or the economy. To be clear: shelter women are not always critical of the school system; yet, they are not complimentary either. In fact, many times the education system means next to nothing to them. If they are mothers, they may concern themselves with their children's welfare in the schools. Without invitation, shelter women, like other women and men, may think rarely or never about the school system as an important piece of the puzzle of their lives. This is an important issue in itself; until they reflect, school doesn't matter. Other women are clear and sure about the influences, positive or negative. Whether they think good or ill of their experience in the schools, once invited to call forth memories and stories, they begin to see the patterns. As Lydia put it: "I never realized . . . until I started talking." There is meaning here for literacy workers.

The Meaning for Schools

Many Americans do believe schools prepare children and young adults to take their place in civil society and the economy. Yet the meaning of schools to shelter women is not about good jobs or increased income. Joel Spring reminds us that "the value of an education depends on social conditions" and the "returns on investments in education vary among racial groups and between sexes because of prejudice and social conditions. . . ." He adds, "The difference in income between women and men is greater than the racial difference" (97). Neither Spring nor shelter women romanticize the school system.

In recounting memories of school days, the meaning of school education to many shelter women is not increased human agency. Personal power, writes Barbara Hart, is based on factors such as "education, income, economic security, employment skills, marketability, class, age, religious experience, physical power, health, social skills, and networks" (176–77): a tangled and fluctuating confusion of factors. In any event, women who use shelters to escape from violence do not score well on these criteria. Typically they are undereducated, poor, unskilled, distressed, sometimes hostile or cynical, and isolated. And, as we've already noted, women, and particularly shelter women, can often be characterized by low self-esteem, feelings of self-blame and failure, economic dependency, fearfulness, anxiety, and depression.

In other words, the profile of women from high school to domestic situations of life-threatening violence does not much change. It can be said that if the schools prepare girls for anything, they prepare them to accept and internalize further oppression. Hence, many women perceive daily life in institutions, such as in shelters, as more of the same.[32] Noelie Rodriguez writes, "Bureaucratically organized shelters staffed by a hierarchy of professionals that treat battered women as clients within rule structured constraints tend to reproduce the stratified relations of the larger society and perpetuate the submissive status of battered women" (226). This is the relationship that exists between the school life of girls and the adult life of battered women: a climate that systemically perpetuates sexism (and, as the voices of women in this essay make clear, racism and classism). Obviously, not all women find themselves in shelters later in life, survivors of violence. Women, however, are frequently socialized—in schools, in families, in shelters, and in the streets—into submissive roles. Rather than contributing to the injustice, schools must intervene.

Shelter women tell us that women look toward one another for intervention. As literacy workers in schools and other educational forums, we should learn from them. We should heed their words of wisdom by developing critical pedagogies that facilitate and foster a collective sense of the self through networks, alliances, and partnerships. Networks are one way, notes Barbara Hart, that a sense of personal power increases (176–77).

I try to do this by using emancipatory pedagogy in my university classes and literacy work in the shelter. Hierarchies are leveled as much as possible: from planning to (in the case of my university students) grading. In lieu of competitive learning, shifting networks of collaborative and cooperative learning are sought. To use Jay Robinson's metaphor: "conversation-centered" schooling replaces teacher-centered or student-centered schooling.

Even more specifically, we should learn from the women's own desire for mentors who, acting as co-agents, show them the way to the power of collective agency. A school girl recognizes the value of a mentor and often will seek one out: in the schools, in the streets, among kin or kind. I do not believe a literacy worker can choose to become an individual's mentor. This is a formative and transformative relationship enkindled by a confluence of characteristics, events, and timing. But a teacher can create forums in which dynamic, dialogic mentoring might happen. Team work, peer partners, service learning, community connections, Internet technology, and parent aides are all opportunities to create alignments, fusions, alliances, between people of diverse backgrounds, interests, and needs who might enrich one another.

The mentor must be a co-agent: one who listens deeply and uses a people's language (as heterogeneous and conflictive as it is guaranteed to be), rather than an elite language. This is an utterly essential point. Jay Robinson speaks of it in terms of a "common language" (266). The academy-trained staff woman Kim met in her first shelter encounter did not bear the humility, openness, and grace a genuine mentor or co-learner needs:

> Kim: I had a friend who was an academic. It took a long time to get close to her. The academics don't know about loving people. Me, I'm a girl from the 'hood. Academics talk about theory, not feelings. My friend was an academic. It's all theory. It's not about the way it is. When I told the intake person[33] my views on my husband, we had a disagreement. The intake person said: "I studied domestic violence." So I said: "Okay, now I know." I saw how it was gonna go. . . . But the intake person, an academic, is part of a scholastic movement on domestic violence that is the dividing line.

Kim went back to school to seek more literacy training. She wants to write her memoirs, a story of domestic violence. Perhaps she will be able to find at the university the mentor she could not find in school or in the shelter. The lucky teacher among us might be able to work with a student like Kim who clearly has a sense of her own views.

The primary function of the mentor, such a teacher would know, is to invite learners into a notion of literacy as an endeavor for collective agency. The one-on-one interaction we most readily imagine when we imagine mentorship relations transforms into triads, teams, classes, and communities. In this way, we can work to enable the collective voice of women.

To do so, each literacy worker must analyze her or his own resources and situations. Clearly, however, we must cut across the lines of class, race, and gender. I seek ways to connect my wealthy white female and male university students with women living in the shelter. My students perform "community service" in the shelter.[34] They go to do what I did: talk, listen, and learn. On computers given to me for the shelter, the students show women how to use the Internet to access bulletin boards on violence against women. If they wish, the women can peruse advertisements for jobs, housing, and community events. They can continue conversations begun in the shelter with students through our class newsgroup. Perhaps alliances will be created that will outlast the semester.

Hopefully, unusual alliances will be enabled, new languages will be formed, and new learning will take place for all of us. Jay Robinson writes, "We will in no way achieve a just society if we do not talk to those alien to us" (267). He speaks in particular of the fragmented languages of the academy, but he may as well have been addressing Kim's academic friend or the many educators who have not yet listened to the way girls experience—and women remember—school. He surely speaks to the experience of my students, the shelter women, and to me. In the end, the participants in the alliances I am trying to enable through border-crossing activities such as service learning and computer technology may discover that, across the barriers of class and race, their apparently alien voices are not alien at all. Indeed, their problem is a common one: the gender discrimination that harms all human beings.

The story I tell here of my relationship with shelter women is just a beginning, but I am learning from them. Just as surely, the shelter women are learning from my students and me. In the end, I do not claim to know the many layers of meaning of the words of women documented here. I wish only to add the voices of shelter women to the current debates on literacy and schooling in America, for the voices of the marginalized are missing from our academic forums. While we listen to them, let us not fragment the language on violence against women. Racism, sexism, and classism is violence, and violence—whenever it surfaces and of whatever sort it may be—is all of one fabric.

So too, I wish to add another dimension to the ever-widening conversations about domestic violence. Woman-battery crosses the classes and races in America; however, it seems that the kind of violence and neglect that characterizes the culture of woman-hatred in our nation does not begin with the kicks and blows of an angry domestic partner. The violence begins long before. Sexism through gender bias and neglect in the schools is violence against female students. The oppression of it is compounded drastically by racism and classism. Violence, Linda Gordon notes, stems from "power struggles in which individuals are contesting real resources and benefits" (3). This happens in the schools just as well as in families. It is the disadvantage many girls face long before they become victims or survivors of domestic violence. Race, class, and gender biases in the schools affect the capacity of women to see themselves as independent agents in the worlds of home and work. That they resist, often in solidarity with others and sometimes in dynamic mentoring relationships with each other, is a tribute to the courage of women.[35] For the sake of social justice, let literacy workers resist, too.

Notes

1. The "Women's House" is a pseudonym for the shelter. It is funded by a variety of sources, including city, state, federal, and donated resources.

2. To be clear: From my first day in the shelter, my role as an ethnolinguist was established with staff, but until I altered my stance from general volunteer to literacy worker, a move I will describe shortly, I tried to maintain, and still do, a non-obtrusive presence in the shelter with the women. In short, I did not and do not parade my position. In fact, general volunteers are required by policy not to share some types of personal information, but my point ultimately has to do with the undesirability of wielding unnecessary power. As anthropologists and linguists are well aware, people are often intimidated and alter their language when they learn of our professions. This is a long-standing problem in linguistic inquiry and the subject of much conversation in sociology and anthropology. The women who participated in this research did so voluntarily and with informed consent; however, the issue I am trying to suggest here has to do also with the delicacy of anthropological inquiry and the false distinctions traditional researchers try to make between their personal selves and their professional selves. It was never possible for me to listen to shelter women as a non-linguist or to act as a linguist without feeling gender commonalties with shelter women. That is, there is no stance that is "objective" or non-interested, either in the social sciences or, as feminist researchers are making clear, in the empirical sciences. See Punch (1994) for a review of issues and influential works in the politics and ethics of anthropological field-work. See also Reinharz (1992), Sieber (1992), and Gubrium and Silverman (1989). See Punch (especially pp. 92–95) for a succinct survey of contending views on issues of privacy, harm, identification, and confidentiality.

3. The activity is voluntary and each phase of it is decided by the women themselves. That is, the women decide the topics for discussion. Individually and sometimes collectively, they decide whether to write at all. They decide whether to share their writing in conversation or in text form. They revise their written or oral texts as they wish. In short, the pedagogical rule is ownership of their own processes. As such, the group is quite different from any other group in which they are involved and the reviews of it by participants have been very encouraging.

4. Feminist pedagogy seeks to level hierarchical power dynamics in classrooms and other learning communities. This woman walked into the session after introductions had been made. Like other shelter women, she was accustomed to attending groups led by middle-class social workers who use more traditional pedagogies to teach. Such group processes tend to replicate typical school culture with respect to teacher-centered pedagogy.

5. They nearly never change their words. On one occasion, an African American woman asked me to clarify a statement she made about an Appalachian

woman. She did not want to be misunderstood as prejudiced. The change was made.

6. One of the points I wish to make is that researchers who study the lives of people living at the margins can seek to avoid exploitation by undertaking their work in the interest of social justice and by inviting people in the field into their research as co-investigators and teachers, thus co-activists for social change. I also believe that feminist research activity, at its best, is always dialogic. The inverse of Maurice Punch's *mutual deceit* (93–94) or mutual exploitation by researcher and researched is social activism by joint partnership in research.

7. The statistics vary depending on the source. The sources for these figures are Sewell (19) and the National Center on Women and Family Law, USA, 1988, cited in *The New York Times* on 19 October 1994. See also *Violence Against Women*, particularly Chapter 6: "How Widespread is the Problem of Rape?"

8. The shelter is located in a city which has strong neighborhood units or identities. A number of the women who come to the shelter know one another through neighborhood and family networks.

9. The *evaded curriculum* is the term used to name the critical subject matter teachers typically do not attend to or acknowledge in schools. See *How Schools Shortchange Girls*, Part 4.3. This chapter concerns the health and well-being of schoolgirls. Topics include substance abuse, sexual activity, STDs, body image, eating disorders, suicide, and feelings. Notice it does not address the pervasive violence witnessed or experienced by girls.

10. Shelters such as the Women's House open their doors to women who have suffered a range of physical, mental, and emotional abuse. The meaning of battery, its causes and solutions, are conflicted areas of policy and research. One particular conflict is between systems theorists and feminist theorists. Family systems researchers (including exchange/social control theorists and symbolic interaction theorists) typically study interaction and seek to explain the problem of family violence by way of (dysfunctional) communicative patterns. Feminist researchers view the problem as a sociocultural issue of power and control sustained through patriarchal domination. Richard J. Gelles (1983, 1990), an exchange/social control theorist, rejects patriarchal or feminist theory as single-factor macrolevel theory. Rebecca Dobash and Russell Dobash (1979, 1992), among many other more recent theorists, reject microlevel theories which, instead of considering sociocultural factors, attribute the causes of violence to individual pathology or malfunctional family communicative patterns. In the 1990s, these two camps, among others, are still vying for control of the field and the subsequent authority to help policymakers allocate resources. See Bersani and Chen (1988) for a discussion of the main sociological theories on family violence, including these perspectives: resource; exchange/social control; symbolic interaction perspectives; subculture of violence views; conflict perspectives; patriarchal; ecological; and general systems.

11. Cf. Lenore Walker's *cycle of violence*. Walker, a pioneer in domestic violence research, charted a chronology of violent behavior that begins with tension, climaxes with violence, and resolves with contrition. The cycle repeats itself over and over with escalating frequency and intensity. The *cycle of violence* paradigm has been criticized for its lock-step pattern which does not seem to characterize all violent domestic relationships. See Walker (1979).

12. This is not to say that battered women do not demonstrate heroic efforts to protect themselves and their children from the onslaught of physical, mental, and emotional cruelty. On occasion, they form solidarity with other women to fight abusive partners. Earlier in the century, for example, Irish women would signal for help from neighbor women by hanging pre-arranged clothing items on the backyard or balcony clothesline when they anticipated trouble with spouses. Clearly, however, the full human agency of women is distorted by abuse. Here and following, the notion of limited human agency is meant to signal unequal sociocultural, economic, and political life situations in which girl-children and women are not encouraged to fully develop their human potential. I do not mean to suggest that persistent, spirited women cannot or do not develop their human potential—often under adverse conditions or in non-supportive environments. On the contrary, I will argue shortly that women seek out mentoring relationships (to take one example) to help them do so.

13. A note on method: clearly this study is not meant to express institutional perspectives, although it does express the ideas of some shelter workers and teachers I have encountered. It is meant to look at literacy in the context of violence and power issues through the eyes of the poor, the assaulted ones. While the charge is impossible for a middle-class researcher such as myself to fulfill, I am attempting here to do so by providing space for the voices of poor women. In as much as it can be, given my own standpoint, it is meant to be a grass-roots or bottom-up view rather than a top-down view. Paulo Freire, the renowned literacy worker, theorizes on the method for popular education in his classic work, *Pedagogy of the Oppressed,* but see also Brackley (1992) and his respondents for an enlightening discussion of the ways in which research and its reception change when researchers consider their subject matter from the eyes of those who live at the margins of society.

14. Among the many real and imaginary factors making it difficult for some women to define their situations as cases of "domestic violence" are these: the remorse of the batterer after the violence, the shame and guilt of the victim who believes she may have triggered the violence, the frequency of violent incidents, the absence of physical assault, and the gender of the batterer (i.e., there are cases of same-sex violence among lesbians and rare cases of women battering men to the point of injury).

15. Many families living below the poverty level are headed by women who have fled violence from partners. The Congressional Budget Office reports that 14 percent of American families live below the poverty level. These figures were reported in the *St. Petersburg Times* (September 13, 1995) and the 1992 Census Report.

16. It behooves us, however, to take the figures and labels used to categorize women in perspective. Like the recent trend toward the medicalization of violence against women (i.e., casting domestic violence as a medical or health issue for women), the psychologizing of the problems of shelter women tends to diminish the economic or structural origins of the violence. By and large, the health problems of low-income women are caused by their economic situations: from the constant stresses in their lives and the lack of resources to effectively deal with those stresses. As Belle puts it: "Women will continue to be overrepresented among the depressed as long as they are overrepresented among the poor" (145). This being said, shelter women often are fit into a therapeutic framework in which they are most often characterized as depressed. See also J. Bernard (1976).

17. See Luttrell (1989) for an elaboration of "schoolwise" and "streetwise" knowledge.

18. Researchers have attempted to draw direct relationships between actual school problems and abuse. In homes where women experience violence at the hands of partners, child abuse is also elevated (Gelles and Cornell 77) and children who are abused perform poorly in school (Starr 137). Other researchers note that battered women may suffer a type of "shock" or "terror" syndrome that negatively affects their ability to perform a variety of tasks, including cognitive ones. See Judith Lewis Herman's *Trauma and Recovery*. The point I am trying to make is that sexism and misogyny affect female performance before, during, and after the school years.

19. See Part 2.3: "Race, Sex, Socioeconomic Status, and Academic Achievement." I mean to emphasize the economic disparity between males and females as much as and more than the AAUW study.

20. I mean this in an affirmative sense. MacLeod uses a sophisticated version of reproduction theory (i.e., the attempt to explain the mechanisms by which class structures are maintained and reproduced in contemporary, free-market, and/or democratic societies), but he writes with clarity. He contributes to the line of social reproduction literature by Pierre Bourdieu, Jean-Claude Passeron, Basil Bernstein, Paul Willis, Michael Apple, and Henry Giroux. Like Bernstein, MacLeod is concerned about the seeming element of choice in the career decisions of working-class high school students. Jane Gaskell (1985) also takes into account the element of choice in her study of course and career selection patterns of working-class girls. The point is that ideology operates at the level of the individual.

21. The Wellesley College Center for Research on Women was commissioned by the American Association of University Women Educational Foundation to report on girls and education in *How Schools Shortchange Girls* (1992). The AAUW report is extensively documented and a rich source for further detailed reading. While I do not espouse a theory of women's ways of knowing, some researchers do. Of the *women's ways* theorists, some writers worth reading are Gilligan (1982); Belenky (1986) and, of more current interest, Luttrell (1989, 1992). Some other writers worth reading on the topic of girls' education are Maureen Barbieri (1995); Dorothy C. Holland and Margaret A. Eisenhart (1990); Myra Sadker and David Sadker (1994); Carol Tavris (1992); Lois Weis (1988; and Michelle Fine 1993); and Leslie R. Wolfe, ed. (1991).

22. You may understand something else altogether from the voices: this is the way that it must be because reading and knowing are processes of co-creation.

23. Both Michelle Fine (1991) and the AAUW report on the complexity of dropout rates. Girls more frequently than boys finish school, but female dropouts have higher poverty rates and lower school return rates. Eighty-two percent of girls who drop out cite school-related reasons and most hold traditional gender-role stereotypes. See the 1992 AAUW Report, Part 2.6. With respect to representation—dropouts typically are represented as having personal, familial, or culturally based deficiencies. For a critique of this view, see Stevenson and Ellsworth (1993). See also Ogbu (1988) for an account of how racial barriers and poor job opportunities cause African American dropouts to blame the schools. These authors argue, and I agree, that critical voices are silenced by attributing deficiencies to the dropouts themselves rather than to the schools; however, neither

Stevenson and Ellsworth or Ogbu focus on girls. Further, Stevenson and Ellsworth argue that interviewees in their sample continue to blame themselves. The shelter women do not blame themselves. Nor do they, as Ogbu's dropouts do, reference a cultural history of racial discrimination. Rather, shelter women seem to have a good sense of how several cultural factors—including race, class, and gender—interact to oppress girls in schools and, later, women in the workplace. See Sarup (1986) for an account of the politics of multiracial education.

24. See Linda Grant (1984) for an account of the "place" of black girls in desegregated classrooms.

25. See Little (1990) on the theoretical problems and issues of mentoring and Merriam (1983) for a review of earlier literature on mentoring. See also Bey and Holmes (1992) and Daloz (1986) for institutional and idealistic views of mentorship respectively. Rather romantically, Daloz writes, ". . . mentors are creations of our imaginations, designed to fill a psychic space somewhere between lover and parent" (17). I disagree with this miasmic, eroticized view. Although the shelter women sometimes conceptualize mentors as mother-figures, mentors are valued for the specific, concrete assistance they render.

26. In the public school system of the city in this study, for example, some schools have no librarians, teacher's aides, or school nurses. For lack of funding, the schools are understaffed in all areas. This is sheerly a pragmatic and economic issue.

27. I would like to make it clear that this is not a shortcoming of individuals in particular; rather, this is a shortcoming of the culture. Girls and women form strong friendship networks, create images of heroes or heroines, and tell stories about women who have survived or thrived in a misogynist culture. What I do mean in the present context is that shelter women do not have readily available accounts of mentors who, in the school years, prepared them to assume economic independence through careers or encouraged them to seek higher education. In my view, the problem is one of the function of unemployment or unpaid labor in a patriarchal capitalist economy, not a moral shortcoming of the adult women with whom girls live or study. Not surprisingly, the well-being of girl-children was a focus at the 1995 United Nations Fourth World Conference on Women, in Beijing, China. The link to capitalist economy was made clear by NGOs in attendance whose sentiments were suppressed in documents, most prevalently by the United States government.

See Penelope Eckert (1989) for a parallel view of social categories in high schools. Eckert argues that white working-class students form strong networks with peers and adults outside of the high school as part of their class socialization.

28. See Horn (1994) on the relationship between violence against women and their economic status. Not only do men under economic stress strike out more frequently at their wives and children, but women without an alternative source of income cannot escape the blows. This does not mean, of course, that domestic violence appears only in the lower or under classes. The risks are simply increased.

29. The politics of naming is important, of course. Sometimes I introduce the word "mentor" into conversations when women are describing a "friend" who is clearly mentoring them. On other occasions, the women introduce the term entirely on their own accord.

30. This is one of the basic benefits of shelter life. Women in shelters perform short-term and sometimes long-term mentoring roles for one another: they advise one another, console one another, and sometimes seek housing arrangements, permanent relationships, and the like together.

31. I do not mean to suggest males cannot intervene. Many women have had positive role models of both genders. In the previous excerpt, Lydia attributes her success in English to a male teacher. I wish to suggest, however, that it does not generally appear as if male mentors figured in the lives of most shelter women, whether they are of Appalachian, African American, or other ethnic descent. By and large, they reserve their admiration for women who helped them negotiate their way through difficult life experiences. The spirit of interpretation, I believe, should be one of words to ponder and not to essentialize or to sex or culture stereotype.

32. I do not wish to suggest that the shelter of this study or shelters in general are not extremely important in the ongoing struggle to ensure women's safety in life-threatening situations. On the contrary, they are critical. What I mean to suggest is that the rampant violence against women derives from entire cultural systems in which the semiotics of unequal power distribution find expression in our basic institutions and organizational structures. As feminists, liberation theologians, and other scholars frequently note, violence against women and the marginalized is structural in origin.

33. This particular staff person was from a shelter Kim resided at before she came to the Women's House. Kim was dismissed from this first shelter for rule infractions regarding curfew. An "intake" person interviews battered women when they arrive at a shelter. She fills out paperwork concerning abuse history, medical history, etc., for house records and federal, state, and local assistance. More and more frequently, as shelters pass from the hands of grass-roots feminist activists, these staff women have some university education, often degrees in social work.

34. See Robert Coles's *The Call of Service* for an account of a community service program at Harvard University. Coles focuses on the transformation of the individual, and he is less concerned about concerted social action. Teachers will find his account both thoughtful and useful, however.

35. As I conclude, I would like to acknowledge the many women, clients, staff, and volunteers at the Women's House who over the years have shared stories and given me hope for women's struggle worldwide. All names have been changed here to preserve anonymity. Beth Hamilton, a community volunteer, has been most helpful to me in facilitating the literacy circle. Harriet, a woman in search of a peaceful life, terror-free, has been a particular inspiration and challenge to me; that is, a mentor to me in this study. Finally, Jay L. Robinson has been a wellspring of inspiration to me through the years since my teacher-student relationship with him at the University of Michigan.

Works Cited

Barbieri, Maureen. 1995. *Sounds from the Heart: Learning to Listen to Girls.* Portsmouth, NH: Heinemann.

Belenky, Mary Field, et al. 1986. *Women's Ways of Knowing: The Development of Self, Voice, and Mind.* New York: Basic.

Belle, Deborah. 1984. "Inequality and Mental Health: Low Income and Minority Women." *Women and Mental Health Policy.* Ed. Lenore E. Walker. Beverly Hills: Sage. 135–50.

Bernard, J. 1976. "Homosociality and Female Depression." *Journal of Social Issues* 32.4: 213–38.

Bersani, Carl A., and Huey-Tsyh Chen. 1988. "Sociological Perspectives in Family Violence." *Handbook of Family Violence.* Ed. V. B. Van Hasselt et al. New York: Plenum. 57–86.

Bey, Theresa M., and C. Thomas Holmes, eds. 1992. *Mentoring: Contemporary Principles and Issues.* Reston, VA: Association of Teacher Educators.

Brackley, Dean, S.J. 1992. "The Christian University and Liberation: The Challenge of the [University of Central America.]" *Discovery* 2: 1–34.

Coles, Robert. 1993. *The Call of Service.* Boston: Houghton Mifflin.

Daloz, Laurent A. 1987. *Effective Teaching and Mentoring.* San Francisco: Jossey-Bass.

Dobash, Rebecca, and Russell Dobash. 1979. *Violence Against Wives.* New York: Free Press.

———. 1992. *Women, Violence, and Social Change.* New York: Routledge.

Eckert, Penelope. 1989. *Jocks and Burnouts: Social Categories and Identity in the High School.* New York: Teachers College Press.

Fine, Michelle. 1991. *Framing Dropouts: Notes on the Politics of an Urban Public High School.* Albany, NY: SUNY Press.

Freire, Paulo. 1986. *Pedagogy of the Oppressed.* Trans. Myra Bergman Ramos. New York: Continuum.

———. 1973. *Education for Critical Consciousness.* New York: Continuum.

———. 1987. *Literacy: Reading the Word and the World.* South Hadley, MA: Bergin and Garvey.

Gaskell, Jane. 1985. "Course Enrollment in the High School: The Perspective of Working-Class Females." *Sociology of Education* 58: 48–59.

Gelles, Richard J. 1983. "An Exchange/Social Theory." *The Dark Side of Families: Current Family Violence Research.* Eds. D. Finkelhor, R. J. Gelles, G. T. Hotaling and M. A. Straus. Beverly Hills: Sage.

Gelles, Richard J., and Clair Pedrick Cornell. 1990. *Intimate Violence in Families.* London: Sage.

Gilligan, Carol. 1982. *In a Different Voice: Psychological Theory and Women's Development.* Cambridge: Harvard University Press.

Gordon, Linda. 1988. *Heroes of Their Own Lives: The Politics and History of Family Violence.* New York: Penguin.

Grant, Linda. 1984. "Black Females 'Place' in Desegregated Classrooms." *Sociology of Education* 57: 98–111.

Gubrium, Jaber F., and David Silverman, eds. 1989. *The Politics of Field Research: Sociology Beyond Enlightenment.* Newbury Park, CA: Sage.

Haraway, Donna J. 1991. "A Manifesto for Cyborgs: Science, Technology, and Socialist Feminism in the Late Twentieth Century: An Ironic Dream of a Common Language for Women in the Integrated Circuit." *Simians, Cyborgs, and Women: The Reinvention of Nature.* New York: Routledge. 149–81.

Hart, Barbara. 1986. "Lesbian Battering: An Explanation." *Naming the Violence: Speaking Out About Lesbian Battering.* Ed. Kerry Lobel. Seattle: Seal Press. 173–89.

Herman, Judith Lewis. 1992. *Trauma and Recovery.* New York: Basic Books.

Holland, Dorothy, and Margaret Eisenhart. 1990. *Educated in Romance: Women, Achievement, and College Culture.* Chicago: University of Chicago Press.

Horn, Patricia. 1994. "Creating a Just Economy Will Reduce Violence Against Women." *Violence Against Women.* Ed. Karin L. Swisher. San Diego, CA: Greenhaven Press. 182–88.

Little, Judith Warren. 1990. "The Mentor Phenomenon and the Social Organization of Teaching." Ed. C. B. Cazden. *Review of Research in Education* 16: 297–351.

Luttrell, Wendy. 1993. "'The Teachers, They All Had Their Pets': Concepts of Gender, Knowledge, and Power." *Signs* 18.3: 505–46.

———. 1989. "Working-Class Women's Ways of Knowing: Effects of Gender, Race, and Class." *Sociology of Education* 62: 33–46.

MacLeod, Jay. 1987. *Ain't No Makin' It: Leveled Aspirations in a Low-Income Neighborhood.* Boulder, CO: Westview Press.

McLaren, Peter. 1989. *Life in Schools.* New York: Longman.

Merriam, S. S. 1983. "Mentors and Proteges: A Critical Review of the Literature." *Adult Education Quarterly* (Spring): 161–73.

Mishler, Elliot G. 1986. *Research Interviewing: Context and Narrative.* Cambridge: Harvard University Press.

Ogbu, John. 1988. "Class Stratification, Racial Stratification, and Schooling." *Class, Race, and Gender in American Education.* Ed. Lois Weis. Albany, NY: SUNY Press.

Pipher, Mary Bray. 1994. *Reviving Ophelia: Saving the Selves of Adolescent Girls.* New York: Putnam.

Punch, Maurice. 1994. "Politics and Ethics in Qualitative Research." *Handbook of Qualitative Research.* Eds. Norman K. Denzin and Yvonna S. Lincoln. London: Sage. 83–97.

Reinharz, Shulamit. 1992. *Feminist Methods in Social Research.* New York: Oxford University Press.

Robinson, Jay. 1990. *Conversations on the Written Word: Essays on Language and Literacy.* Portsmouth, NH: Boynton/Cook.

Rodriguez, Noelie Maria. 1988. "Transcending Bureaucracy: Feminist Politics at a Shelter for Battered Women." *Gender & Society* 2.2: 214–27.

Sadker, Myra, and David Sadker. 1994. *Failing at Fairness: How America's Schools Cheat Girls.* New York: Scribner.

Sarup, Madan. 1986. *The Politics of Multiracial Education.* London: Routledge.

Sieber, Joan E. 1992. *Planning Ethically Responsible Research: A Guide for Students and Internal Review Boards.* Newbury Park, CA: Sage.

Sewell, Bernadette Dunn. 1994. "Traditional Male/Female Roles Promote Domestic Violence." *Violence Against Women.* Ed. Karin L. Swisher. San Diego: Greenhaven Press. 19–25.

Spring, Joel. 1991. *American Education: An Introduction to Social and Political Aspects.* 5th ed. New York: Longman.

Starr, Raymond H., Jr. 1988. "Physical Abuse of Children." *Handbook of Family Violence.* Ed. V. B. Van Hasselt et al. New York: Plenum. 119–55.

Stevenson, Robert B., and Jeanne Ellsworth. 1993. "Dropouts and the Silencing of Critical Voices." *Beyond Silenced Voices: Class, Race, and Gender in United States Schools.* Eds. Lois Weis and Michelle Fine. Albany: SUNY Press. 259–71.

Swisher, Karin L., ed. 1994. *Violence Against Women.* San Diego: Greenhaven Press.

Tavris, Carol. 1992. *The Mismeasure of Women.* New York: Simon & Schuster.

Walker, Lenore. 1979. *The Battered Woman.* New York: Harper.

Weis, Lois, ed. 1988. *Class, Race, and Gender in American Education.* Albany, NY: SUNY Press.

Weis, Lois, and Michelle Fine, eds. 1993. *Beyond Silenced Voices: Class, Race, and Gender in United States Schools.* Albany, NY: SUNY Press.

Wellesley College Center for Research on Women. 1992. *How Schools Shortchange Girls: A Study of Major Findings on Girls in Education.* Washington DC: American Association of University Women.

Wolfe, Leslie R. 1991. *Women, Work, and School: Occupational Segregation and the Role of Education.* Boulder, CO: Westview Press.

6 Imagining Neighborhoods: Social Worlds of Urban Adolescents

Colleen M. Fairbanks
University of Texas at Austin

And in weaving texts, we weave lives, thereby composing a classroom neighborhood, filled with the distinctive sounds of child voices.

—Anne Haas Dyson

In *Social Worlds of Children Learning to Write in an Urban Primary School*, Anne Haas Dyson describes the various worlds that young children bring to and construct within a primary classroom. She details, in this study, the ways in which students negotiate the boundaries of home and school, official and unofficial worlds, as they attempt to make sense of their early literacy learning. She likens the students' forays into imaginative and representative worlds as constructing "neighborhoods" and documents the kinds of social work students accomplish through their texts. In this way, Dyson illustrates how "children's voices articulate who each thinks he or she is relative to particular others in particular historical moments" (211). To hear students' voices requires that teachers are there to listen, to invite sharing, and to create what Dyson calls a "permeable" curriculum (217). Such curriculum ought not be limited to primary grade students, however. By inviting students to portray their many neighborhoods—those real and imagined places students inhabit—teachers create opportunities to learn from their students, whose lives are often very different from their teachers'. By extension, teachers also then open the classroom to students' lived experiences and the possibility for negotiated classroom interactions.

In this essay, I trace what my colleague Kathie Smith and I, two middle-class, white teachers, learned from our predominantly African American tenth-grade students over the course of one school year. Teaching at an urban high school in Saginaw, Michigan, we focused our curriculum upon the question "Who am I?" and offered students invitations to explore their lives in a variety of contexts.[1] It was our intent and our hope that such invitations would encourage them to see greater connections between their high school and their community. Through this joint exploration of community, we sought to examine and to understand the lives of our students as well as to provide broader and deeper opportunities for their literacy development. By analyzing the range of texts and the ways in which students represent their social worlds, I aim to describe both students' representations of themselves and their community and the diversity of perspectives within this relatively homogeneous population. As the analysis of student texts will illustrate, the students in these two classrooms constructed diverse portraits of their neighborhoods and struggled with the personal and moral dilemmas associated with adolescence. Their texts also displayed an array of values and beliefs in relation to their community experiences. While the students' lives are clearly shaped by the broader social and cultural issues of their racial and economic circumstances, their texts also provide important windows into contemporary adolescence. In other words, the students' social worlds consisted of complex local relationships among family, friends, residents of their neighborhoods, and larger social and cultural forces.

The student texts I have chosen to highlight here were responses to assignments offered as opportunities to learn, occasions to articulate beliefs and values, or ways of understanding specific phenomena. Kathie and I constructed particular assignments that consciously elicited personal connections to the themes we studied and that were directly tied to our commitments to community-based literacy. As teachers, we wanted the students to use reading and writing as ways of describing and understanding the lives they lead; at the same time we wanted to learn how students use language to describe their worldviews. Students wrote these texts for various instructional purposes as well: to learn about formal business letters, to develop certain writing abilities such as the use of descriptive language, or to learn about reader response. The specific journal entries or writing assignments were embedded in other classroom activities which dealt with the overall theme of study and arose from discussions or readings. Some were formal classroom projects; others informal responses to class discussions or reading material.[2]

As students explored their various neighborhoods, they read about, wrote about, and discussed a wide range of social issues that concerned them. In my analysis of their texts, I found that their writings, whether formal essays or journal topics, could be grouped under two broad themes: (1) Imagining Community Life and (2) Exploring Personal Relationships. The students did not write about these topics in this order. Depending upon the larger curriculum task, students chose to write about some aspect of their personal life or the community, not necessarily because we asked them to but because their response to a question or an assignment prompted them to do so. There is also a certain degree of overlap between the topics; students often included personal anecdotes in their writing about community issues. This overlap appeared to be consistent with the ways students' social worlds intersected. However, a topic-centered focus for the presentation of students' texts in this essay allows the diversity of the student group to emerge more clearly. In the two classes under study, the student population was almost exclusively comprised of African American students. (There were two European American students in our classes and one Mexican American student.) The two classrooms were heterogeneously grouped with reference to past academic performance; the socioeconomic status of the students varied within the school population as a whole. These variations, but more centrally, the variety of personalities that made up each classroom, created a mosaic of actors, actions, opinions, abilities, and temperaments very different from pictures which emerge from many studies of ethnically homogeneous populations.[3] I want to begin with a brief history of the community, because this history has shaped the students and forms the backdrop for their texts.

The Community and Its History

Located on the east side of Saginaw (Michigan), the students' neighborhoods have become a predominantly African American enclave in the aftermath of racial unrest that gripped many cities during the 1960s. When the riots exploded in Detroit in the summer of 1967, Saginaw officials, fearing similar violent activity, closed the bridges spanning the Saginaw River and connecting the predominantly African American east side with the predominantly white west side. Even prior to the events of 1967, whites had begun the trek across the river to the west side and Saginaw's newly developed suburbs, but the process accelerated rapidly after 1967. By 1969, for example, African American students represented 23 percent of the school district's population, but on the east side the African American population had reached 51 percent (Purvas). In 1971, the figures had increased to 36 percent for the district as a whole and 72 percent at Saginaw High School (a figure representative of the east side school population as a whole) (Watson). In 1976, the enrollment of minority students surpassed that of white students in the whole district (Watson).

A large section of the east side is comprised by the First Ward, a neighborhood adjacent to the Chevrolet Gray Iron Plant, built in 1926. During and after the foundry's construction, the First Ward became a tenement area where African American men, recruited by General Motors from the South, lived. Houses in the First Ward, bought by real estate companies, were divided into rooming houses shared by the men who worked in the foundry (Thompson). As southern migration continued during the 1930s and 1940s, the African American community steadily expanded its borders—west toward the river and south toward the newer Malleable Iron Plant that General Motors built during post–World War II economic expansion. As more African American auto workers settled on the east side, more whites moved across the river.

Economic forces have shaped the east side as much as racial politics. The Saginaw community has drawn upon the General Motors Corporation for its economic survival since the Gray Iron was built in 1926. Employment at one of its plants brought many members of the African American community a measure of economic security throughout the 1960s, allowing them to buy homes and settle on the east side. Those who could do so abandoned the First Ward tenements, leaving them to the indigent. But during the recession of the 1970s, Saginaw experienced the dramatic economic downturn characteristic of other rust-belt cities and has, in some ways, never fully recovered. For example, in 1967, 56 percent of the student population came from homes that met federal low-income standards. In 1987, even with the economic recovery of the 1980s, 69 percent of the students met these criteria. In the First Ward and its adjacent neighborhoods targeted as a high-risk area, 75 percent of the households qualified for federal money to help students deemed at-risk in 1969; in 1987, 91 percent qualified (Stern).

Imagining Community Life

Knowing, however, that students often see things in a different way than their teachers or other outsiders do, we asked the students to tell us how they saw their neighborhoods. When they closed their eyes and envisioned their neighborhoods, what did they see? What time of day was it? Who was out? What were they doing? What did it feel like? In response, the students wrote neighborhood sketches in their journals like the ones that follow.

> In the summer when it's hot, sunny, and bright, the wind is usually blowing warm and soft. My neighborhood is filled with activity. . . . If you listen long enough you would hear lowriders cruising up the nearby streets with music booming out of their trunks, or someone's dog barking at a car, or an intruder lurking in a closeby back yard, or you would probably hear cars drag racing down the back streets, and near the edge of the hood the sound of an expressway. During

the evening freight trains blow their horns and come creeping into the Saginaw Freight Yard which also borders my neighborhood. Around the block you can see teenagers standing around in small groups, talking, smoking cigarettes or just dancing to the music. . . . Not too far away you can get a glimpse of small children running and jumping through a water sprinkler to cool off.

Ronnie

The neighbor next door is always busy, busy, busy. He's money-hungry. Look he's on his way to work now. It sure is hot out here. I better get off of this banister thing before my mom start hollering . . . . It's old and wiggly. I told my brother a million times to fix this thing. We gotta lazy landlord. Just look at that yard it's a mess. Our yard needs a crew cut. Oh, there's Shawn she lives next door. She's motioning me to come over now. . . . I hate them little bad dirty kids across the street. I don't see why Shawn let her little sister play with them. Now look at ol' Antuan across the street washing his beautiful precious car. I hope it rust. Me and Shawn sit on the curb when we gossip. Oh, I better watch the crack so I won't break my moma's back. Now look at Shawn everytime we do she got on pajamas. I wonder is they dog out. If it is I'm goin' back home. She always say he don't bite, he don't bite. I say he got teeth don't he. Sittin on this curb makes my butt hurt. No cute boys never ride down our dull street. Gossip time—She tell me a lil'—I tell her a lil'. We put them together and talk about it. She always has better gossip than me. Dang! That's my moma calling me soon as it start gettin good! I'll step on all the crack now. . . .

Nyesha

I picture us outside co-lampin' against the trees in the gansta-gansta lean. Our hats on backwards to the left shoulder with the starter sign the other way, sweatin' every girl in biker shorts. . . .

Quentin

It is a nice summer day. I see nothing but blue in the sky. My friend Tiffany is across the street washing their cars. Our next door neighbors are sitting on the porch listening to some music, talking and playing games. My friend and I are about to go play basketball over my cousin house. My father is cutting the grass. Mom is upstairs watching t.v. laying down on the couch. Everything is nice and smooth. My brother is over my sister's house around the block, playing with my nephews. No one is angry at anyone. Everyone is nice to each other.

Cariton

These sketches provide a glimpse, I think, of students' everyday lives; they portray some of the images which shape students' sense of their own neighborhoods. And they stand in sharp contrast to the public statistics and news reports about the neighborhoods which surround Saginaw High School. These public reports speak to the poverty of the east side, the very real social problems that exist as a function of poverty, the lingering myths about race, and not enough in the way of municipal support, and they paint a gloomy picture of the east side community. There is, indeed, crime and violence. Drug houses plague even the more prosperous neighborhoods. But, if these were the only stories about such neighborhoods, there would be little hope in the lives of its residents or the teachers working in its high school. Instead, while the portraits the students painted do not as a rule ignore the community's problems, these problems do not make up the central themes of the students' sketches. Ordinary city life—gossiping on the curb, posing for young girls, cutting the lawn, and running through sprinklers in the summer—occupy center stage. These are not desperate portraits, nor desperate kids, even if their prospects are not as bright as they, in their youth, might believe.

The neighborhood sketches also reflect the imaginative and discursive resources students used to portray their sense of neighborhood. Each student simultaneously draws upon memories and the generative possibilities of language to construct an image of his or her neighborhood. For example, Ronnie's sketch takes a realistic approach. His text draws upon serial strategies; he catalogs the activities that occur in his neighborhood, making a collage with words. In his sketch, we see the many landmarks of his neighborhood: the cars, trains, pets, and the people, young and old, who live out their lives in this neighborhood. He captures the sights and sounds that constitute neighborhood life for him. All of these images, including the lurking intruder, are part of his experience of community life. They echo what have become the predominant themes of the city: industry, popular culture, and people living in close quarters.

Nyesha and Quentin take a more personal, conversational approach. Nyesha's sketch presents a kind of personal, interior dialogue that both describes the events around her and offers a running commentary. Her next-door neighbor does not just go to work; he's "money-hungry." Shawn's dog does not merely exist as a fixture of the neighborhood; he is a source of irritation and some measure of fear. The rickety banister leads to a commentary on family relations and tenant-landlord disputes. Underlying this commentary is Nyesha's mother, who, ever present but unseen, is both loved and reviled, depending upon the current situation. From the curb in front of her house, Nyesha talks to herself, and to her readers, about daily life in the neighborhood and the range of emotions it evokes in her. In her text, the reader sees Nyesha's view of the shifting and often uncertain terrain of urban life.

Quentin's sketch is full of the hip-hop sounds of his contemporaries. He mouths the language of the rap music blaring from the trunks of Ronnie's lowriders. His short piece both imitates and imagines his neighborhood in the current language of his generation. It is not so much about the neighborhood, but an imaginative description of some of its residents. For Quentin, it is he and the home boys who are central to the community, and he chooses to portray them on their own terms, not so much as they are, but how they imagine themselves to be (or perhaps how they would like to be): reflections of contemporary popular culture. He takes a BET (Black Entertainment Television) view of the world around him, not a localized one, but a media-inspired, national one, which takes its metaphors from the music and culture emanating from cities across the country.

Finally, Cariton presents us with the "happy family." The world is sunny and bright, family members are nice to one another, no one is angry. It is not clear whether this description is how Cariton really sees his family or if it is his wish. The comment, "no one is angry at anyone," hints that the "happy family" is not his only experience. Cariton's depiction of neighborhood life strikes me as an idealized portrait of a social world that could be drawn from anywhere in America, most typically as seen on television. Unlike Nyesha, Quentin, or Ronnie, Cariton does not present us with the starker or more ethnically enriched visions of neighborhood life. There are no neglectful landlords or lurking intruders. Instead, he portrays a Saturday afternoon filled with everyday family activities that are "smooth and nice."

Each of these neighborhood sketches reveals as much about the individual authors as it does about the neighborhoods they describe. The frame of reference each student assumes gives us a glimpse of their personalities and their attitudes toward community life. Presented with such diversity, the landscape of urban life that these students describe takes on more contours. These kids are not immune to the real violence that pervades their lives, but it is not the all-consuming concern that is so often displayed in newspapers and discussed in the teachers' lounge. Within the community, some neighborhoods are more dangerous than others; some are more stable than others. Some families are more secure than others; some more fragmented. The students who attend Saginaw High exemplify this diversity, and all of these portraits stand in contrast to the grim newspaper accounts of Saginaw's eastside community.

These sketches, as well as the various texts that follow, are also instructive to both students and teachers. As imaginative representations of lived experience, they invite students to "shape and reshape their lives, imagining what could have or should have, as well as what did happen" in their neighborhoods (Dyson and Genishi 2). By taking up their teachers' invitations to share their experiences, students further invited their teachers to learn from them. As Maxine Greene writes, "each time [a person] is with others—in dialogue, in teaching-learning situations, in mutual pursuit of a project—additional new perspectives open; language opens possibilities of seeing, hearing, understanding" (21). The students' texts not only open possibilities for them to understand better, through the act of constructing a text, the lives they have led and might lead, but these texts also open possibilities for teachers to see, hear, and understand better the students sitting in classroom desks in front of them. Greene's sense of the mutuality in dialogue, the teaching and learning that attend social interactions, also points toward the future. She suggests that as an individual shares perspectives and discovers multiple realities, "each person reaches out from his/her own ground toward what might be, should be, is not yet" (21).

In their responses to another classroom activity, the students from Saginaw High School reflected upon the future of their community by addressing community members. Reading a newspaper article, "Survival of Blacks Depends on Events in Next 10 Years, Local Leaders Claim" (Verburg and Osborn), the students wrote letters to several community members who addressed in the article what they perceived as the critical issues facing African Americans in the 1990s. The interviewees identified education, economic conditions, and crime as central aspects of the community's "survival." In their letters, the students drew upon past and present experiences to formulate their own sense of the community's needs and its prospects for the future.

In the following letters, the variety of their concerns is indicated both by the individual they chose to write to and the topics they chose to write about. Moreover, they outline an additional dimension of students' constructions of community.

> Dear Dr. Crawford [former Mayor of Saginaw]:
> My name is Michael, I am a sophomore at Saginaw High School and a concerned citizen of Saginaw.
> In your comments in The Saginaw News on January 28, I believe that you missed one critical problem, "crimes on blacks committed by blacks." I've seen blacks shoot blacks, blacks sell drugs to blacks, yet nothing is being done about it. This concerns me because how do I know I won't be the next person to get a bullet from a "Brothers'" gun?
> I agree with the whole article about the economic problems of blacks. Even with a college degree I, being a black male, might have a harder time getting a job than my female counterpart. A company

can kill two birds with one stone if they hire a black female and at the same time meet certain hiring requirements.

Education of black children depends on the parents. My parents constantly remind me of my goal to go to college. In my room I have a step by step process and at the end of it is my goal to become a lawyer.

I really hope that I can make people understand that just talking about these problems won't make them go away, we have to work together to get rid of them.

My classmates and I would like you to come to our class and talk about these problems of our race and how we can get them out of our community. Please let me know if you are able to come. Thank you for your time.

> Your friend,
> Michael

For Michael, the threat of black-on-black crime was very real. Early in our study of the community, Michael came to school and announced that he had seen someone shot the night before. He was obviously and appropriately upset by the incident, raising the issue frequently during classroom discussion. On another occasion, he related an incident which occurred at the music store where he worked. Outside the store, in a rough part of the city, a fight broke out involving several men. He called 911 to request police assistance and waited for twenty minutes locked in the store for a single police car to arrive. Unable to subdue the fight, the police stood and watched until the fight was settled on its own.

Michael's concerns were not limited to the violence he had witnessed; he was also concerned about his future prospects, raising such issues as affirmative action and hiring practices as well as personal goal setting. His fears about employment opportunities echo the frustration that Ogbu found in the perception among some African Americans that even with a good education, economic chances for this population are limited at best. Michael's letter, by its depiction of his "step-by-step" plan for the future, emphasizes individual preparation and goal setting as a means toward a better future. In essence, his personal project is the construction of a social world where he can prosper and where he can struggle against the violence of his present circumstances.

Another student, Latasha, questioned the real investment of these community leaders in east-side neighborhoods. Having watched crack deals transacted on street corners, Latasha was skeptical about the depth of these leaders' knowledge of neighborhood conditions:

Dear Rev. Hall:

I'm a student at Saginaw High School and our class had to do a project that involves this letter.

I was wondering about the comments you made in the Saginaw News, The title was, "Survival of Blacks Depends on Events in the next 10 years Local Leaders Claim" (January 28, 1990).

I just wish you would stop, think for a minute, and ask yourself, "have I been out or seen enough to say the things I said in the newspaper?" I mention this the way you was carrying on about the situation, you acted like there really is not a drug problem, but ther is a problem.

Sincerely yours,
Latasha

Latasha's letter and her response to the article stem from Rev. Hall's comments that students need to get a college education and the stress he placed upon "the urgency of the community responding to the worsening economy" (Verburg and Osborn 1A). Latasha did not seem to see a connection between the local economy and increasing drug use and worried that even African American community leaders were out of touch with the real problems in the east-side neighborhoods. She intimates that she and her classmates are far more aware of the daily experience with drug dealers in her neighborhood than these community leaders, infusing her letter with a degree of cynicism and a plea for adult commitment to improve conditions. Finally, underlying Latasha's letter, there seems to be a sense of panic in her concern about the prevalence of drugs in her neighborhood. Many students voiced deep reservations about the ability of community institutions or community leaders to combat crime and drugs in the neighborhood. "We're just killing ourselves," students often commented, "they don't care about that."

A third student, Lady, argues that children themselves bear responsibility for their lives, placing the responsibility for crime and drugs on kids themselves.

Dear Dr. Crawford:

The future is going to be difficult their are so many thing going on in the world. There my be children coming up with the right tools maybe not. The parent do raise their children in the right environment it's the kids who on themselves. now a days kids hang with their friends and if their friends are bad that makes them blend in to be bad also. Life is hard and some kids feel that they are living for themselves so they sell drugs hang in gangs, all that kind of rapture, and it's mainly because their friends do, and that makes them do it also. Some kids may have dreames ahead of them, such as becoming a basketball player or football player. I myself have the attitude where i feel that life is to short to be trying to kill one another, I'm trying to get an education and learn about life. The parents try to help there children, but they don't wan't to be helped' they only have the answer to their own problems Some suffer from their parents getting a divorce or something like that. There is ways some kind of problem to make their children do what they do. All they have to do is try and with the work that you are doing they will succeed.

Sincerely,
Lady

Although Lady qualifies her response by indicating that some children have to deal with problems, like divorce, which makes their lives more difficult, she sees the real problem as peer pressure. In Lady's world, having dreams for the future and a common-sense approach provides the way to a better life: children "only have the answer to their own problems," and it is up to them to overcome the problems that life puts in their path.

Lady's belief in self-reliance was endorsed by many students. One of the themes in classroom conversation was the need for students to be strong and focused. Michael's "step by step process" in his room is a manifestation of personal goal-setting and responsibility. In these student letters, the way to a better future lies diversely in personal strength and community cooperation. The balance for each student changes, but throughout their letters and in their conversations, these two aspects of social life play an important role. Even Lady concludes with a nod toward the community programs that Dr. Crawford advocated in the newspaper interview.

The neighborhood sketches and the letters to community leaders offer surprising contrasts and an interesting profile of the students. When asked to describe their daily lives, many students emphasized the positive aspects of children growing up, playing games, and enjoying themselves. However, when asked to comment upon the current conditions of the community, their fears and frustrations were vividly expressed. The dichotomy between daily living and community politics is not as surprising as it might first seem. The students conduct their lives in the midst of crime and violence, but they manage to find ways to grow up that include "ordinary" childhood experiences. Conflicting experiences characterize their lives, and what they are willing, sometimes eager, to say depends both upon the questions they are asked, the rhetorical conditions these questions evoke, and their sense that someone is listening. As their teachers, Kathie and I became privy to the variety of their responses to community life, because we extended genuine invitations to bring students' experiences into the classroom and allowed them to be the focus of the literacy curriculum.

We discovered in both sets of texts that the students' social worlds were imbued with themes of critique and concern. They continually vented their frustration at the inability of city officials, parents, the schools, and children themselves to improve the neighborhoods. Yet, their voices also evinced concern that people in the community work together to recognize and resolve community problems. In their eyes, the decline of the neighborhoods cannot be arrested without the commitment of all residents, a responsibility that each member had to assume if their neighborhoods were to become safe once again. These students shared many similarities with the teenagers in a study of adolescent moral development conducted by Bardige and her colleagues. In this scheme, adolescents, both male and female, displayed justice and caring concerns when faced with moral dilemmas. According to Gilligan, justice concerns "focus on problems of oppression, problems stemming from inequality, and the moral ideal is one of reciprocity or equal respect." Caring concerns "focus on problems of detachment, on disconnection or abandonment or indifference, and the moral ideal is one of attention and response" (xvii). The Saginaw students' responses to community problems displayed an overriding inclination toward caring. They worried about neglect by the city and its police force, about the inability of parents to adequately raise their children in such conditions, and about the indifference of those people who had escaped the neighborhoods to the severity of the drug problem the students faced. Yet, they assign, to differing degrees, the role of personal responsibility and community action.

By contrast, justice concerns surfaced infrequently in the letters the students wrote, occurring more often in their classroom discussions. In their discussions students cited police corruption, heightened media attention to east-side crimes (as opposed to the west side), and racial discrimination as the impediments to real change in their community. The relative absence of these concerns in the students' letters most likely stemmed from the students' attention to audience and rhetorical considerations. These letters were written to African American community leaders by African American students. Despite certain criticisms about the leadership of the black community, the students recognized that Mr. Holiday, Dr. Crawford, and Rev. Hall could not be held responsible for racism. The letter-writing exercise involved students in the opportunity to build community rather than address inequalities across communities, even though students seemed to understand that unfair treatment by the white community played a role in the community's problems. That students were willing and open to discuss issues of race and community conflict suggests that they felt safe in talking and writing about such issues with their teachers. Considering the urgency instilled in many of the students' conversations and letters, the students also seemed to indicate the importance they placed upon the conditions of their community.

Exploring Personal Life

Equally important to the students' constructions of their social worlds, personal relationships emerged as a central theme in the lives of these Saginaw students. Providing opportunities for students to explore their relationships with others through reading and writing was also an underlying aim of our curriculum. As a consequence, students' classroom activities included biographies of family members, autobiographies, and journal entries which explored students' relationships with others. In these writings, the teachers could begin to see the range of personal experiences which shaped the students' lives:

> One of my best friends almost killed our other friend over some crack, cause both of them sold it. So they was selling it together like. They was going half and half. The one of my friends, can't give his name but anyway, we went over his house one day and we seen him chopping up some crack. To try to get more then my other friend. So they started to fight and all of a sudden my friend pulled out his gun and shot at my other friend. He missed, but he didn't shoot again cause he thought about what he was doing. So he just told him, that they couldn't be friends anymore, and they just ended their friendship. And he begged for their friendship back, cause in a way he was jealous of him. Cause he had a lot of money and got almost anything he wanted. And without him my other friend would take all of the things that he bought for the other back. So you could say he was jealous. Cause he told me one day hisself. I was kind of too. But not really, cause I almost got a lot of the things I wanted.
>
> Mac

> I had a close relationship with someone. He was my uncle, but he was more like a friend to me. His name was Henry Quentin _____. Quentin would let me hang out with him, he would teach me Tae Kwon Do. Quentin taught me everything I know all the way from basket ball, girls to fighting. He wouldn't let noone mess with me. He didn't just take time with me he also took time with my brother. When Quentin graduated he moved to Los Angeles with his girl friend, but he come here every year to visit the family. When he gets here he always tells me whats going on in L.A., and I'll [tell] him whats been going on here. By the way he's named after his father or my grandfather, and he named his son after him.
>
> Stephon

> Well I had a friend name Ometita. She is 15 teen years old we grew up together. From 1st grade to now. We went to church, school, parties, name it we did it together. But when we started to grow up about 13 teen I was in the 7th and she didn't pass she was in the 6th. But she thought I was going to change but I didn't. So we used to go places and most would try to talk to me. So she loves boys she had

a baby in the 6th grade and he didn't even claim it. So I used to babysit and I still was her homie. But this boy she went with in the 12th grade and she was in the 8th I was in the 9th. She always wanted me to go over his house with her. But when he tried to talk to me I just wouldn't so he told her I tried to talk to him but I really didn't I swear. So she asked me and I said no but she started calling me all kind of names Bitches, hoes, and everything you name it. And she ran in the house crying I was going in the house after her but she grab her mother big knife and stabbed me in my leg and then I start to fight her back. But he really didn't like her and she didn't know it. But I had 16 stitches. And she came out there to see me and I didn't won't to see her. So the next day she came to my house and I said come in she told me she was sorry and I said why did you go off like that she said because she was pregnant again I said what did I have to do with it she said she wanted him to stay with her not leave her but they still broke up and we stayed friends.

Evelyn

Evelyn, Mac, and Stephon show us some of the personal encounters which have marked their young lives. Even though the violence that Mac and Evelyn depict is chilling, their stories still display a sense of loyalty and a concern for the bonds of friendship. Evelyn is emphatic that she resisted the advances by Ometita's boyfriend, and she remains friends with Ometita even after the knife attack. Mac's friend, the cheating drug dealer, might beg for forgiveness but cannot mend the breach he has caused. As a result both he and Mac are no longer the recipients of the other dealer's largesse. Less dramatic, but no less important, Stephon's uncle remains an important friend to Stephon despite his move to Los Angeles, sharing stories and lessons on his annual visits to Saginaw. Over and over again, our students wrote about such friendships and the necessity of loyalty. When place of residence, unexpected death, and economic uncertainty claimed so much of these students' attention, the bonds between individuals took on great importance for our students.

Similar themes emerged in students' responses to the texts they read. For example, the first reading assignment of the year asked students to choose selections from *The Bridge*, a collection of often compelling stories about growing up in Saginaw authored by students from the city's two high schools.[4] After reading a selection, students wrote informal letters to their classmates or teachers in response. In these letters, students identify with characters and events of the stories, revealing experiences that have shaped their relationships with others. In the following exchange, Anthony had just read a poem by Ernie Mitchell entitled "Should I Hate Them?" It is a stark poem of parental neglect and abuse in which the speaker wonders aloud if he should hate his parents. Anthony chose to write his response letter to Kathie Smith, discussing his own circumstances and answering the poem's question for himself:

> Dear Ms. Smith the story I read really got to me because I fill sorry for Ernie if that was my father I think I would not want to see or talk to him, but I take that back. I would try to find some love for my mother and father. Because when I was born my mother and Father were not married and everybody thinks he is my step-father and sometimes when I really think about it, sometimes it hurts to know he's your father but on you Birth certificate it says step-father. But I know my parents love me vary much and I love them. But I will never hate my parents.
>
> Sincerely,
Anthony

Sorting out his conflicting feelings about parenthood became a personal theme for Anthony throughout the academic year. It first appeared here in his attempt to resolve the uncertainty and pain he felt about his own father not being named on his birth certificate. He concludes his letter, however, with a re-affirmation of the mutual love that exists between him and his parents.

In the following letter, Ebony writes a response to "E" that could have been directed to Anthony. In it we see both Ebony's determination to survive hardship and the messages she uses to overcome personal adversity:

> Dear "E" I think everyone feels a little unwanted once upon a time in their life's there have been so many times I could just crawl up under a rock and stay there. I can't count. Just to think all the times I have been hurt. but you have to pick yourself up, dust yourself off and go on about your business.
>
> Ebony

Letters like Ebony's and Anthony's, stories like Mac's, Evelyn's and Stephon's written as journal entries, take on conversational tones: for example, Anthony says he would not want to talk to Ernie's father, but then "takes it back," just as Evelyn "swears" to her readers that she did not "talk" to Ometita's boyfriend. Ebony uses a nickname, "E," to begin her letter and sprinkles adages and conversational phrases throughout it, and Mac tells his audience in a narrative sidebar that he cannot reveal the names of his friends. The overall tone of the responses, because of their informality, take on the cadences of conversation, echoing the students' everyday talk and displaying the storytelling patterns they use in ordinary conversation. The students talked to each other through writing as though they were chatting at lunch about personal matters, even though these conversations had been elicted by their teachers in class-room assignments. Through such informal writing, the students shared with their teachers bits and pieces of their lives as well as their reactions to these experiences. The students revealed, at least partially, the issues that were important to them, their joy or worry about friends and family, and the despair they sometimes felt.

Other activities encouraged students to write more deeply about family life. In biographies, students investigated the life history of a family member and shared in their texts what they had learned through interviews with the family member. Most of the biographies also included statements of praise or admiration for the person portrayed. For example, Deshawnda ends her biography by telling about a memorable day spent with her aunt:

> I remeber the first time me and my aunt spent time together we had lots of fun. We went out to eat at a resturant we arued the whole time we were there at the resturant but we were only playing. I love her. She is one of my favorite aunts.

Deshawnda's aunt spends time with Deshawnda, "plays" with her in mock arguments, and as Deshawnda wrote earlier in the biography, "is a nice understanding lady."

For other students, adult family members were important if stern sources of guidance. Tomika, whose own child was born just prior to the school year, writes that "Her [mother's] childhood memories are of how she was taught to be very responsible and how to accept hurt and pain in the hard way which makes her the person she is today." Later in the essay, Tomika elaborates on the way her mother treated Tomika's pregnancy and the respect she has since acquired for her mother:

> Most people would be glad to have my mother because she is a mother who understands and accepts things in life. For the fact that when I got pregnant at first she was hard on me but as everything fell into place and things happened as they did she began to accept and understand it. That was a great memory I have of my mother for the person that she is.

Tomika acknowledges that her mother was very disappointed in her, but she also admires her mother's insistence that a person take respon-sibility for his or her life. Tomika's mother seems to be inculcating these values in her daughter through the interview itself. These values also had special import for Tomika—they were clearly incorporated into her worldview—even though she often felt the burden of motherhood and the constraints it placed on her life.

Not all students described their family life with such warmth or ad-miration. Dulani's biography of his mother hints at but does not elabo-rate upon the less secure nature of his family circumstances:

> Two years after [my mother, Marilyn] had finished school she got
> married to my father and the[y] settled down and we lived in a
> brick house in Tennessee, Then when my ant got shot we moved
> back up here to stay.
>
> A year later my mother went to college for two years a[nd] got a
> job as a secretary she was always working so she didn't see me too
> much because I was staying with my daddy.
>
> After some months my mother found out she was pregnant again
> with my little sisters.

Dulani leaves so many unanswered questions in the reader's mind: What
happened to his aunt? How did he feel about staying with his father
and not seeing his mother because of her work? What was it like in
Tennessee? Always a struggling writer and often absent from school,
Dulani does not share the intimacies of his family relations beyond basic facts, even though these facts in and of themselves give clues to his
family life. Nor does Dulani share his reactions to these events. It is uncertain whether he chooses not to share more about his family, he is not
interested in sharing more, or his writing abilities limit what or how he
chooses to share. His biography nonetheless adds to the range of the
students' family circumstances. It contributes in this way to understanding the diversity of life experiences that students brought with them to
the classroom.

Reading students' personal writing as a collage, Kathie and I often
found a sense of their values, their relationships with others, and the
variety of their experiences. In other words, the students allowed us to
glimpse various facets of their social worlds. Parents and older family
members (aunts, uncles, or grandparents) held an important place for
most of the students. They are seen as caregivers, supporters, and teachers of life even though students describe these roles in different ways.
Stephon's uncle, Quentin, teaches Stephon about girls, basketball, and
fighting, making sure that no one "messes" with Stephon. Deshawnda's
aunt takes Deshawnda out for dinner and has fun with her. Tomika's
mother teaches her important life lessons. The Saginaw students reserved
a great deal of respect for parents, even though their relationships were
not always clear or stable.

Similarly, friendships were highly prized, even when they caused
trouble or were lost through disloyalty. Evelyn maintains her friendship
with Ometita despite her friend's accusations and attack. For Mac, however, cheating a friend causes an irreparable breech in the friendship.
The difference in these two stories may have its source in gender differences. Girls seem to be less willing to abandon friends, despite crises
and disappointments (Bardige, Ward, Gilligan, Taylor, & Cohen 1988).
They tend to find ways to understand the actions of others that allow
them to maintain their attachments. The value of attachments to friends

and family may have allowed Evelyn to maintain her friendship with Ometita. Boys, on the other hand, seem less inclined to prize attachment over integrity. Thus, Mac maintains his friendship with the "cheating drug dealer," but both Mac and his friend lose the generosity of the other dealer. Perhaps Mac maintains his friendship because the dealer cheated not on Mac, but on someone else.

Finally, personal responsibility played an important role in both the students' portrayals of personal life and their constructions of community life. Although Evelyn's story recounts Ometita's violent response to her situation, Evelyn does admonish Ometita for taking out personal problems on her friends, instead of accepting responsibility for her actions. The students send the implicit message that even though they may not control the external circumstances of their lives, they must take control of their responses to those circumstances. In uncertain conditions, our students seemed to believe that they must draw upon their own resources and make their way as best as they can. Yet, each of the students approaches his or her sense of personal responsibility differently, because the stories they tell focus on different issues and span the variety of their life experiences. It is a long way from Evelyn's and Mac's stories of violence to Michael's desire to become a lawyer or Tomika's responsibilities for her child. Each student responded to an activity by drawing upon their individual constructions of the activity and the personal experiences it brought to mind. In this sense the students constructed both themselves and the activity which helped account for the diversity of issues, experiences, or events that students described. As a result, the students created an increasingly complex image of urban adolescence, one that Kathie and I as their teachers could learn about most fully through the students' own portrayals.

Conclusion

In her address to the Nobel committee, Toni Morrison tells a story about an old, blind, wise woman who is approached by a group of children. One of the children asks her, "Old woman, I hold in my hand a bird. Tell me whether it is living or dead" (10). From the perspective of both the old woman and the children, Morrison considers the task and the circumstances presented by the story. Morrison writes that she "choose[s] to read the bird as language and the woman as a practiced writer," and through the ensuing dialogue between the old woman and the children, explores the responsibilities of adults to children and of children to adults in the uses of language. At the end of the story, when both the old woman and the children have asked their questions, made their replies, and told their own stories, the old woman says, "Look. How lovely it is, this thing we have done—together" (30). In my reading of Morrison's story, this lovely thing they have done together is to "grasp," as Geertz writes, "what is in front of [them]," the concrete circumstances of lives initially separated by age, history, and the varieties of experience (123). The old woman and the children use language to lay open their joys and concerns, the events that have shaped who they have become and are still becoming, creating a new story together.

Such new creations depend upon the willingness of adults to see, hear, and at least to try to understand lives different from their own. For teachers, the classroom affords a place where students can begin to tell their stories or assert their opinions and a place where teachers can begin to understand their students better. As Shirley Brice Heath argues, "Stories, when they can be told in safe places, are [young people's] theories, ways of testing what others feel and think and how they and their friends stand in contrast to others" (216). Depending upon the rhetorical context, these Saginaw High School students presented us with their theories of adolescence, describing their lives in their own and others' language. The language of others—media clichés, rap music, and adult wisdom—percolates through their texts as the students struggle to find their own words, their own voices to construct images of their lives. The students' language is entangled in their individual efforts to define themselves, their community, and their place in school. Quentin's imitation of rap music to portray his neighborhood, Lady's comment that "life is hard," and Ebony's guide to survival all borrow from the language of others as students begin to articulate their individual experiences. The reliance on others' language is not surprising, since the students were continually surrounded by the words of adults whose opinions they valued and by various forms of media. Yet, the appropriation of language from others is also a generative act. As they shape and reshape experience, "The young can be empowered to view themselves as conscious, reflective namers and speakers if their particular standpoints are acknowledged, if interpretive dialogues are encouraged, if interrogation is kept alive" (Greene 57).

Students' stories and portrayals are also instructive: they help teachers consider the interests, values, concerns of their students in making curricular and instructional choices. Moreover, listening well helps teachers create what Anne Haas Dyson calls "curricular spaces" for students who have their own "social skills and cultural roots" ("Confronting the Split" 26). They provide the ground upon which teachers can make connections through dialogue, open avenues to keep "interrogation alive," and construct curriculum in collaboration with students. Once opened to students, such curricula try, as Robinson and Stock assert, to "fashion in the classroom an inhabitable world for students, one in which they might safely raise such voices as they have to make meanings for themselves and others, voices that will be valued for what agency they can manage" (312). Robinson and Stock further argue that teachers need to:

> read [students'] words about their worlds, to circulate them, to respond to them . . . , to read through those words toward human and humane interpretations of the selves *in situ* who have composed them, to read in texts from the margins attempts to recompose a sense of self, to reconstitute the meanings of self in relation to others. (313)

As young, urban adolescents, the Saginaw students are at once growing into adulthood and struggling to understand the meanings they can make of their lives at present as well as what they may make of them in the future.

The growing-up process takes place with or without teachers' participation, with or without the opportunity to use literacy as a means of exploring and appropriating language to name one's world. By engaging students in a process of self and community discovery deliberately focused on students' evolving perceptions of their relations in community life, we attempted to create the curricular space through which students could teach us about their social worlds. Our learning consisted in interpreting what students revealed about their lives through their texts in the context of our knowledge about community history and from the perspective of the events students shared and interpreted for us. In this process, we learned to see the complexity of our students' lives, some of the issues they grappled with, and the great diversity of their experiences. That our students so willingly shared their lives and opinions gives testimony to their desire to use the curricular spaces available to them to interrogate these social worlds.

Such interrogation engages students in both critical and imaginative exploration of lived experience, an essential element in the development of agency. It also requires, however, that teachers begin to construct classrooms that "partake of the spirit of a forum, of negotiation, of the recreating of meaning" (Bruner 123). For urban adolescents who confront daily the struggle to enjoy "ordinary" childhood pastimes in the midst of poverty and crime, recreating the meanings of experience presents both a daunting task and generative moments. As our students demonstrated to us through their texts, they are more than able to cast their experiences in the bright light of critical reflection as well as in the softer shades of fond reminiscences. This range of reflective capacities reveals to teachers, when they observe carefully, students' resilience, their hope, their wisdom, and the depth of these resources. Within the context of the literacy classroom, these resources, when tapped, become the seeds from which to create lovely things—together.

Notes

1. This curriculum for tenth graders invited students to read and write about their lives in various contexts (e.g., home, school, community). It was also a part of a larger, three-year high school curriculum, "Inquiry and Expression," that resulted from the partnership between the University of Michigan Center for Educational Improvement through Collaboration (CEIC) and the School District of the City of Saginaw. Jay Robinson, the director of the CEIC, provided the theoretical "heart" of the center and made it possible for university and school faculty, graduate students, and high school students to construct literacy projects such as the one described here.

2. The students displayed varying degrees of writing proficiency, and the texts used in this essay represent a variety of formal and informal writing activities. They have not had the benefit of editing for publication.

3. It is important to note that this essay examines the themes, counter-themes, and images students articulated to their teachers over the course of the year. It does not focus specifically on cross-cultural interactions, especially those involving student-teacher relations; nor does it focus on the growth of writing or other literate abilities.

4. *The Bridge* was published in 1988 as the culminating activity for twelfth-grade students who participated in the first collaboratively constructed and taught curriculum project of the CEIC and the Saginaw schools. This curriculum became the model for subsequent collaborative projects. For further details about this curriculum, see Robinson and Stock (1990) and Stock (1995).

Works Cited

Bardige, Betty, Janie Victoria Ward, Carol Gilligan, Jill McLean Taylor, and Gina Cohen. 1988. "Moral Concerns and Considerations of Urban Youth." *Mapping the Moral Domain*. Eds. Carol Gilligan, Janie Victoria Ward, and Jill McLean Taylor. Cambridge, MA: Harvard University Press. 175–200.

Bruner, Jerome. 1986. *Actual Minds, Possible Worlds*. Cambridge, MA: Harvard University Press.

Dyson, Anne Haas. 1994. "Confronting the Split between 'the Child' and Children: Toward New Curricular Visions of the Child Writer." *English Education* 26: 12–28.

———. 1993. *Social Worlds of Children Learning to Write in an Urban Primary School*. New York: Teachers College Press.

Dyson, Anne Haas, and Celia Genishi. 1994. Introduction. *The Need for Story: Cultural Diversity in Classroom and Community*. Eds. Anne Haas Dyson and Celia Genishi. Urbana, IL: National Council of Teachers of English. 1–7.

Geertz, Clifford. 1986. "The Uses of Diversity." *Michigan Quarterly Review*: 105–23.

Gilligan, Carol. 1988. "Prologue: Adolescent Development Reconsidered." *Mapping the Moral Domain*. Eds. Carol Gilligan, Janie Victoria Ward, and Jill McLean Taylor. Cambridge, MA: Harvard University Press. vii–xxxix.

Greene, Maxine. 1995. *Releasing the Imagination: Essays on Education, the Arts, and Social Change*. San Francisco: Jossey-Bass.

Heath, Shirley Brice. 1994. "Stories as Ways of Acting Together." *The Need for Story: Cultural Diversity in Classroom and Community*. Eds. Anne Haas Dyson and Celia Genishi. Urbana, IL: National Council of Teachers of English. 206–20.

Morrison, Toni. 1994. *The Nobel Lecture in Literature, 1993*. New York: Knopf.

Ogbu, John. 1987. "Opportunity Structure, Cultural Boundaries, and Literacy." *Language, Literacy, and Culture: Issues of Society and Schooling*. Ed. Judith A. Langer. Norwood, NJ: Ablex. 149–77.

Purvas, John. A. 1969. "Whites Rush to Suburbs Causing School Problems." *Saginaw News*, 5 December: A3+.

Robinson, Jay L., and Patricia L. Stock. 1990. "The Politics of Literacy." *Conversations on the Written Word: Essays on Language and Literacy*. Jay L. Robinson. Portsmouth, NH: Boynton/Cook–Heinemann. 217–317.

Stern, Avi. 1989. "More than 500 'at-risk': More Students Fitting Drop-Out Profile." *Saginaw News*, 27 August: B1.

Stock, Patricia L. 1995. *The Dialogic Curriculum: Teaching and Learning in a Multicultural Society*. Portsmouth, NH: Boynton/Cook–Heinemann.

Thompson, Mike. 1990. "Chronicle of Blacks in Saginaw—The Seldom Told Story." *Saginaw News*, 18 February: A1.

Verburg, Steven, and David Osborn. 1990. "Survival of Blacks Depends on Events in Next 10 Years, Local Leaders Claim." *Saginaw News*, 28 January: A1.

Watson, Rod. 1981. "The 'New' Student Picture: Schools' Racial Mix Gradually Reversed over 10 Years." *Saginaw News*, 13 December: B1+.

7 Conflicting Interests: Critical Theory Inside Out

Roberta J. Herter
Henry Ford High School

Introduction

"To be or not to be. That *was* the question. We're going to change the question." Victor, a seventeen-year-old African American male, set the scene for the first night of his English class at Henry Ford High School in Detroit.[1] Victor had chosen "to avoid the hassles" of day school, as he put it, by enrolling in night school. He was well-known and well-liked among the three hundred fifty night school students, many of whom had also dropped out of the crowded, anonymous day school of over two thousand students. Along with seven other night school students, Victor had volunteered to take part in a special semester-long theater workshop in collaboration with a college class from the University of Michigan. With his turn of Hamlet's phrase, Victor eagerly introduced himself to Sally, Susan, and Paul, three of the college students who came to his night school classroom once a week on Wednesday evenings during the winter semester of 1994. The college students were white, middle class to affluent, enrolled in a 300-level English course entitled "Theater and Social Change." Like Victor, the high school students were working-class African Americans enrolled in a required night school English course and quite different from the college students with whom they would collaborate. The goal of the project for the college students, as defined by the course description at the university, was to "form small groups to perform, in nontraditional spaces, street, action, and guerrilla theater pieces advocating social change." The goal for the high school students was to substitute something a little different for the traditional American Literature course required for these night school students: English 56, "Theater Workshop."

I had been teaching night school at Henry Ford for ten years when Buzz Alexander, a professor of English at the University of Michigan and an experienced political organizer, began looking for another project

site in which to continue his ongoing outreach work. An urban night
school class had potential to provide an interesting alternative setting,
he suggested. For many high school students, night school has become
a viable choice for those who select it as an alternative to mandatory
day school. Further expanding choice into course selection for these students, it seemed to us, might mitigate the stigmatizing labels sometimes
attached to those who enroll in night school. As well, as both a teacher
at the high school and a graduate student at the university, I welcomed
the collaboration. From a teacher's perspective the student-to-student
interaction promised a unique learning opportunity for my students and
for me, and so I viewed the theater project as an invitation for curricular
change rather than as an intervention program.

The college students, obviously interested in issues of social change,
were encountering authors like Freire for the first time, and they had
had minimal real-world experience in settings that were culturally different from their own. Their texts for the course included Kohl's *36 Children*, Clyde Taylor's *Dangerous Society*, Freire's *Pedagogy of the Oppressed*,
Boal's *Theater of the Oppressed*, and Myles Horton's *The Long Haul*. However, as the college students soon discovered, these readings could not
quite capture the complexity of the group of students they would meet
at the high school; neither had their suburban high schools prepared
them for an inner-city classroom.[2]

Not surprisingly, the weekly workshops produced tensions from the
beginning—some typical of any classroom encounter and some created
by the unique situation this particular collaboration presented. For example, in the process of collaboration, the high school students' interests proved different from the college students'. Victor's opening declaration is characteristic in its implication that the high school students
understood theater differently from the social action thrust of the college students' readings and interests. For Victor and others, theater was
defined in terms of its conventions of scripts, characterization, and performance. Knowledgeable about theater and a regular at Detroit's Attic
Theater, Victor's expectations of the course were that it would emphasize those conventions: students would read plays, study dramatic form,
write scripts in terms of those conventions and perform scenes. In contrast, the college students designed a course which emphasized such
elements as warm-up exercises, theater games, journal writing, and oral
script composition based in the students' own lives, culminating in "performance pieces." Victor had intended to use his writing ability in the
theater class but was repeatedly defeated by the college students' insistence, instead, on extemporaneous performance. In their writing and
conversations with me, the high school students expressed their expec-

tation that the theater project would teach them principles of acting, would give them a chance to perform and have fun, and would allow them to meet new people. In contrast, the college students expressed a desire to learn from the high school students, to "help" them in whatever way possible, and to make a difference in their lives through the theater encounter. In this paper, I will explore how these differing expectations and backgrounds played out in this collaborative venture.

From the perspective of the college students, the project began with theoretical readings rather than with an immersion in the culture of the night school. The primary text for English 319 was Augusto Boal's *Theatre of the Oppressed* (TO), a polemic analyzing western aesthetic philosophy while explicating political theater. Boal's vision of theater is based on Freire's broader ideological perspective. Born of the political struggles in Latin America during the 1960s, its technique is dramatic confrontation in order to display everyday complicity in various forms of oppression. As I viewed and reviewed videotapes of the students' weekly meetings and transcribed their dialogue into text, I began to wonder how the underlying critical theory of the project supported the college students in their attempts to make visible the complicated structures of an everyday life they were only beginning to see. As these college students struggled to negotiate the high school students' expectations of theater while at the same time trying to enact Boal's ideological theater, they were faced with the complex dynamic of being students from a powerful elite institution attempting to collaborate within the institutional constraints of an urban public school.[3] While the collaborative constraints represented one form of conflict for the students, they were additionally constrained by Freire's categorical constructions of "oppressor" and "oppressed," which framed the project.

As a practitioner of critical pedagogies, I began writing this paper with the intention of describing the students' interactive processes in an attempt to identify the sources of their conflicts. What I found was a pattern of discourse which threatened equitable negotiation. Selected excerpts from the student interactions will illustrate features of the project discourse which not only revealed sources of conflict but identified broader conflicting interests between the two groups of students.

The Project Begins

At the outset of the project I had discussed with both groups of students that I was interested in looking at how they worked together in producing their final performance pieces. Each of these sessions during the winter of 1994 was videotaped by a stationary video camera which the high school students set up in the corner of the classroom before their sessions began. I was teaching a class next door, and the project workshop was designed to be conducted by students for students in an adjacent classroom.

During the course of the semester, I was able to review the videotapes with the high school students to discuss their reactions to the class. Transcripts of the videotapes created a text that further enabled the high school students and me to view and discuss their workshops. Their initial take on theater, as Victor interpreted it, was a theater of expression, of imagination, of re-creation. In contrast, they saw the college students as focusing on a more overtly political construction of theater. While Boal's TO presented an opportunity for critical self-reflection, the high school students were not equally informed of its methods, and consequently found their lived experience subject to exposure rather than having their more technical concerns, such as the conventions of scriptwriting, addressed. For example, after two weeks of introductory theater games designed to loosen up and engage students in the process of creating scenes, the college students began asking Victor, Diego, Eve, and the others to talk about themselves. The invitation was met with confusion by the high school students who were unclear how their lives and theater came together, but they were willing to try. The first scenes the high school students put together included depictions of police brutality, rape, domestic violence, and substance abuse, based in their lived experiences. The college students' lives, in contrast, went unexposed as they participated in the scenes by playing roles assigned them by the high school students.

Contributing to this issue of unequal exposure were a number of occasions of disjunctures of discourse. As members of different discourse communities, the college students' interactions with the high school students produced a discourse defined by the negotiation necessary to accomplish weekly work. On the surface, their working discourse was characterized by the push and pull of classroom conversation, but when I looked deeper, I saw a discourse revealing some of the complexities of theoretically based cross-cultural communication in a school setting.[4]

Global vs. Local Questions

In attempting to locate the sources of tension in the students' interactions, I viewed and reviewed both the videotapes and their transcripts. As I mentioned above, the college students faced a dual dilemma by having to negotiate the theoretical constraints of Boal's theater with the conflicting interests of the high school students. They were, as Mady Schutzman points out, like all North American practitioners of Boal's theater, "working with groups to which they themselves do not belong, and thus represent, ironically, the very element of oppression the exclusion of which the group is founded upon" (141). Despite this dilemma and for all their differences, their common identities as students seemed to enable their dialogue and foster a commitment to the performative aspects of their work. In fact they did produce final performance pieces at the end of the project. The most persistent feature emerging from and intruding upon the students' interactions, however, was their different use of questions. My focus on the use of questions developed out of a close reading of the transcribed texts in response to the high school students' belief that they were not being heard when they suggested scenes for the workshop. The dialogues which I reviewed demonstrated an intricate form of resistance by the high school students when questions were used—by both groups—for multiple purposes and for achieving multiple goals.

Typically the conventions of asking questions in school settings are to elicit information, to check students' knowledge and understandings, and to pose problems for students to solve. Those teacherly uses, however, were notably absent in the interactions of these two groups of students. During the course of their interactions over the seventeen-week semester, the high school students generated almost twice as much talk in real time as measured by the text generated in transcripts of their videotaped interactions with the college students, but the college students asked twice as many questions as the high school students. However, numbers alone don't reveal the way questions were used by the students to inquire, speculate, philosophize, challenge the project's purpose, express desires, control opposition, silence one another, and assert authority.

Victor, Diego, and Eve stood apart from the other high school students as they used questions to undermine the college students' intention of exposing the high school students' lives for critical, reflexive examination. Through their resistance, the high school students not only reiterated their understanding of theater as imaginative play, but they also contrasted the everyday level of their lives with an imagined ideal. In a form of Heideggerian self-consciousness, the high school students elected to act out ideal lives in order to create and take on new characters often connected to their own lives, but occasionally in opposition to their lived experience (Heidegger 82–83). As I will explain in a moment, this insistence served in opposition to the college students' vision of this class.

By contrast the college students used questions very differently, at times in ways theoretically inconsistent with liberatory pedagogy. These questions became a way of controlling the behavior of the high school youth, limiting their responses, and contradicting the declaration of shared authority that the high school youth had rejected. Eve spoke for the high school group when she announced, "We talk freer when you all not here 'cause you all older." This prompted Sally, one of the college students to respond, "This is *our* class. We're all teachers here." In fact, some of the high school students were older than the college students, but Eve's message attempted to communicate something more complex than age. For example, one week when the college students were absent, Eve served as facilitator of the group, using the occasion to compare medical treatment she had received at two clinics. When the college students returned the following week and she tried to pick up both the thread of the conversation and the role she had taken on, she was ignored. Instead of even inquiring about what had happened in their absence, the college students began the class with "Well, let's get started," almost as if they hadn't been absent the week before. The stated shared authority of the group faced similar repeated challenges within the critical theoretical framework when the college students seemed frustrated in their attempt to respond openly to the high school students. The focus on lived experience suitable for performance put the college students in the position of judging what life experiences were valid and available as products of classroom conversation.

Changing the Question: Diego and Victor

Sally, Paul, and Susan's plans for developing scenes continually bumped up against some of the expressed desires of the high school students. When it came to developing scenes depicting significant events in their lives, some of the high school students elected to envision scenes from their imaginations. Both Victor and Diego argued that they didn't want to be themselves in scenes. They felt that they were already familiar with their own experience and wanted to try on new ways of being. Diego in particular wanted to imagine a role in which he reacted differently to a situation where he knew he would be forced into a fight. He imagined a character named Silvio, a tough kid, always ready to fight— unlike the real Diego who prided himself on talking his way out of trouble. For him the freedom to put himself in a real-life situation, but as an imagined self, allowed him to try on new ways of being which he said would permit him "to think differently." Sally, however, offered resistance to Diego's conceptualization of the scene. Through her questions, she remained faithful to Boal's political theater, but obstructed Diego's search for real life alternatives to his existing way of dealing with conflict.

When Diego proposed exploring alternatives to fighting in a real-life situation by examining his own first response with an imagined possible response, the exchange went like this (the college students' voices are in bold print):

> **Paul: One of the things that's important about acting is that you use your life to fuel it. You can't . . .**
>
> *Diego:* That's why I want to be different, a totally different person in a role than I am in reality, do something I've never done before. I want to be a totally different person. Somebody talk about the way I look, I don't fight. I don't really care what you think, but Silvio does. That's why I picked Silvio because me and him is two different characters. He wouldn't even be sitting here. He wouldn't be in this group. His bike would be up on Schoolcraft. He would be meeting. Silvio cares what other people think about him. I don't. Silvio end up being bad at school.
>
> **Sally: Isn't that still too close?**
>
> **Paul: Could . . .**
>
> **Sally: Ebony, what do you think of the situation? Put Silvio in the situation.**
>
> *Diego:* . . .
>
> **Sally: Because it's so powerful. What do you think? You want to do something completely different?**
>
> *Diego:* No, 'cause like I said, an actor is his work.
>
> **Sally: Ebony, do you like that?**
>
> (Diego turns his back and walks away from Sally.)

Diego's insistence on trying on a new and different persona met resistance from Paul and Sally in the form of questions, but he was resolute in identifying himself as an "actor." Diego reasoned that the character of Silvio was so unlike himself, that Silvio wouldn't even participate in this group. Diego emphasized Silvio's difference by contrasting his combative nature with Diego's more cooperative character. In addition, Diego acknowledged that Silvio "was bad in school" and that he probably wouldn't be involved in this project. Diego offered these rationalizations to persuade Sally and Paul that his choice was legitimate and based on his understanding of theater and the character of Silvio that he had created, but his suggestions were rejected. The gap between what Diego chose as his form of self-representation conflicted with the genre constraints of theater as the college students constructed it. In part, this gap occurred because of the lack of shared knowledge: Diego had not read

Freire, and the college students had not directly shared their understanding of liberatory theater with the high school students. The college students had not adopted an "inclusive or a critical orientation" in their interactions with the high school students (Burbules 111). Their dialogue illustrates the more "separate knowing" that Belenky and her co-authors identify. This lack of understanding and rejection of the high school students' choice of characters as different from themselves occurred throughout the project: as you will see shortly, Victor, for example, experienced the same diversion when he insisted on imagining life as a Colombian immigrant.

Paul and Sally searched for ways to bring the students' lives into the scenes the group was preparing, but they didn't support the students when they chose to reimagine their lives, to think alternately of their own lived experience or to invent what Markus and Nurius refer to as "possible selves." Neither Victor nor Diego needed any prompting in their imaginative turn. Both students argued their cases persuasively; however, Paul and Sally were caught between the project's goals being appropriated by the high school students and enforcing their conceptualization of the project—or negotiating a compromise. While other possibilities for defining mutually agreed-upon goals could have resolved the conflict, the absence of negotiated differences prevented all of the students from expressing their personal constructions of the project.

On another occasion Diego searched for an alternative portrayal of himself, this time as a character distanced from the reality of a friend's recent death. Sally and Paul again attempted to persuade him to reconsider his choice. Diego held firm, and justified his choice.

> *Sally:* **How about something doing with school?**
>
> *Diego:* I thought of a dialogue.
>
> *Paul:* **Do you want to do a monologue or do a dialogue?**
>
> *Diego:* You know how you get all of a sudden?
>
> *Sally:* **What happened to you this week, uh, you had a very strong reaction to that and I think if you wanted to, maybe portray that?**
>
> *Paul:* **Why not?**
>
> *Diego:* No, [shaking head] no, uh I mean if this was another time, but the way the situation is now, it'd be kind of hard. You know how if you were doing a play with a death in it? Now if you had just been to a funeral, and you went to play that you just went to a funeral, it be kind of hard 'cause you know you'd see no one but that person you saw in that casket, and then you want to be in a play? That would have a big impact on your mind. You know, you'd think, dang!
>
> *Sally:* **Do you think it would help you work through some of these feelings?**

Diego: Honestly what I told I didn't want to throw it away, but basically in the back of my mind, calming myself down, having a fantasy or dream because I know her as a friend.

Paul: You could . . .

Diego: I want to be a totally different person in a role, and then a totally different person in reality because when you think about it, if I'm going to be a punk like Silvio, I don't want to *be* like that. Silvio end up being bad. See? That's why I picked Silvio because me and him is two different people.

Diego held his ground, but Sally and Paul's questions attempted to coerce him into making a choice between a scene out of his own life or one in which he reimagined his own life building on his sense of possibility. Interestingly, though, it was because of their questions that Diego found himself defending his creation of Silvio's character.

Like Diego, Victor had an interest in performing, as indicated by his interpretation of Hamlet's soliloquy. He was the most enthusiastic participant among the high school students, first to enter the classroom each night, eager to set up the camera and do a check by taping himself sending messages to me. Throughout the semester Victor both facilitated and frustrated the group's efforts by consistently resisting the attempts of the college students to persuade him to abandon his imagined character for one based on his own life, when in fact, Victor saw the complex relationship of drug dealing and stereotyping young black males as his own life dilemma. Victor held fast to his idea and developed it into a performance by the end of the semester. How did he manage to resist the influence of the college students, and how did he persist in the creation of his imagined character? A partial answer rests in Victor's understanding of theater and his appropriation of the college students' agenda.

Victor not only knew what he wanted to perform, he expected the college students to support his choice and show him how to create his character. What he met instead was resistance to the role he created of a Colombian importer who is mistaken for a druglord. The following scene was developed and performed by Victor at the final performance. The questions raised and implied by the piece indicate Victor's interest in stereotypical representations of men in his community.

Victor's Druglord Scene

Real Time: Three minutes, twenty seconds

Setting: An office in a large city

Victor: One thing that troubles me as well as all people on this earth at one time or another. My problem is stereotypes. Why do people judge each other negatively and treat each other differently just because of the way they look or the things they do or the things they wear. This is sort of hard for me to explain to you, Sir, but if I could have a moment of your time . . . I can . . .

Sir: (from behind a newspaper) Go on, go on.

Victor: You see, Sir, I came to this country for a business meeting, and I didn't like the things I heard or I saw. I heard things like, "The big drug man is in town" or "Look! That must be the druglord." People even acted afraid of me!

Sir: What?

Victor: You see sir, I run a transport company in Colombia. A man asked another man at a meeting that I attended, what I did for a living. This man told him. I ran a transport company in Colombia. This man treated me bad. He acted strange towards me all because of what I did. I don't understand why he did this, Sir. Tell me why. Why did he do this?

Sir: Uh, uh. Well, uh, I don't know.

Victor: Well how about the time when I went to the store to buy a candy bar? I saw how the man behind the counter treated these kids. They were nothing but neighborhood kids who just came in from the street. Little urban kids. The man treated them like they were going to steal something.

Sir: Why does that concern you?

Victor: This concerns me because I realize now it's not just the people I deal with, but everybody treats each other differently just because of who they are or where they're from. This man treats these kids just like this just because of where they came from. Everybody's doing' this now, it's not just the people I deal with. People cannot survive if we continue to treat each other badly just because of who you are or what color you are or where you came from. Why, Sir, why do people do this? Why?

Sir: Well, uh . . .

Victor: Sir, are you listening? See? (to audience) You all see? Sir is reading the newspaper. A newspaper, a newspaper! I bet it's the media. People let television and newspapers control their minds, tell them what to wear, what they should think. A brown box made of wood and plastic should not decide what you should wear, who you should be friends with, what you should think. It's not right. Then again, the media ain't the same in all countries. There's a lot of difference in countries. Media ain't. Countries, government. What's the same in all countries?

Sir: Yeah, I'm listening.

Susan: (walks through set, grabs Victor's arm pulling him off stage) Time's up.

Victor: But . . .

Susan: Time's up. (continues pulling him off stage)

Victor: (from off stage) Answer me, Sir. Sir. Sir.

Victor's scene depicts his frustration at not engaging answers to his big question: "Why, Sir, why do people do this [stereotyping]?" Victor invokes "Sir" as an unresponsive moral authority. In their self-conscious and deliberate choice to fictionalize their character in opposition to the "real-life" story the theater project encouraged, both Diego and Victor attempted to find in their imaginations a new identity, a possible self, a moral "I." In so doing, they disclosed and defined themselves ontologically as they sought respect, dignity, and compassion through the lives and life situations of the characters they created.

Where the theater project began for the college students with Freire and Boal's theory of conscientization, for the high school students it began with their imaginings of other ways of being as a way of delving more deeply into their known lives. Thus, the project's purposes were contradictory and complex. In part because the purpose centered on the generation and enactment of theory grounded in the resistance of the high school youth, critical theory, from the outset, supplanted the needs and desires of the theater project participants.

According to Usher and Edwards, "For us, it is about reconfiguring emancipation/oppression in favour of the excluded and oppressed. In this, we need to recognize, however, that the oppressed might also become oppressors, that there is always a danger of simply replacing one totalising, oppressive discourse with another" (213). The college students created scenes which revealed the high school students' lives but didn't implicate themselves equally in the process. The absence of reciprocal openness and inquiry placed the high school students in the vulnerable position as object of a "critical" project.

Questions of Control

Their shared social identity as students was a point of interest and connection where the two diverse groups aligned themselves, and yet they persisted in contradictory constructions of one another. As the two groups of students struggled to identify and negotiate project goals, their interactions revealed other sources of conflict. Again by looking closely at their discourse, some of the less obvious differences between the two groups of students emerged. In order to get a sharper picture of the group's interactions, I narrowed my look at the project by focusing on the discourse of their interactions.

"We're not your teachers, we're all teaching," Sally announced, attempting to equalize her authority by this declaration. The following interaction took place the second week of the course and illustrates the use of questions to silence the high school students.

> *Paul:* **Does anyone have any questions right now, er, like just . . . ? Anything you want to ask about us or next time?**
>
> *Cory:* Yeah, which came first, the chicken or the egg?
>
> *Victor:* The egg.
>
> *Sally:* **Chicken.**
>
> *Paul:* **The egg. You said first, you go ahead.**
>
> *Victor:* Why'd the egg come first? I don't know. I just feel that way, the egg came first.
>
> *Cory:* Where'd that come from?
>
> *Victor:* The egg just magically appeared. The eggs just magically appeared?
>
> *Cory:* Why?
>
> *Charity:* I believe the chicken came first because when God made earth he put two of every kind on this earth.
>
> *Victor:* How'd you know there weren't two eggs? How'd you know there weren't two eggs? There could have been two eggs that might have hatched and then there were two chickens.
>
> *Eve:* No. You . . .
>
> *Victor:* You know chickens don't just appear, they have to hatch.
>
> *Eve:* You have to understand. God created the sun and earth first. Then he created people, a man and a woman, nah. Then he created two chickens. . . .
>
> *Victor:* Does the Bible specifically say God created two chickens? How do you know he didn't create two eggs?
>
> *Eve:* (raised voice) Read the Bible, boy!
>
> *Sally:* **Anyone have any other questions? (pause) Can we go around and say names again? I'm Sally.**

Where Cory's question is used to entertain and humor his peers, Sally uses her question to shut down the banter. The high school students could have kept this up for a time, but Sally's two questions allowed her to regain the floor and redirect the conversation.

Power relations in schools are often constructed in terms of teacher/ student authority; however, there are other forms of power exerted less visibly and more ambiguously on both teachers and students through a largely bureaucratized system of teaching and learning. Foucault proposes the interrogation of institutional discourses as a way of revealing forms of bureaucratically rationalized domination, while Pierre Bourdieu in *Outline of a Theory of Practice*, "Systems of Education and Systems of Thought," and *Reproduction in Education, Society, and Culture,* argues for the analysis of personal discourse as a way of coming to understand social interactions and power dynamics in interpersonal relations. Each of these can help us rethink the use of questions by the college students, burdened by their cultural and institutional representations as outsiders.

The following exchange revealed another way in which the college students used questions in shaping the high school students' responses. The previous hour had been filled with playfulness and unproductive activity. This led Susan to attempt to get the group back to more focused activity.

> *Susan:* **Victor, what do you think?**
>
> *Victor:* Y'all not organized.
>
> *Sally:* **Do you guys think we'll be able to produce a play if we keep working like this?**
>
> *Ken:* No.
>
> *Susan:* **So what helped you last time?**
>
> *Victor:* Like you got to learn to, OK, *act* it.
>
> *Susan:* **So?**
>
> *Victor:* Just tell me that Jose is about to die.
>
> *Sally:* **That's what we're trying to say.**
>
> *Eve:* And tell us what part to act out. Let them . . . You all didn't say . . . You just tell them. Most plays that you're directing . . . You going to say what you done read. Most people . . . You . . .
>
> *Victor:* That's not really true though 'cause last week when we went to the play in Ann Arbor. He had to figure out how he was going to act as a gay person. The lady, she was supposed to have that, she was uppity or whatever.
>
> *Eve:* She didn't tell us, you know how to investigate . . . What the meaning of the investigator? How do a murderer act? How do a murderer think?
>
> *Susan:* **How did you feel when you were playing that role or is that how you would have really acted? What? How do you know that?**

Susan's questions served to place blame. A literal reading of Eve's questions, for example, might be interpreted as seeking information; however, in the given context, they are accusatory. Rather than replying with information which would not be an appropriate response here, Susan fires back with a string of questions to again rebuild the floor.

The familiar Freirean notions of power, empowerment, and invention (or the college students' understandings of these notions) conflicted with high school students' expectations of the project. When seen through their eyes, these notions become, in one sense, objects of a theoretical and ideological gaze fixed on them through the college students' understandings of community service as a mode of empowering the high school youth. Through this unintentional "othering," the college students undermined the theoretical foundations of the project with their attempt at "teaching" theater as a form of empowerment to the high school students.

The premature leap to Theater of the Oppressed, without adequate preparation for the high school students to understand how this form of theater is designed to contribute to a deeper understanding of one's self in relation to a highly politicized world, left the high school students confused about purposes and their role in making self-determining choices within the context of the project. As Kincheloe and Steinberg point out, "problem detecting and the questioning that accompanies it become a form of world making in that the way these operations are conducted is contingent on the system of meaning" (305). Theater as a form of meaning making and interpretation of lived experience requires more time and orientation than the project first allowed.

Various current constructions of community service learning use language like the "doers and the done-to," "helpers and the helped," "agents and clients," "reformers and reformed."[5] These unilateral and nondimensional descriptors diminish the reciprocity and potential for mutual growth that could benefit both groups of students. Since the college course, like my high school class, is informed by various interpretations of Freirean critical theory, the outcomes for both groups of students have been institutionally defined by the roles they have assumed and been assigned as students enrolled in a credit course, either at the high school or at the university. In some measure these student roles conflicted and constrained the possibilities for participants since their work responded to course requirements.[6] Had all the students been reading Freire and Boal while openly discussing the theory underlying the project, their goals could have been more mutually constructed.

The Social Life of the Group

The social life of this group was defined by particular kinds of interactions. As mentioned above, questioning played a central role in defining how individual students interacted within the group. Asking questions not only served a gatekeeping function throughout the course of the project by redirecting the high school students toward a construction of theater congruent with the project's intention, but the questions also determined roles that the college students rejected but enacted nevertheless (Erickson and Schultz 151). The types of questions asked largely determined the social and political roles the questioner served in the life of the group. My analysis displays the ways in which questions were used to control conversational turn taking, to divert issues of control, and in some measure, to reveal the contradictions in Freirean critical theory as the students struggled to meet one another's needs as members of a group. The college students experienced even more difficulty in abandoning the rules of classroom discourse by denying their teacherly roles.

Critical theory challenges practitioners to "find forms within which a single discourse does not become the locus of certainty and certification" (Giroux 201). The theory supporting the collaboration simultaneously disrupted its process when critical theory's discourse imposed beliefs on the college students which they were not experienced enough to share or challenge. Victor, for example, saw the relevance of his choice to his life and wanted to examine it more globally. The college students interpreted this as a step away from his own experience without realizing just how close it really was. Rather than questioning their resistance to his choice, the college students questioned Victor's choice.

Kincheloe and McLaren identify "the hybridity endemic to contemporary criticalist analysis" (140). Given my questions about the portability of a critical theory project in a particular school setting, Freirean critical theory is itself being interrogated. From inside the high school, critical theory must be "ground(ed) contextually," in the words of Kincheloe and Pinar (20). The larger institutional forces that shape the local school culture—social, economic, linguistic, and political—form the project's backdrop. Words like "oppressor" and "oppressed" make collaboration impossible because they disempower the "other" group. This mutual "othering" or objectifying of the other reduces one's ability to act. In order to enact a liberatory pedagogy, some shared assumptions about goals and mutually constructed goals are necessary. Nancy Fraser's work in postmodern feminism supports this view. Fraser's postmodern critical theory helps us see the "overlapping alliances" and "vocabularies of contestation" which were generated by the students' discourse in their collaboration. By looking at critical theory (Freire's in particular as interpreted by Boal in *Theater of the Oppressed*) as it was applied in a local and particular context, I am responding to calls by Gore (1990), Ellsworth (1989), and Lather (1991) for more reflexive applications of a critical theory more broadly constructed. A useful enactment of critical theory will view collaborating partners as "agents involved in interpreting their needs and shaping their life-conditions rather than as potential recipients of predefined services" (Fraser 174).

Critical theory from inside the high school generated a dialectical relationship with the project which was designed outside the high school. The difference between critical theory as theory and critical theory as praxis emerged through looking at the way theory framed the college students' ideological orientation and understanding of their responsibilities to their high school counterparts and the requirements of their course. The roles they shared as students were complicated by the disproportionate responsibility the college group took upon itself for shaping the final outcomes of the project without sharing the reading, rationale, or open dialogue about the ideology behind the project. They also had a disproportionate investment in the outcome of the project, because the academic stakes were higher for the more privileged group, while the life stakes may have been greater for the high school students. At various points in the project, particularly at the beginning, the street theater politics disrupted the high school students' understanding of theater as imaginative play. While this was intentional, it ignored what the high school students brought to the project. Their understandings of theater, while conventional, were useful to their own enactment of identities which moved them beyond what students like Victor and Diego demonstrated were significant enactments of new "possible selves." At the same time, such an emphasis left the college students in the position of advocating for and coercing the high school students into a type of performance which conflicted with their preference and their understanding of theater and theatrical performance.

The confusion over and struggle with terminology is one of the difficulties expressed by the college students in their journals. I share a concern with Michael Apple that there exists a "danger of our own kind of mystification" (177). Victor, Diego, and Eve expressed their needs as students, often in ways that conflicted with the goals set and articulated by the college students. Nevertheless, the completion of the project depended in part on their knowledge and ability to act on that knowledge.

Choice, Chance, and Change

For months I wrestled with my conflicted writing about the struggle the college students had in negotiating the terms of their course objectives with the needs of the high school students. In a conference paper, I repeated this story, including my own partiality, by putting a negative spin on the lopsided collaboration which was consistent with a literature review on collaborations between urban schools and more powerful institutions. But the causes of collaborative failure and remedies for improving collaboration were not identified.

Likewise, my initial response to the project focused on the college students' difficulty in working under the political and ideological frame of Freirean critical theory. I too had failed to account more precisely for the problems. The part that questions played in obstructing their under-standings of their roles emerged in my rethinking the effects of their difficulty in working within a theoretical frame imposed on their social relations with the high school students. Subsequently, their interactions were negotiated around the liberatory discourse of critical theory. On the other hand, the high school students' participation, investment, and agency in the theater project was measured by their willing interactions with the college students, a much less complicated assessment.

Since my initial attempt at writing about the project was filled with contradictions and biased assumptions, it seemed valuable to rehearse that turnaround in the interest of articulating what Gloria Anzaldúa calls the "in-between" worlds of academic and work cultures in which theo-ries have the power to silence as well as empower. My roles as teacher, graduate student, and project collaborator not only gave me multiple perspectives on the project but complicated my reading of it as well. Since the project continues to grow and mature with each semester, what we as a group are learning about how language helps open us to possi-bilities, contributes further to our understanding of how best to encour-age more openings within the project.

Implications

What difference did this project make in the lives of the students in-volved, the school in which it was set, or to the teachers who planned and revised it? While I've spent time over the past five semesters re-viewing its goals and strengths, its shortcomings and failures, I've learned in the course of the project that collaboration requires constant rebuild-ing and ongoing revision if it is to fulfill goals of social change.[7]

The project informs other school/university collaborations by dem-onstrating the need to modify initial goals in order to align insider and outsider conventions. The implications of this work impact educational research in a number of ways. First, it raises questions about the use of critical theory and "empowering" pedagogies. Related studies on criti-cal-theory-based writing pedagogies already exist, and to some extent inform this study.[8]

In turn this study informs sponsors of projects by offering an insider's perspective on a school-based collaboration. From inside schools, em-powering pedagogies depend as much on the agency of those we seek to empower, particularly when they may or may not share beliefs or values with sponsoring partners. Carole Edelsky points out how "all projects are necessarily partial and contingent" (7). To take advantage of the existing potential within projects, it is essential to rethink the practices within them and to challenge even partially hegemonic practices.

Freirean critical theory itself became the object of interrogation as the analysis of student discourse probed the social organization of the project, discovered the friendships which developed between some of the students, and precipitated shifts in relations of power throughout the project. The discursive practices of both groups of students revealed ways in which they experienced the project differently as they learned about themselves as well as about one another. The high school students took advantage of opportunities throughout the project to try on various identities and imagine new ways of being. From a teacher's perspective, this reinventing of life stories created a sense of possibility the high school students expressed through the roles they chose for their performances, illustrating what Giroux calls "emancipation of the imagination." The high school students' discourse made the importance of imaginative play evident throughout the project.

And finally, why is it that this group of night school students continued coming to school, determined to make it? In spite of a 50 percent dropout rate, what kept the other 50 percent actively pursuing an education? What did they see in that education that the others didn't? Why aren't we hearing more of their stories? When we read about successes in urban districts, it is often in the form of institutional innovation—Central Park East, for example. But we know that there are thousands of young people who succeed in the thousands of other urban schools as well, in spite of the institutional failures loading the odds against their success. What compels them to persist in systems that are not consistently serving them well? Why don't we know more about them?

In a word, this story is a rebuttal to the *Last Chance* syndrome that constructs school and schooling as the last frontiers of hope for urban youth whose intelligence, resilience, and willfulness often defy the odds against them, yet find too little representation in the literature. I am not denying the harsh realities of many students' lives and the often difficult conditions of their schooling. I am, however, attempting to hear their stories of school as told by them from the inside in spite of these conditions. I hope it is a re/vision of school as a place students see as meaningful and useful to their needs as they take their places in the world.

We read one story after another accounting for failure in urban schools: Why there "Ain't No Makin' It," how dropouts are framed, why blacks are resistant in high school, the "Savage Inequalities" of the conditions of schooling, and how minority youth are silenced and oppressed. With few affirmations in the stories coming out of urban schools, there is little surprise that those of us working in these schools feel harassed by research, as often as not, and have to struggle to maintain dispositions which reject the totalizing failure so often described, documented, and displayed in research. At what point does the bad news become a self-fulfilling prophecy of hopelessness and despair? As a researcher consumed by the passionate voices of desperation in the literature, and as a classroom teacher equally passionate in her concern and commitment to those who return to the classroom day in and day out with an expectation that being there makes sense, I wanted to tell a different story from inside one urban classroom. It is not a simple story. If failure is as complex as research documents, success under the circumstances that these students achieved it is equally complex and equally important to study and document.

Notes

1. Henry Ford High School is a comprehensive public school with grades nine to twelve. At the time of the project the school offered two alternative programs to accommodate students in addition to day school, Extended Day School and Night School. In 1996 Governor Engler and the Michigan legislature cut funding for adult education, thus eliminating these alternative programs.

2. For a comprehensive discussion of students in alternative school settings, see Stevenson and Ellsworth (1993).

3. LeCompte (1995) writes about community organizers in the critical tradition who take into account their own power, agenda, and voice when entering collaboration. Her work in Chicago Public Schools illustrates the complexity of collaboration.

4. Sinclair and Coulthard (1975) introduce the discourse of questions in classrooms focusing on teacher/student interaction. Later studies by Cazden and Hymes (1982), Cazden (1988), Gumperz (1986), Goffman (1963; 1981), Tannen (1988), Gee (1990), and Schiffrin (1994) further explore the use of questions in classroom interactions between teachers and students.

5. Separate and distinct bodies of literature have developed around collaboration and service learning. Although they may intersect or overlap at various points, their motives, affiliations, and outcomes are different. See Radest (1993) for a broad discussion of service learning and community service. Gartner and Reissman (1993) address problems surrounding "help" as a concept in intervention programs. Karasik (1993) focuses on the traditions within existing communities for successful organizing rather than on white middle-class volunteerism. The theater project was not viewed as a service learning course by the instructor Buzz Alexander or by me, but the language used by the college students in their journals and final papers indicated that *they* constructed themselves in the discourse of service learners.

6. Both groups of students were enrolled in classes for credit. While criteria for grading students was determined separately, the primary expectation was that students would attend all sessions, and participate fully in the weekly workshop and final performance.

7. I have not come to new understandings of the project's conflicting interests alone. Through conversations with both high school and university students in the project, parents of project participants, school and district administrators, and with my collaborator, Buzz Alexander, I have gained a much broader perspective on the outcome of the project. The implications for research which addresses ongoing and replicable projects depend on examinations of theories which ground both projects as well as theories developing out of their process.

8. For example, see Lensmire (1994).

Works Cited

Anzaldúa, Gloria, ed. 1990. *Making Face, Making Soul: Haciendo Caras*. San Francisco: Aunt Lute Foundation.

Apple, Michael. 1993. *Official Knowledge: Democratic Education in a Conservative Age*. New York: Routledge.

Belenky, Mary Field, et al. 1986. *Women's Ways of Knowing: The Development of Self, Voice, and Mind*. New York: Basic.

Boal, Augusto. 1979. *Theatre of the Oppressed*. Tr. Adrian Jackson. London: Pluto Press.

Bourdieu, Pierre. 1992. *An Invitation to Reflexive Sociology*. Pierre Bourdieu and Loic J. D. Wacquant. Chicago: University of Chicago Press.

———. 1977. *Outline of a Theory of Practice*. Trans. Richard Nice. Cambridge: Cambridge University Press.

Bourdieu, Pierre, and J. Passeron. 1977. *Reproduction: In Education, Society and Culture*. London: Sage.

Burbules, Nicholas C. 1993. *Dialogue in Teaching: Theory and Practice*. New York: Teachers College Press.

Cazden, Courtney. 1988. *Classroom Discourse: The Language of Teaching and Learning*. Portsmouth, NH: Heinemann.

Cazden, Courtney, Vera P. John, and Dell Hymes, eds. 1972. *Functions of Language in the Classroom*. New York: Teachers College Press.

Edelsky, Carole. 1991. *With Literacy and Justice for All: Rethinking the Social in Language and Education*. London: The Falmer Press.

Ellsworth, Elizabeth. 1989. "Why Doesn't This Feel Empowering? Working through the Repressive Myths of Critical Pedagogy." *Harvard Educational Review* 59: 297–324.

Erickson, F., and J. Schultz. 1981. "When Is a Context: Some Issues and Methods in the Analysis of Social Competence." Eds. J. Green and C. Wallat. *Ethnography and Language in Educational Settings*. Norwood, NJ: Ablex. 147–60.

Foucault, Michel. 1980. *Power/Knowledge: Selected Interviews and Other Writings, 1972–1977*. Ed. C. Gordon. New York: Pantheon Books.

Fraser, Nancy. 1989. *Unruly Practices: Power, Discourse and Gender in Contemporary Social Theory.* Minneapolis, MN: University of Minnesota Press.

Freire, Paulo. 1981. *Pedagogy of the Oppressed.* Trans. Myra Bergman Ramos. New York: Continuum.

Gartner, A., and F. Reissman. 1993. "Pitfalls of Help: Making Sure Helping Helps." *Social Policy* 1: 36.

Gee, James P. 1996. *Social Linguistics and Literacies: Ideology in Discourses.* London: Taylor and Francis.

Giroux, Henry A. 1988. *Schooling and the Struggle for Public Life: Critical Pedagogy in the Modern Age.* Minneapolis: University of Minnesota Press.

Goffman, Erving. 1963. *Stigma: Notes on the Management of Spoiled Identity.* Englewood Cliffs, NJ: Prentice-Hall.

———. 1981. *Forms of Talk.* Philadelphia: University of Pennsylvania Press.

Gore, Jennifer. 1990. "What Can We Do for You! What Can We Do for You? Struggling Over Empowerment in Critical and Feminist Pedagogy." *Educational Foundations*: 5–26.

Gumperz, John. 1986. *Discourse Strategies.* New York: Cambridge University Press.

Heidegger, Martin. 1966. *Discourse on Thinking.* Trans. John M. Anderson and E. Hans Freund. New York: Harper and Row.

Karasik, Judy. 1993. "Not Only Delicious Bowls of Soup: Youth Service Today." *Visions of Service: The Future of the National and Community Service Act.* Washington, D.C.: National Women's Law Center and American Youth Policy Forum.

Kincheloe, Joe L., and Peter McLaren. 1994. "Rethinking Critical Theory and Qualitative Research." Eds. N. Denzin and Y. Lincoln. *Handbook of Qualitative Research.* London: Sage.

Kincheloe, Joe L., and William Pinar. 1991. *Curriculum as Social Psychoanalysis: The Significance of Place.* Albany: SUNY Press.

Kincheloe, Joe L., and Shirley Steinberg. 1993. "A Tentative Description of Postformal Thinking: The Critical Confrontation with Cognitive Theory." *Harvard Educational Review* 63: 296–320.

Lather, Patricia. 1991. "Staying Dumb? Student Resistance to Liberatory Curriculum." In Lather, Patricia, *Getting Smart: Feminist Research and Pedagogy With/in the Postmodern.* New York: Routledge. 123–52.

———. 1991. *Getting Smart: Feminist Research and Pedagogy With/in the Postmodern.* New York: Routledge.

LeCompte, Margaret D. 1995. "Some Notes on Power, Agenda, and Voice: A Researcher's Personal Evolution toward Critical Collaborative Research." Eds. Peter L. McLaren and James M. Giarelli. *Critical Theory and Educational Research.* Albany, NY: SUNY Press. 91–112.

Lensmire, Timothy. 1994. *When Children Write: Critical Re-visions of the Writing Workshop.* New York: Teachers College Press.

Markus, H., and P. Nurius. 1986. "Possible Selves." *American Psychologist*, 41: 954–69.

Radest, H. B. 1993. *Community Service: Encounter with Strangers.* Westport, CT: Praeger.

Schiffrin, Deborah. 1994. *Approaches to Discourse.* Cambridge: Blackwell Publishers.

Schutzman, Mady. 1994. "Brechtian Shamanism: The Political Therapy of Augusto Boal." Eds. M. Schutzman and J. Cohen-Cruz. *Playing Boal: Theatre, Therapy, Activism.* London: Routledge. 137–56.

Sinclair, J. M., and R. M. Coulthard. 1975. *Towards an Analysis of Discourse: The English Used by Teachers and Pupils.* London: Oxford University Press.

Stevenson, R. B., and J. Ellsworth. 1993. "Dropouts and the Silencing of Critical Voices." Eds. L. Weis and M. Fine. *Beyond Silenced Voices: Class, Race, and Gender in United States Schools.* Albany, NY: SUNY Press. 259–71.

Tannen, Deborah, ed. 1988. *Linguistics in Context: Connecting Observation and Understanding.* Norwood, NJ: Ablex.

Usher, Robin, and R. Edwards. 1994. *Postmodernism and Education.* London: Routledge.

Weis, Lois, and Michelle Fine, eds. 1993. *Beyond Silenced Voices: Class, Race, and Gender in United States Schools.* Albany, NY: SUNY Press.

8 Writing Back: The Research Writing of a Freshman College Composition Student

Sylvia G. Robins
Delta College

> When teachers raise their voices in the heteroglossia that constitutes the current discourse of education, and especially the discourse of public education, theirs are likely to be anxious ones. Teachers of language use particularly—those who teach things that are named by others "basic skills," "reading, writing, spelling," skills identified as fundamental to making it in the world—find it difficult to use a language that is anything other than a language of anxiety.
>
> —Jay Robinson and Patricia Stock

The anxiety which Robinson and Stock describe above receives mention also in the closing paragraphs of Roberta Herter's paper in this collection, an anxiety teachers feel in reaction to the depiction of themselves and their classrooms by some journalists, politicians, academic scholars, and leaders in education. Those countervailing voices to whom Herter reacts sometimes describe that work as ineffectual because of those we teach and the conditions under which we teach. Other countervailing voices depict the teachers themselves as practitioners of a pedagogy which ignores "the basics," the "skills identified as fundamental to making it in the world," thus perpetuating the failure of our students. As Robinson and Stock point out, this anxiety is particularly experienced by teachers of reading and writing, those deemed responsible for the nation's literacy.

In a sense, though, this anxiety wells up in the natural course of learning, in the struggle to transform the self, equipping oneself for a life as yet unknown, unfamiliar, and filled with contradiction. Teachers, of all people, ought to recognize this anxiety as that which accompanies learning, all the bewildering contradictory voices which deafen the learner, making it at times virtually impossible to know how one's own voice sounds or where it fits in, if, indeed, one can be said to have a voice. But teachers have been conditioned to perceive themselves as those who should quell anxiety, who should introduce their students to the clear, bell-like tones of a single truth. And to help the teachers, textbooks and encyclopedias offer monologic renditions of the one story which can be told, the one set of lessons which can be learned in predictable stages through packaged activities. The slowly increasing number of teachers who invite their students to participate in the cacophony of voices that makes writing engaging and learning possible often struggle against a sense that they are ignoring "the basics," particularly when the writing their students produce reflects the nuances of their spoken voices and reveals the conflicts in their lives. We cannot demonstrate beyond a doubt that what we are doing is superior to weekly spelling tests and daily punctuation exercises. The data just does not accumulate that swiftly, nor does it compute that neatly. It is well known that those who teach English in grade schools and community colleges seldom generate any sustained prose of their own. Confronted with heteroglossia, uncertain of our proficiency, our anxiety silences us.

I teach basic reading and writing and freshman composition courses at a community college in Saginaw Valley, Michigan, some one hundred miles north of the high school in Detroit where Roberta Herter teaches. Some of my students come from an inner city which resembles in minia-ture, though with perhaps a stronger sense of community, that of De-troit, and others are drawn from rural communities, peaceful small towns, and a middle-class community dominated by a huge corporation. When my students name a high school teacher, I can often put a face and a personality to the name. I have been inside many schools here and met many of the teachers, with some of whom I have developed long and beneficial relationships. I feel closer to my communities and the teach-ers who send their students on to me than I do to those whose research and writing shape my discipline. Consequently, when I write it is largely, and inevitably, with the heteroglossia of my communities and with a lingering doubt that my voice has a place in "the heteroglossia that con-stitutes the current discourse of education." The "current discourse" is changing, but very slowly, and the forms it is taking still offer insuffi-cient guidance for classroom teachers, mainly because we contribute little to the direction of that change.

Teachers whose working lives consist largely of hours in classrooms and hours reading student prose still consider themselves to be poten-tial subjects of research rather than researchers themselves. Our language, after all, cannot be the conventional language of academic scholarship. We converse and write more with our students and within our commu-nities than with colleagues or within the community of our disciplines. Silenced, then, by anxieties derived from perceptions about our work and the conventions of our discourse communities, we must find some path along which teaching and writing can occur in spite of the critical gaze we perceive to be levied on both activities.

By the same token, our students, too hastily judged as the flawed outcomes of their flawed lives and our flawed pedagogies, themselves must struggle to compose through their own anxiety. It is perhaps significant to realize that students themselves seldom get their prose read with a view to discovering potential directions for change in academic discourse. One reason could be that students in high schools and community colleges are deemed to be incomplete and inconsequential sojourners through academia, their writing necessitating much correction and refinement, a washing away of dialects and local knowledge, before their expertise and linguistic versatility acquire a form that academia, and indeed the entire professional and business world, can pay attention to. How do our students write back to these constraints? How do they respond to their own anxieties, those that threaten to silence them and those that beset them as they write?

My students and I confront our shared anxiety at the moment when I invite them to write a documented paper, one which integrates the voices of others with the voice of the student writer in the context of formal academic writing. When writing of this kind is called the research paper or term paper, the emphasis for students is frequently upon the search for sources and documentation and the mechanics of write-up rather than upon concerns centering upon the mingling of multiple voices. For many of my students, a research paper is an instrument for reporting facts, not a repository of voices. On being asked to write a brief self-evaluation of a research paper written for an advanced composition course, one student wrote of the assignment, "I think this is more of an opinion paper and observation paper, rather than a research paper." To this student, the research paper is a genre all its own, separate from other genres that are, in turn, separate and distinguishable from each other. Writing in this discrete genre, many students feel, demands omission of personal opinions or experiences. Students invariably report having been told in high school to omit personal pronouns from their research papers. The "I" has no place in such a setting. According to such approaches, in academic writing it is the subject matter more than the people who do the writing which forms the nexus of academic communities.

And their thinking is not altogether mistaken. Their thinking about research writing corresponds to a version of academic discourse, exemplified by a certain kind of research paper, which can be described as detached, objective, focusing on subject matter to the exclusion of the self. That there are other ways of documenting information, ways which question the separation of self and subject matter, seems to college students to be a dubious and unbeneficial insight. Understandably, students want their composition teachers to teach them the ways to succeed in their other college courses, and one of those things we can teach is the way to write that research paper. Not to do so, to teach anything else, is to withhold from them privileged information, the key to their success. On the other hand, I have good reason to persuade them away from that model of writing up information. The I-search and research papers I assign to my students invite them to perceive subject matter not as one entity but as multiple expressions of insight, many voices interacting with their own writing voices and all emanating from what one of my students called "the reality of it all."

Yet persuasion and invitation often seem to earn rather limited returns. I constantly seek better ways to persuade my students of the value of this approach and to persuade myself that what I am doing does indeed prepare students to approach those research assignments in other courses which appear to separate self and subject matter. Like other teachers, I rely heavily on student texts as models for the writing I want my students to undertake, but I often wonder to what extent I am fully describing, to my students and myself, precisely the features of those texts which make them worthy of emulation. To help me acquire this more precise description, I have found one student paper which suggests to me ways to present this assignment to future classes and some of the textual features to look for as students work through this process. In the case of this student, I found in his successful research paper the use of personal narrative, of sources taken from popular rather than professional journals and books, of heteroglossia in abundance, and of a stance which explicitly unites the student with a personal community, the use of "we" in a very particular way, accompanied by a rejoinder to his detractors, the "not we" imagined in his text. All these features may serve, in some circles, to describe a text which is unconventionally academic, perhaps even unacceptable. Yet it is a text which skillfully moves between multiple voices, appropriates outside sources as reinforcement of a clear unifying point, introducing those sources to readers in a manner which reflects an awareness of what it means to communicate with strangers, and reflects upon the meaning of the source material at some length, thereby serving as a mediator between the reader and the information offered. All these qualities, it seems to me, are integral to successful research writing.

The student whose paper I am analyzing wanted at first to make his project one that was filled with facts he did not possess at the outset of his paper. This student, whom I will call John, had earlier written a narrative describing the way in which annual deer hunting expeditions bring three generations of men in his family together and create a valued tradition among them. For his later research paper, I had asked him and his classmates to search for two or three sources of information that would permit them to reinforce, question, and elaborate upon their earlier narratives. That assignment itself left the students bewildered. They did not see the point of adding to something they already knew about, nor did they see the value in becoming more knowledgeable about something they had experienced. John wanted to write about the history of hunting.

History is narrative, and I warned John that his idea for a historical paper entailed the risk of his composing a narrative that would contain no central point. Assuring me that there was no danger of that, he proceeded with his library search and drafting of the paper. The freshman composition course in which John was enrolled included two extra classroom hours each week to permit workshop time. For this paper, some of that workshop time was spent in the Computer Laboratory, permitting students access to and assistance with word processing software as well as allowing me an opportunity to read drafts as they were first being composed. I looked over John's shoulder as he completed page one of his paper on the computer, and I told him that he had fallen foul of the dangers I had earlier warned him against. He was copying passages from his three sources, mingling them to form a neat patchwork of facts and descriptions without any attempt to tell his readers what they all signified to him. What he was doing precisely matched what Rebecca Moore Howard calls "patchwriting," defined in her words as "copying from a source text and then deleting some words, altering grammatical structures, or plugging in one-for-one synonym-substitutes" (788). In my experience, plagiarism of this sort seems to arise most commonly from students' misconceptions about the objective nature of research writing and the primacy of information over response.

John was willing to alter this paper so that it did make a point. I read the rough draft once more with him and looked at some of his sources, asking him about his impressions of the information he had acquired, which told him about changes in hunting behavior from the late nineteenth century to the present date. He told me that deer hunting seemed to him now to be more attentive to the suffering of the deer and to the well-being of deer herds. Thus armed with a point, he turned to his computer, calling me over some half hour later to read his first page in order to be reassured that he was proceeding in the right direction. I read over his revised first page and gave him the reassurance. This is what I read (For full text of John's work, see Appendix):

The 1995 deer season was Michigan's 101th year of licensed and well controlled deer hunting. As we Michigan hunters begin our 1995 white-tailed deer hunt, either archery, firearm, or muzzleloading, we begin to prepare our blinds to shoot that big trophy buck. Our ways of hunting are a lot different from 1856. We hunt for the sport not the profit. We respect the deer and try to maintain them, unlike what they did to deer in 1856.

When I first read this paragraph, I wondered about possibly borrowed language. On much later and much closer examination, I noticed John's later use of quoted material from an article written for *Michigan Out-Of-Doors* by Kenneth S. Lowe. This is a sentence from the quoted passage: "On November 15, Michigan will mark the start of the 100th year of licensed deer hunting, a land mark in wildlife management" (54). Clearly, John is patchwriting here, and if I had noticed that his paper actually contained the passage from which he was borrowing, I would have shown him how to make the quotation an impressive part of his introduction. It is also clear that John was writing with no intention to deceive his readers. Often students borrow from published texts because they feel defeated by what they think is the paucity of their own language. They do not have words to express the meaning of the text. In this case, though, I think the borrowing occurs precisely because John communicates often and articulately on the subject of hunting, incorporating insights from magazines frequently and smoothly into his discourse. Lines often blur between what is generally known within a discipline and what is additional knowledge, between language that has been absorbed from many readings of similar texts and language only now appearing in one's lexicon. (Indeed, some readers may hear echoes of Clifford Geertz in my casual mention of "local knowledge" earlier in my paper.) On my first reading, I decided to accept the possibly borrowed language in this first paragraph as one appropriated and not borrowed wholesale, thereby having no need of attribution. Having seen the borrowed text, I can now see an opportunity I missed for teaching John how to embed a quoted source into an introductory paragraph. As it is, this opening still possesses the two virtues of appealing to a general readership and of containing a central point to which John could direct his material.

Over the course of the next few days, I saw John frequently, making his way to the Computer Lab early in the morning and leaving late in the afternoon, always seated at the same corner terminal, putting in hours of work on his revision. Although he worked alone, seldom requesting feedback from others, he was often acknowledged by others in the Lab. I greeted him whenever I saw him, and I felt anxious on his behalf, but

I was never invited to read over his shoulder, and I never asked if I could do so.

It occurred to me as I watched this prolonged effort at revision that few community college students have the luxury of uninterrupted time to devote to one task. Few also can physically locate themselves in a site so well suited to composing for hours at a time. Our relatively small English Division Computer Lab offered John a quiet, private location in which he was surrounded by others who understood and were supportive of his project. His body was thus enacting the two-fold nature of composing, that one is at once alone and part of a community. Time, both intensive and extensive, a suitable location, and suitable equipment are more commonly absent than present in the college lives of too many of our students.

Late on the Friday afternoon of that week, John asked me if I would read his completed draft. Since I shared his anxiety as to the outcome of his efforts, I agreed to read the paper with him. I noticed that in this draft much of the factual information from the original essay remained, this time treated quite differently. His second paragraph commingled factual information with narrative. It read, in part and with all the errors included, as follows:

> In 1989 my father filled out an application for a doe permit. He paid 3 dollars for it without any guarantee of receiving one. In every given season the DNR will hand out a certain number of permits, with only a few hunters receiving them. About 150,000 doe permits are handed out each year. With about 700,000 to 750,000 hunters entering the woods each year, many of them go up north where the deer herds are larger. There is usually about one million deer or less in the U.P. compared to about 350,000 and 450,000 in the northern Lower Peninsula and about 250,000 to 350,000 in the southern Lower Peninsula. My father is one of those hunters who stays home and hunts. Within 4 weeks my father received his doe permit. My father also purchased an antlered deer permit from "Bare's Sports Shop" in St. Charles Michigan for $12.85. On Thanksgiving day, Michigan received a snow storm that dropped seven to ten inches of snow. This made my father and probably many other hunters happy. It made it good tracking weather and the deer tend to move when there is snow. On the Saturday after Thanksgiving my father entered the wood about 4 miles from were we live. Within 30 minutes after the sun casted its light on the earth, my dad shot a doe.

The statistics John includes in his second paragraph bring to mind the impressive details absorbed by individuals, particularly children, who are taken up with a hobby. Mary Louise Pratt, in "Arts of the Contact Zone," describes her son acquiring similar knowledge from his fascination with baseball cards. Through his hobby, Pratt observes, her son "learned the meaning of expertise, of knowing about something well enough that you can start a conversation with a stranger and feel sure of holding your own" (33). While Pratt is satisfied that schooling offered her son the essential skills to complement his growing knowledge of baseball and the ways of the marketplace, she complains, "schooling itself gave him nothing remotely as meaningful to do" (33). This complaint is echoed by Cathy Fleischer, who describes school literacy as "a kind of literacy constructed by and for the schools" (36), a literacy divorced from the richly meaningful knowledge and literacy acquired outside the classroom.

Teachers responsive to complaints of that sort endeavor to bring the lives of their students into the classroom, to offer participatory, social avenues to learning and to create smooth pathways between what the student knows and what academia has to teach. But students like John come to their college courses convinced that school is of necessity and by its very nature an abstracted experience discontinuous with everyday life. John had to struggle against this conviction when I informed him that his research paper might require personal narrative. In writing back to this requirement, John told a narrative that offers his readers his own credentials as an expert on hunting. John's father exists not as a character in a story but as an enactment of expertise, someone who knows how to follow procedures and practice his skill. He is faceless in the same way that Pratt, Stock, Robinson, Fleischer, and John himself are faceless in my text, supporting my insights with their words. The father represents also the community with which John is identifying himself, the "we" of his text. This is a form narrative can take when it serves the purpose of detached exposition, a form different to that which might possibly be deemed appropriate for personal narrative.

Having described present hunting practices, John creates a transition to the past as follows:

> The only thing the 1995 hunters used to see the deer is the area the deer like, bait piles, and buck grunts. In 1856 hunters used several methods to get deer, some of which are described by Ed Lengenau, our Michigan Department of Natural Resources (MDNR) President who wrote an article in *Michigan Out-Of-Doors* called "Michigan's Deer Management Centennial." He stated this report: . . .

It is difficult for many inexperienced students to understand how lengthy and explicit must be the wording which introduces quoted or summarized material. John's introduction to his quoted passage acknowledges his responsibility to inform the strangers who will read his work; he invites us into his world of expertise. By selecting a source which is part of his regular out-of-school reading, John can act as an authority in relation to his readers, validating Lengenau's textual authority not only by virtue of Lengenau's status within the world of hunting but also by virtue of John's long familiarity with the man's texts.

That familiarity with his source also grants John the authority to call to judgment the practices described in Lengenau's paragraph. In this paper, John immerses his readers in a heteroglossia that he has practiced, quite possibly, for as long as he can remember. He now brings that heteroglossia into another context, the academic context which involves conversing with strangers. This new context leads to an important understanding, that there is no one-to-one relationship between text and reader, no single way to read a text. As a hunter, John's reading of Lengenau's passage probably differs from the way a nonhunter might read the same words. Immediately following his quoted passage, John offers his readers his own reaction to Lengenau's depiction of deer being slaughtered wholesale by teams of hunters. He writes:

> These were cruel and harsh ways to kill deer. These hunters looked at the deer hides and venison as profit like the forests that stood before them. But like the forest the deer also became rare sights in Michigan.

Whereas in the original draft of this paper Lengenau's historical information had been reproduced in a neutral fashion, without comment, it now becomes vulnerable to judgment, something to write back to.

Later in his paper, John addresses his imagined opponent:

> Michigan spends millions of dollars to build or clean up areas for wildlife, where do you think they get that money? Not from the taxpayers, but from hunting licenses. If we outlawed hunting you would see regions of land be destroyed from companies, housing developments, and pollution. The only way they could possibly take care of nature is by raising taxes because there would be no licenses to pay for it. Since we do have hunting in Michigan we hunters are able to enjoy ourselves and nature without someone like anti-hunters looking over their shoulders saying "Save the animals, what did they do to us? My response would be, *if it doesn't effect you shut up*.

I was naturally taken aback by the outburst appearing in this passage. John had typed it in italics and underlined "shut up" for additional emphasis. Having had time to reflect on it, I can now understand its inclusion in this text, but before commenting on it, I would like to describe the successful features in this passage (which is not to say that the outburst is unsuccessful for John's purposes).

John writes as one of "we hunters" in response to "anti-hunters," addressed as "they" but also implicated in the "you" who is commanded to think about the consequences of lost revenue from hunting licenses.

He has, on this occasion at least, made a transition in research writing from pure textual reduplication, information for its own sake, to what Gordon Harvey describes as "an interesting idea and structure, bringing general insights out in the particulars . . ." (648). John's escape from pure reduplication involves restoring the self to his text, this time subsumed under the collective identity of deer hunters whose interests he seeks to justify.

About the outburst, on that Friday afternoon I read the entire paper while John sat beside me. To assuage his anxiety, I did what most teachers do when conferencing individually with students on a brief paper. I tried to include him in the reading by holding the text before him as I read certain passages aloud, expressing enjoyment of features I liked. When I finished and offered my evaluation of the paper, I suggested to John that he might consider rewording that outburst. I indicated to him that it represented a departure from conventional public writing and that the same emotions could be expressed by more subtle means. John listened to me, nodding but making no comment as to where the outburst came from or why he worded it as he did. He then went away, no doubt to a weekend devoted to making up hours of work and study lost to those two days spent writing a research paper.

John's next major assignment for my course was a portfolio accompanied by an extensive self-assessment report. Students were told that they could revise any major papers they included in that portfolio, and I fully expected to see that outburst altered in the version of his research paper that appeared in John's portfolio. To my surprise, the paper had undergone no alteration at all. I thought at the time that press of time and satisfaction with his grade for that paper might have had something to do with the decision not to revise, but a revision would have taken no time at all. It was a simple matter of rewording a sentence or two or omitting the passage altogether. Again, John did not volunteer an explanation for retaining the outburst, and I did not press for an explanation. I felt it to be a slight anomaly in an otherwise successful text.

Since that time, I have been able to think more deeply about the outburst. I have also been able to return to a paper written by Jay Robinson and appearing in *Conversations on the Written Word*. In that paper Robinson reveals the manner in which classroom conversation influences a high school student's text so as to render it vulnerable to the judgment that it lacks focus or signs of critical reasoning. When the classroom conversation is recalled, however, Robinson could recognize the text as the writer's use of "language to constitute character, community, and culture in order to make meanings that are expected to be meaningful to others" (101).

Robinson has offered me a way of understanding John's text as a form of writing back not only to what David Bartholomae and Anthony Petrosky call the "presence and pressure of the institution in the writing of an individual" (39), but also to his classmates, one of whom had, much earlier in the semester, publicly refused to respond to his first essay, a personal narrative, because she was opposed to hunting. Her refusal had created an awkward moment in the classroom, making it memorable for me. I responded with the lame request that, in this setting, we respect the writing of our fellows regardless of our feelings about the subject matter. Other students more helpfully suggested that the young woman ought to become better informed on the subject and that John's essay might furnish an opportunity to do so. Throughout the discussion, John remained silent, no doubt hurt and angry at such an unexpected reaction to a class assignment. Recalling that incident leads me to understand the purpose for the outburst of John's later research paper. Seen one way as a jagged rent in the fabric of his text, these italics now become the emotional force driving John's desire to inform his readers that they are beneficiaries of the hunter and his contributions to the environment. Through this paper, John reconstitutes himself as authority on a subject about which he had previously been a teller of tales. His anger joins him once more with the community that had earlier threatened to reject him, this time with history to sustain his argument. There was a time, he can now tell this young woman, when he too would have been opposed to hunting, so "cruel and harsh" were the ways in which the deer were killed, but now hunters practice their sport under controlled conditions, permitting deer herds and wilderness areas to flourish. If all this touches you at all, he can add, it is only to save you taxes and offer you more ample spaces for recreational activities. If none of this touches you, he might conclude, then my text and what it contributes to your understanding must surely silence your complaints.

In offering the above explanation, I do not wish to ignore the troubling aspects of this outburst. When John's paper came up for feedback in class, I pointed out that some of our best reforms have materialized as a consequence of individuals involving themselves in issues which do not necessarily affect them directly. (I record this comment with some trepidation since I know I sound preachy.) At the time I interpreted the outburst as a threat, a demand to be silent, but I think that, when read as a rejoinder to the thoughtless young woman, it is no more than she deserves. She really should have kept her mouth shut. When read as directed at John's readership in general, then it becomes more akin to undifferentiated rage reflecting a desire to be less criticized, less governed, less aware that he is watched and talked about by people who do not

share his values. Not surprisingly, he wants all that to go away, yet if
that is the meaning behind his outburst, it gives an interesting impetus
to this paper. There is more than hunting practices being addressed in
this paper, and there is much that John could examine about himself, his
world, and the world around him if he could be given the opportunity
to do so.

Following his outburst, John writes a paragraph which commingles
statistical information with narrative. He writes:

> Through the sportsmen's help we have seen a major increase of deer
> and hunters. The deer population just this year got to about 1.9 mil-
> lion to 2.1 million deer according to the reports in the newspapers,
> and on the news. Just 95 years ago the deer population was 50,000
> in the entire state according to Lengenau. According to Bob Gwizdz
> of *Field and Stream* the 1995 deer "Season will almost certainly top
> last year's deer harvest total . . . of 362,490 . . . the sixth highest deer
> season ever. Their record harvest was 452,490 deer in 1989" (80), my
> dad's year. Just this year six bucks were taken on my grandmother's
> land. On the first day of deer season my cousin Mike shot a 12 point
> at about 9:00 a.m. Half an hour later my other cousin was helping
> his brother drag the other one up, when about 150 yards out in the
> field wandered two bucks. One was a 6 point and the other an 8
> point. My cousin Ken shot the six point and the neighbor shot the
> other. On the second day of deer season my father shot a 4 point in
> Ken's blind at about 9:30. On the third day my cousin Ken shot his
> second buck, a 5 point, out of his blind. On the fourth day my uncle
> Jim shot a 3 point. It would have been a 6 point but one half of the
> rack was gone. You could say that it was mercy hunting since that
> buck had a cracked skull probably from a fight or a car. From what
> I heard from my Uncle and my father there are probably more than
> 60 deer running around in a 10 acre area—that's small. There are
> probably more deer than that in the woods, but 60 was all they saw.

His family's successful deer season testifies to the validity of the statistics he quotes, the anecdotal and the official responding to each other as
smoothly and energetically as the talk of sports enthusiasts recounting
seasons, games, and players. There is a sense too in which, his opponent
having been vanquished, he returns to his own people and speaks their
language. It is precisely this eloquence, it seems to me, that we desire
from our students when we send them out to find information and record
it in writing. That we so seldom receive it may very well stem from our
narrow concept of what it means to write for and to academia. It may
also derive from distinctions we are failing to make between what it
means to find information and what it means to be informed. None of
the information John mentions in that long paragraph is new to him. It
is part of his lore. His purpose here is not to tell us what he has learned
(he has already done that); it is to inform us, to correct our ignorance

and make us aware. Imagining an audience not so much of opponents as of individuals in need of enlightenment, he constitutes himself as educator. He also, quite effectively, invites us to participate in his community (perhaps retracting his earlier outburst), thereby much enlarging it.   John ends his paper with the following paragraph:

> As you can see there were a lot of changes in hunting since 1895. All of them were contributed from sportsmen (mercy) hunters. Every man and woman have things they like. Remember you would not like it if a person who did not like what you like interfered with it. Have the same courtesy for others.

Clearly a rebuke, and not a little condescending, this conclusion nonetheless weaves together the substance and purpose of the foregoing paper. We can indeed see from his text "a lot of changes in hunting since 1895." That much has been fully established. We can also clearly see from his paper John's personal affiliation with this sport that is such a large part of his life. His final piece of advice to his readers revises his earlier outburst (which might explain why he ignored my suggestion to revise). Himself reconstituted as authority rather than student and his readers re-imagined as students rather than opponents, John's tone can now be more conciliatory, more in the vein of a suggestion that we please remember to be courteous.

This was not the paper John had originally envisioned when he received the research assignment. I am not certain that, even after composing this successful text, he feels that what he has done here is an authentic or "real" research paper. It was, in a sense, a writing back to an assignment he might well have had little faith in. There is some doubt, after all, that the composing strategies he employed for this paper could be applied to subsequent research assignments for other courses. Because of that discontinuity, John cannot be said to have reached a level or passed through a stage which readies him for the next level or stage. We require institutional changes and changes in our valuing of information in order for this piece of work to become a learning experience, something which transforms future behavior.

In "Arts of the Contact Zone," Mary Louise Pratt points out that we have no verb form of the word *pupil*, no way to suggest what being a pupil entails (38). Perhaps this is the reason why I am unable to describe the kind of learning which has led John to compose, virtually by himself, a fully authentic and interesting paper against all his convictions of what such a paper should look like. He wrote back to "the presence and pressure of the institution," and he wrote back to his critics. Through narrative he introduced his own community, and through research he constructed a framework for their practices. Writing of literary texts,

Bakhtin describes the work of composing them as an ongoing historical struggle "to overcome the official line with its tendency to distance itself from the zone of contact, a struggle against various kinds and degrees of authority" (345). From this passage, Mary Louise Pratt developed her insight into what it means to enter into the contact zone as a writer, and from it I take the metaphor of struggle as one perhaps more apt than "level" or "stage" for what I see John accomplishing with this paper. To compose his text, John struggled against "various kinds and degrees of authority" and refused to distance himself from the contact zone. He entered the fray, and in his text can be discerned many of the qualities Pratt attributes to writing in the contact zone, among them "critique, collaboration, . . . mediation, . . . denunciation, imaginary dialogue, and vernacular expression" (37). Such struggles engage one's consciousness, permitting greater awareness when the work is finished.

Struggles that enlarge one's consciousness can occur only with permission and encouragement. When I engage my students in the struggle to "overcome the official line," I must have at my disposal texts which are doing the same thing so that my students and I have something to emulate. Such a text, written by Mary Catherine Bateson and occurring in her book *Peripheral Visions*, explicitly expresses her struggle as she writes:

> Adults are freer than schoolchildren in their writing, but I am in defiance of scientific convention and much of literary history when I claim the freedom to begin many of my sentences with the word *I*. Yet it rescues me from the temptation to be categorical. The word I want is *we*, but there are limits to the assumption of agreement, so I "personalize" as a more honest way to be inclusive. Impersonal writing often claims a timeless authority: this is so. Personal writing affirms relationship, for it includes these implied warnings: this is what I think at this moment, this is what I remember now, continuing to grow and change. This finally is contingent on being understood and responded to. (75–76)

This is a passage I could show to my students. They would understand it, and they would understand from it that their puzzlement with changing rules is a puzzlement shared by other academic writers. No longer obliged to be a "timeless authority," a student must now handle the more complex task of writing in order to "affirm relationship," to reconstitute self and community through language. John chooses the pronoun "we" because he can assume an agreement between himself and other hunters that is impossible in academia. The shift, though, to any kind of personal pronoun in a research paper represents an insurmountable obstacle for many students, so convinced are they that to be scholarly is to be nonexistent in one's own text. I am still at a loss as to how those students can be convinced otherwise, although John's paper, supplemented by Bateson's paragraph, offers much by way of validation. It is interesting to me also that Bateson insists upon understanding and response as a crucial component of this relational writing. Those who write to "affirm relationship" must know how that affirmation is received, and herein lies the rub for teachers whose crowded classes and long days offer few opportunities for the kind of feedback and intervention which launched John into his successful work.

Through his paper, John has taught me ways to approach research assignments such that students identify with a group and then describe the issues confronting that group and its detractors. Referring to themselves and their group as "we," they write a paper which writes back to the detractors on the issue, using a few outside sources to support their ideas but using also narrative to reveal their community to the strangers who will read their work. The sources they use, I now tell my students, can very well be the journals to which they subscribe, the literature of their community. I perceive a confident tone in my writing here, a tone familiar to those who read the texts of teaching. It suggests that as I do all this, I never falter in my conviction that my approach is workable and that the success of my students is guaranteed by this method. It moreover suggests a one-to-one relationship between what we teach and what our students learn or do. Such, of course, is not the case at all. What I have here, unless I am careful, is a formula. Even now, when I am fairly convinced that it is a worthwhile assignment, I have received some dreadful papers in response because it requires some thought and maturity to recognize within one's communities issues that might be of significance to a wider public. And there are still those students who beg permission to write about Mozart because they have to learn about him.

Am I doing the right thing? I do not know. John has taught me much, but I have much to learn, and I have my own critical voices ringing in my ears as I make his text and mine public. On the other hand, I have the supportive voices of Robinson, Stock, Bateson, and many others, people who write about the contingent nature of learning and the anxious nature of writing. For teachers to reconstitute themselves as writers in the academic community would demand a textual approach not unlike that adopted by John: personal narrative, local experts, and multiple discourses combining in the context of shared, if contested, community values. When others observe our teaching and devise practices from what they see, we become their texts, and no matter how sensitive, knowledgeable, or perceptive those texts may be, the fact that they were not composed by us limits their usefulness. Reading closely and writing about John's paper has altered my teaching of this one kind of assignment more dramatically than all the papers on research writing I have read and all the workshops I have attended. For this reason alone, we must compose our own texts, no matter how shameful it is to reveal the contradictions and lapses in judgment which are a natural part of every teaching day. We must also write in spite of our limited scholarship. Our own observation is our scholarship, and we should not permit anxiety to keep that from public view. John has taught me the enormous power of an intellectual endeavor driven by emotion, of anxiety confronted. I wonder if I can follow his teaching as courageously as he followed mine.

Works Cited

Bakhtin, M. M. 1981. *The Dialogic Imagination*. Trans. Caryl Emerson and Michael Holquist. Austin: University of Texas Press.

Bartholomae, David, and Anthony Petrosky, eds. 1986. *Facts, Artifacts, and Counterfacts: Theory and Method for a Reading and Writing Course*. Upper Montclair, NJ: Boynton/Cook.

Bateson, Mary Catherine. 1994. *Peripheral Visions: Learning Along the Way*. New York: HarperCollins.

Fleischer, Cathy. 1990. "Re-forming Literacy: A Collaborative Teacher-Student Research Project." *Conversations on the Written Word: Essays on Language and Literacy*. Jay L. Robinson. Portsmouth, NH: Boynton/Cook. 35–48.

Harvey, Gordon. 1994. "Presence in the Essay." *College English* 56.6: 642–54.

Howard, Rebecca Moore. 1995. "Plagiarisms, Authorships, and the Academic Death Penalty." *College English* 57.7: 788–806.

Lowe, Kenneth S. 1994. "A Deer Hunting Chronology." *Michigan Out-of-Doors* (November): 54–56.

Pratt, Mary Louise. 1991. "Arts of the Contact Zone." *Profession 91*: 33–40.

Robinson, Jay L. 1990. "Literacy and Conversation: Notes Toward a Constitutive Rhetoric." *Conversations on the Written Word: Essays on Language and Literacy*. Jay L. Robinson. Portsmouth, NH: Boynton/Cook. 93–113.

Robinson, Jay L., and Patricia L. Stock. 1990. "The Politics of Literacy." *Conversations on the Written Word: Essays on Language and Literacy*. Jay L. Robinson. Portsmouth, NH: Boynton/Cook. 271–317.

Appendix: John's Paper

Hunting Changes

The 1995 deer season was Michigan's 101th year of licensed and well controlled deer hunting. As we Michigan hunters begin our 1995 white-tailed deer hunt, either archery, firearm, or muzzleloading, we begin to prepare our blinds to shoot that big trophy buck. Our ways of hunting are a lot different from 1856. We hunt for the sport not the profit. We respect the deer and try to maintain them, unlike what they did to deer in 1856.

In 1989 my father filled out an application for a doe permit. He paid 3 dollars for it without any guarantee of receiving one. In every given season the DNR will hand out a certain number of permits, with only a few hunters receiving them. About 150,000 doe permits are handed out each year. With about 700,000 to 750,000 hunters entering the woods each year, many of them go up north where the deer herds are larger. There is usually about one million deer or less in the U.P. compared to about 350,000 and 450,000 in the northern Lower Peninsula and about 250,000 to 350,000 in the southern Lower Peninsula. My father is one of those hunters who stays home and hunts. Within 4 weeks my father received his doe permit. My father also purchased an antlered deer permit from "Bare's Sports Shop" in St. Charles Michigan for $12.85. On Thanksgiving day, Michigan received a snow storm that dropped seven to ten inches of snow. This made my father and probably many other hunters happy. It made it good tracking weather, and the deer tend to move when there is snow. On the Saturday after Thanksgiving my father entered the woods about 4 miles from where we live. Within 30 minutes after the sun cast its light on the earth, my dad shot a doe. The only bad thing about it is it would not die; he wounded it. He tracked the deer for about a half an hour. Finally it gave up its life. My dad gutted her and then began to search for a spot to cross the river. When he found the spot he wanted, a buck stepped into view about 8 yards away. The buck did not see him there because he was checking behind him to see what was pursuing him, which was another hunter. My father pulled up his 12-gauge shot gun and shot the buck in his tracks.

Compared to 1856 you would not find one hunter pursuing one or maybe two deer; instead he would be with several hunters pursuing many deer with dogs helping. The only thing the 1995 hunters used to see the deer is the area the deer like, bait piles, and buck grunts. In 1856 hunters used several methods to get deer, some of which are described by Ed Lengenau our Michigan Department of Natural Resources

(MDNR) President who wrote an article in *Michigan Out-of-Doors* called "Michigan's Deer Management Centennial." He stated this report:

> Hunting methods commonly involved snares and deadfalls. Some of the deadfalls were as simple as logs that were propped to fall on deer walking beneath them while others involved intricate pulleys, guillotine-like structures, and fancy trip wires and triggers. Dogs were often used to drive deer out of thickets to hunters who waited along runways or fences that funneled deer movements. Dogs were also used to drive deer into water or deep snow where they could easily be shot. Shining (then called 'Jack-lighting') deer at night was also very successful. Sometimes, fires were built in the front of canoes, and shooters would aim for deer eyes at night, which would shine brightly in reflecting the firelight. Jack-lighting was also used on land by hunters who would carry a torch or blazing pine knot above the head of a shooter who would aim for the eyes in the woods. At times, shooters accidentally killed cattle by using this method. (42).

These were cruel and harsh ways to kill deer. These hunters looked at the deer hides and venison as profit like the forests that stood before them. But like the forest the deer also became rare sites in Michigan. It was said by Lengenau that in 1900 there were about 50,000 deer in the entire state. Most of those 50,000 deer were found in the U.P. and Northern Lower Peninsula. Deer disappeared from the Southern Lower Peninsula in the 1870 as said by Lengenau. Just 20 years before 1900 there was said to be about one million deer in the Upper Peninsula. Market hunters saw this increase in deer and began to hunt them for profit, Ed Lengenau wrote. He also wrote this:

> Commercial interests quickly capitalized on this resource. Professional killers, known as 'pot-hunters,' invade the north as railroads made access easy. Market hunting became a dominant industry in the state. With deer meat and hides shipped to Chicago, Detroit, New York, and other ready markets along railroad lines.
> It was reported that venison brought two cents a pound in Rose City during the late 1870's and early 1880's. The average market hunter could kill 10 to 15 deer a day with an average dressed weight of about 60 pounds for an income of $12 to $8 a day. Maker hunters sometimes killed deer just for the hides and discarded the meat in summer. Often they skipped just the saddles (hindquarters and legs) at other times of the year. (43)

Just as there were market hunters there were sportsmen hunters. Lengenau wrote that at the time of this great increase in northern deer, and the market hunters, sportsmen clubs were formed. They later "organized to form a Michigan's Sportsmen's Association (MSA) to lobby against the market hunting industry" (44). Lengenau also said that the

MSA failed in its first attempt to outlaw the sale of game to other states. They would also not give up their fight to end the marketing hunting style of killing deer. Through the MSA's hard work and dedication they saved the white-tailed deer from disappearing from Michigan. In my opinion if the sportsmen were the ones who saved the white-tailed deer shouldn't we be the ones to hunt them also? Sportsmen are the mercy hunters of deer not the cruel no-hearted people non-hunters think we are. Through our hunting we saved the white-tailed deer from starvation and saved us from high insurance rates brought on by car-deer accidents. An average dressed out deer in the 1880's was 60 pounds compared to about 120 pounds in 1995, that's doubled the average from 115 years ago. Michigan spends millions of dollars to build or clean up areas for wildlife, where do you think they get that money? Not from the taxpayers, but from hunting licenses. If we outlawed hunting you would see regions of land be destroyed from companies, housing developments, and pollution. The only way they could possibly take care of nature is by raising taxes because there would be no licenses to pay for it. Since we do have hunting in Michigan we hunters are able to enjoy ourselves and nature without someone like anti-hunters looking over their shoulders saying "Save the animals, what did they do to us?" My response would be *if it doesn't affect you shut up*. We are animals too, just smarter. We are just like the cat that kills a mouse even though it just ate. That cat has that instinct to hunt just as we do. Man for centuries had to hunt just to feed themselves, just as the cat did. Now we can go to the store to buy the food we need, plus cat food, but that cat still hunts.

Through the sportsmen's help we have seen a major increase of deer and hunters. The deer population just this year got to about 1.9 million to 2.1 million deer according to the reports in the newspapers, and on the news. Just 95 years ago the deer population was 50,000 in the entire state according to Lengenau. According to Bob Gwizdz of *Field and Stream* the 1995 deer "Season will almost certainly top last year's deer harvest total . . . of 362,490 . . . the sixth highest deer season ever. Their record harvest was 452,490 deer in 1989" (80), my dad's year. Just this year six bucks were taken on my grandmother's land. On the first day of deer season my cousin Mike shot a 12 point at about 9:00 a.m. Half an hour later my other cousin was helping his brother drag the other one up, when about 150 yards out in the field wandered two bucks. One was a 6 point and the other an 8 point. My cousin Ken shot the six point and the neighbor shot the other. On the second day of deer season my father shot a 4 point in Ken's blind at about 9:30. On the third day my cousin Ken shot his second buck, a 5 point, out of his blind. On the fourth day my uncle Jim shot a 3 point. It would have been a 6 point but one half of the rack was gone. You could say that it was mercy hunting since that buck had a cracked skull probably from a fight or a car. From what I heard from my Uncle and my father there are probably more than 60 deer running around in a 10 acre area—that's small. There are probably more deer than that in the woods, but 60 was all they saw.

Here is a run down of facts from *Michigan Out-Of-Doors* written by Kenneth S. Lowe:

> On November 15, Michigan will mark the start of the 100th year of licensed deer hunting, a land mark in wildlife management.
>
> A lot of changes have occurred since that first licensed season. For one thing, the firearm license now costs $12.85. [Now it's $13.1 if you're a resident of Michigan and $100.35 if you're not.] And there are a lot more hunters now and a lot more deer. The number of licenses sold in 1895 was 14,477. By last year, the numbers in Michigan had grown to 775,140, of which 722,760 hunted in the firearms season, 334,620 in the archery season, and 177, 920 in the muzzleloading season (the total exceeds 775,140 because many hunt in more than one season).
>
> The number of deer hunters Michigan has grown faster than the population as a whole. From 1940 to 1977, the state's population increased 1.7 times while the number of firearm hunters grew 4.2 times.
>
> Michigan's army of firearm deer hunters passed the 200,000 mark in 1941; 300,000 in 1946; 400,000 in 1952; 500,000 in 1963; and 700,000 in 1975. The highest total was in 1991 when 757,690 hunted deer in the firearm season.

As you can see there were a lot of changes in hunting since 1895. All of them were contributed from sportsmen (mercy) hunters. Every man and woman have things they like. Remember you would not like it if a person who did not like what you like interfered with it. Have the same courtesy for others.

Works Cited

Gwizdz, Bob. "Optimistic Michigan Deer Forecast." *Field & Stream*. December 1995: 80.

Langenau, Ed. "Michigan's Deer Management Centennial." *Michigan Out-of-Doors*. November 1994: 42–44.

Lowe, Kenneth S. "A Deer Hunting Chronology." *Michigan Out-of-Doors*. November 1994: 54–56.

9 Time, Talk, and the Interpretation of Texts in a Teacher Education Seminar

John S. Lofty
University of New Hampshire

Small-group work has become an increasingly popular format in all subject areas and especially so in composition, literature, and education courses. From listening in on small-group conversation, though, many teachers at the high school and the college level, too, report that their students often talk more extensively about their own personal lives than about the assigned task, for example, the meanings of a text. The frequently made observation fails, though, to recognise that talk serving expressive purposes and talk seeking to interpret or analyse a reading can complement and support each other.

By expressive or reader-response talk, I am referring broadly to subjective criticism, what, for example, Robert Probst or Louise Rosenblatt would characterise as self-referential statements marked by varying degrees of autobiographic and experiential content. By text-based, I am referring to statements about features of form—word, image, patterns of organisation—that situate meaning in the text itself as, for example, did the New Critics. Although response and analysis are not mutually exclusive modes of criticism, each does place a strategically different emphasis on the role of the reader and on the text in producing meanings.

In this essay, I will present from my own class of preservice teachers, stretches of student talk about literature. In examining conversations about a play, a poem, and novels, my focus will be on talk that serves different purposes that I will argue are complementary. By describing a classroom in which talk served expressive purposes that support the emotional life of the group, I will argue that such talk can prompt and enhance text-based conversations rather than undercut them. An essential condition for this process to occur, I will argue further, is that we need to encourage students to use class time actively and consciously for both kinds of talk rather than to regard the former as time off-task. For this process to happen, though, we need to recognise fully how clock time shapes and constrains conversation. We need also to reflect on the complex relationships between how we use instructional time and the different kinds and qualities of classroom talk that our students practice.

The occasion and impetus to study each aspect of the time-talk relationship are twofold. First, in the NCTE/IRA Standards for the English Language Arts, "oracy," a term that Britain's Andrew Wilkinson coined in 1965, has received greater attention than ever before. James Britton noted that "writing floats on a sea of talk." The profession is now recognising that we need to focus on the sea of talk both as a mode of knowing—talking to learn—and also to integrate oracy into our instruction in literacy and mediacy. I will use the term talk also to encompass active listening.

Second, the need to document fully the relationships between time and learning in public schools has been established already by the formation of the National Education Commission on Time and Learning. The Commission's 1994 report to Congress opens by observing that "Learning in America is a prisoner of time. For the past 150 years, American public schools have held time constant and let learning vary" (7). A central purpose of recent school reforms has been to find alternative ways to use time more efficiently than in the seven-period school day, for example, through innovations such as modular and block scheduling. As we provide extended periods of learning time, we need also to revise our conceptions of how best to use instructional time for writing, reading, and especially for classroom talk.

By the time students enter college, clearly they have had many years of learning how to determine and meet their teachers' expectations for what it means to talk and write about literature. Students have learned also which kinds of talk the teacher most likely will validate and which kinds will be regarded as time off-task. So even when students are asked to talk about literature—without specific teacherly directions—students' memories of prior discussions in high school and their current work in other college classes always will shape and inform their conversation. In Alton Becker's words,

> Languaging is inherited not as grammatical rules or patterned lexicons but particularly, in particular memories of particular instances of languaging, what I have called prior texts. Knowing a way of languaging means having a repertoire of prior texts—all the particular instances of languaging any one of us remembers, always imperfectly. When we speak or write, we take those imperfectly remembered prior texts and shape them into new contexts. (17)

Memory, then, of our own prior texts, of the many previous conversations about literature that students could remember, was a dimension of time for us to consider in this methods course. In addition, new teachers needed to consider, for example, that talk serving expressive purposes was likely to be occluded by task- and text-based talk when students perceived themselves to have very limited time.

Staging a Play

For this activity, I had asked each group of new teachers to stage a scene from *Death of a Salesman*. Students had been instructed to explore their understanding both of the play—character, themes, situation, and historical context—as well as reading the play in relation to experiences from their own lives. Because I did not want to overdetermine the scope and content of rehearsal conversations, I gave no further directions beyond asking students to be ready to present their interpretations to the class and to explain the decisions taken and approaches adopted. As teacher, I allocated forty-five minutes for the groups to prepare. Given the range and potentials for exploratory talk that emerged, this probably was insufficient time.

A problem in researching talk is knowing how the presence of a tape recorder in a group might influence conversation. Even when absent from the room, teachers are always present in their students' conversations. To a degree, the tape recorder regulates the kinds of conversations that students believe are appropriate to engage in. When I listen, then, to the tapes of my students talking about texts, I hear a duet of voices: the double consciousness of ourselves and of our students speaking. Students speak to satisfy the expectations for literary discourse held by authorities while also attempting to author their own thoughts.

As you read the following transcript from three-and-a-half minutes of conversation in one group, note the several different kinds of talk that occur, for example, personal response, exploring and interpreting the text, and goal-directed, planning talk. Observe also how transitions occur between each kind of talk and how one kind prompts and segues into another in ways that maintain topic continuity.

> *Elissa:* There are a lot of things I would enthusiastically sell. Things related to the arts. (1)
>
> *David:* Hmm. Hmm. (2)
>
> *Elissa:* Education. Things like that. If I had to write certain articles that were about things that I didn't believe in, or something, that would be. Couldn't do that . . . (3)
>
> *Sam:* I don't think everybody would be as limited by that sort of thing. . . . (4)
>
> *Elissa:* Right, so it does depend on your personality. (5)

Cathy: Yes. (6)

Elissa: It's fun to sell. (7)

David: But you know it's interesting too that he does distinguish between he is liked, no, he is well liked, you know, I mean that's, it's really. . . . (8)

Barbara: That's the most important thing to Willy, you know, to be liked, and he is so blinded by it that he can't even see that he has lived his whole life being blind to what really matters and making excuses for his children. I just see his parenting style as no wonder these two thirty-four-year-olds don't know what they are doing in their life. (9)

David: I mean this is my family absolutely, totally my family before I decided to go back to college. It's like this is so scary. Except we were a little younger. But I mean, man. It is so scary. Except my mother wasn't as forgiving as Linda. (voice trails into ironic laughter) (10)

Elissa: And what did you feel like as a child in the family? (11)

David: Well, I was Happy. My brother was Biff. I mean really. I mean I was sort of like well, you know, just don't, just sort of go along. You know it's actually, you learn about family dynamics when you start doing like awarenesses with kids and stuff which you may have already done. You learn about their role models and family and there's the scapegoat, there's the kid who keeps everything together and all that. And the role models in this are so clear, you know. Biff is like the. . . . (12)

Sam: Golden child. (13)

David: Well yeah, he is the golden child. And what is the other one that is sort of quiet, and that's Happy. But then Biff goes between Golden child and scapegoat. So it's real interesting. (14)

Elissa: Well, Happy is well liked by women. He is always selling himself to women. (15)

David: Hmm. There's just many, so many things in this play! (16)

Barbara: So we ought to do that scene. (17)

Elissa: Yes, I know we have another twenty minutes. (18)

Barbara: What scene should we do? (19)

Elissa: I suppose we should make it kind of short. (20)

David: That's kind of a big, big scene. (21)

Elissa: A long scene but we could do a piece of it. Right, what piece stands out in the restaurant? Well, there is the part where Willy keeps on interrupting. He says that he's been fired, and that sort of changes the whole thing. (22)

Sam: Yes. (23)

David: That's pretty important. (24)

Elissa: I can find it. (25)

Sam: I think it's 107 or 109. (26)

Elissa: Oh, boy . . . can you find the line? (27)

> *David:* Actually, my father even got really into organic gardening right before he died. It's like, "Oh my God!" (28)
>
> *Cathy:* (sympathetic laughter.) You know, I was thinking if we did the scene that starts on 107 or wherever where Willy says that he was fired. (29)

We join the discussion above after the group of five already have been discussing for some minutes what they know about sales:

> *Sam:* This is sort of unrelated, but I was looking through the *Sunday Globe*, and I was just looking at the help wanted section for myself and my boyfriend in the pages of sales. It's really bizarre that in this bad of an economy that they still want this many people to try to sell things.
>
> *Cathy:* Most professional salespeople though can sell anything. They don't care what it is. I had a friend whose mom sold AAA memberships. Then she sold prefab-like garage structures, and then she sold farm equipment, right. . . .
>
> *Elissa:* Yes, she could sell anything. And then she sold radio advertising, and so it didn't matter as long as it was a good job, she just liked selling things.

The personal-response theme continues through the first seven exchanges. David then moves discussion from his personal opinions back to the play—without an apparent transition—by recalling Willy's distinction between Charley's being liked but not well-liked. Barbara runs with David's lead by using the liked/not well-liked distinction to examine how Willy's spiritual blindness has arrested his sons' development; her phrase "parenting style" casts her interpretation in the language of popular psychology (9).

The transition from interpretation of character back to a personal connection with the text is made quite abruptly by David (10), beginning, "I mean this is my family absolutely. . . ." This personal response marks David's first public identification with a family that we now might describe as dysfunctional. The affiliation has been foreshadowed, perhaps in David's one isolated comment that occurs immediately prior to Cathy and Barbara's initial discussion of sales: "This play really gets me. This really gets me. Whew." David is unusual in the class in that he is an experienced teacher who is confident enough to make an admission that nevertheless takes a risk with the three younger women in his group. As David's voice trails off into ironic laughter, Elissa, herself a "nontraditional" student, promptly asks him to say more: "And what did you feel like as a child in the family?" Her question serves to extend David's personal exploration by supporting the emotional life of a group member. She thereby validates in her group talk about literature, in addition to yet very different from, the kind of textual analysis about what is "in the text" in contrast to what is "in the reader."

Exchange 12 of the conversation offers a particularly rich example of how, as the group prepares to stage the scene, one speaker moves among kinds of talk that serve different language functions: personal talk, explaining and generalising about behaviour, and analysing and interpreting the text. Is it David's unease with his own very close identification with Happy that moves him to shift the topic from himself to his students' families and finally to the roles that Biff and Happy occupy? "The roles in this are so clear. Biff is like the. . . ." Samantha, who has been listening intently to this point completes David's thought with "golden child." Using the archetypes of scapegoat and golden child, discussion next turns to character analysis of Biff and Happy in exchanges 14 and 15.

David's global reflection that "There's just many, so many things in this play" suggests something of the internal drama going on for him. By reminding the group of the need to select a scene to stage (17), Barbara both acknowledges David's observation while diplomatically returning conversation to the task. Elissa, who up to this point has both made and encouraged personal responses, then herself plays the timekeeper. That David has been continuing to think about his own family in relation to the Lomans is strongly suggested by what appears as the non sequitur (28): "My father even got really into organic gardening right before he died." Cathy's sympathetic laughter is the only public acknowledgement that David has shared a very personal, if not a troubling memory. Yet she keeps the group "on task" by continuing to discuss staging (29): "You know, I think if we did the scene that starts on 107. . . ."

The final selection of a scene is then made swiftly after this segment with each student suggesting possibilities. Barbara closes further selection: "Maybe in the interests of time we should do the restaurant one." David's close identification with the family dynamic between Willy, Biff and Happy prompts him to exclaim, "Let me be Willy, Let me be Willy. I'd like to do that!" David wants a double voice for Biff: Biff number one, who appeased Willy, and Biff two, whose several attempts to speak honestly were frustrated. Elissa is more interested in adding a narrator to orient the audience to the excerpted action, a suggestion that David opposes: "It's too easy in drama to put a narrator in there. I think it makes it more challenging if you don't."

The idea is dropped and discussion turns again to casting. David again volunteers to play Willy. "I wouldn't mind being Willy just because. . . ." Elissa cuts in ironically with "the role of a lifetime." Cathy agrees. David's "Yes, I know," again is followed by the laughter of self-identification and imagined future: "I wish they would put this on at our school rather than *Music Man*." This is his last personal response prior to rehearsing the scene.

After a powerful performance before the whole class, the group discussed their staging decisions to place Willy with his back to Biff and to
the audience. Several character interpretations of Willy follow.

Barbara: Maybe the audience can't think into Willy's head.

Cathy: Willy is very closed off.

David: Willy is like Everyman, you know. Doesn't need to have a
face. He's sort of everybody.

David's closing evaluation of Willy is consistent with, and has been prepared for, by his own several identifications with Willy's family in the
transcript above.

The group also discussed questions of meaning that emerged in the
rehearsal. For example, Cathy did not understand why Happy says, "ter-
rific, Pop" in response to Willy's "I had an experience today." Barbara's
reply ends in a character interpretation. "Willy has like lied throughout
his life to his sons, to his wife and to himself, and Happy kind of does it
back to him . . . none of them really can be honest with each other." Thus
we see that the groups' talk encompasses both simple character analyses as well as talk about self and others; the latter disappears quickly,
though, once planning and rehearsal begin.

Discussion in our class about the kinds of talk engaged in by each
group preparatory to staging *Death of a Salesman* led us to ask these kinds
of questions: As teachers, which intentions or purposes for student-talk
do we validate or approve and which do we discourage? How do the
kinds of talk that occurred in our own conversations affect what we see
as our purposes and rationale for studying literature? When the conversation became oriented to the task set by the teacher—staging a scene—
what happened to the personal thinking and feeling that had surfaced
initially? Can the Pandora's box of memory simply be closed again because students needed time to complete the assignment of staging a
scene? Do remembered images find expression again in their acting? By
encouraging students to explore their personal response, what kinds of
language learning can teachers and students foster? For teachers to generate reflective, open-ended questions is essential to their understanding the complex dynamics of classroom talk.

Reading and Talking about Poetry

For the next example of small-group talk, I will feature students' reflections on their discussion of a poem. Since I want to focus only on selected parts, extended transcriptions are not included as for the play
rehearsal. I asked each group to talk among themselves for twenty minutes about Stephen Spender's poem "My Parents Kept Me from Chil-

dren Who Were Rough." Each group of five appointed one student to record discussion foci and the kinds of talk heard but not to participate.

As students worked their way toward meanings, they picked up and dropped possible interpretive leads. Silences without awkwardness punctuated their questions and responses. Students' personal connections with the situation of a child intimidated by peers were conveyed in lines such as, "If the other kids had only smiled back at him, he would have been fine" and "This poem reminds me of the place I grew up, White Plains, New York." Students sought to interpret the poem by locating and then filling in the gaps of meaning with fragments of talk-words, phrases, but often not complete ideas.

By testing interpretations on other ears, readers risked the smiles and laughter of "No, I don't think the poem is really about that at all." Occasionally I would hear a reader ask, "But did you like it, really like it? That's what I want to know." Another reader remembered a time in his life when, like the character in the poem, he was pinned down squirming beneath the knees of an older brother. Cutting through their discussions after twenty minutes, my own teacherly announcement attempted to channel the flow of talk from the intimacy of a small group back into the more public space of a classroom. "When you are ready, bring your conversations to a close." A few students looked ready to "wrap up," but others immersed in the poem barely looked up to see who spoke of time.

The next stage was for the class to look at students' responses to the poem and then to describe the kinds of talk they had engaged in. Across the four groups, student recorders reported that the meanings of the poems had been determined largely through readers' analyses of images, symbols, and clues inferred about an author's purpose. Members of one group recognised that their particular training in school had shaped strongly how they had approached interpretation: "We started with personal responses but then paused. 'Wait a minute. Don't we need to be analysing this?'" Because the subject matter of the poem invited strong personal connections, I was surprised that reports of students' making personal responses was comparatively rare.

In our seminar discussions about teaching literature, the class had resisted a simple oppositional distinction between analysis and personal exploration. We recognised that certain versions of textual analysis have situated meanings exclusively "in the poem" whereas reader-response theorists have privileged the reader's experience informed by his or her culture in creating meanings. We had explored, instead, a model of interpretation as interaction between text and reader argued for in *The Reader, the Text, the Poem* by Louise Rosenblatt, for example, and more recently by McCormick, Waller, and Flower in *Reading Texts*. On the occasions when personal response did penetrate these conversations about poetry, analysis quickly overshadowed it and was heavily foregrounded.

Our subsequent conversations about the relationship between time and how we talk about literature shaped a series of follow-up questions that we used to push further our analyses of reactions to the poems. For example, we considered how time frames that were clearly limited influenced students' talk. We also considered how such time frames influenced the interpenetration of response and analysis in large- and small-group settings, what students regard as relatively public in contrast to private domains. Our subsequent discussion addressed time in two different ways. First, students talked about how available classroom time shaped their conversation—what they talked about. Second, students reflected on the temporal contours of the discussion itself, on the rhythm or pace of talk and particularly the dimensions and experiences of time that go beyond its common identification with the measure of the clock. (I will later describe these contours in terms of what I call *timescapes*.) We found a close relationship between the form and content of a discussion and how we had shaped its temporal features.

Both the time available for talk and the conversational patterns established by teachers influence the range of students' choices between analysis and personal response. In Tracy's words:

> I learned that personal response is one of the last things conversations turn to. By teachers asking students well-structured questions, talk usually goes in one direction. If you want to leave the possibilities for talk open to see where it goes, it is best to leave a longer amount of time.

Binary, either/or thinking tended to shape much of students' thinking about this topic. According to Kathy, "If a group is given a poem to analyse in x amount of minutes, then the group will tend to cut right to the formal analysis *versus* describing personal connections and exploring different tangents." About the reasons for reading, Michael asked, "Do you want to teach literacy to your students? Do you teach them to read and enjoy reading? *Or* do you want to teach them to read and be able to analyse a book. Like what is literacy?"

Students such as Stephen sought out and would have valued more opportunities than they had in school to talk about a text in terms that had encompassed and had made connections with their own lives:

> I sensed that we all feel a bit cheated by our own experience as students; personal response and the reader's relations to the text, which, we all seem to see as at least important, if not the primary means of constructing meaning, was not part of educational experience.

Because such students had learned to regard the teacher's agenda for dealing with features of a text as the primary one, they seldom saw any kind of a personal response as appropriate to school time.

> Moving beyond the text is what you do when everything else is finished with. And that is next week's class, if we have time. When you go to school with people who are trained in the new critical tradition, there is a meaning here and let's find it . . . and if we have time, we'll talk about your life. (Steve)

In a class of thirty new teachers, I had expected to find a wider variety of talk about poetry than I did. Given the current widespread recognition by English teachers that readers and writers actively make meaning, I would have anticipated that many more students would have practised what McCormick, Waller, and Flower describe as "strong readings" against the text. Yet few students reported ever being in high school or college classes where personal-social talk was valued as being intrinsically worthwhile and encouraged for its role in understanding who we are in relation to others. Neither did students report that such talk was valued for the analytic talk that it might prompt.

Binary thinking also made it less likely that students would recognise and move along the continuum between reader and text, between the close and familiar texts of our own lives and the initially more distant and strange text of a writer. Admittedly, in these conversations, the time limits I set did appear to focus students on the text. Additional time likely might have shifted the contours of conversation to encompass the readers' experiences. I would argue, though, that this move most likely would occur—particularly with poetry—only when students hear their teachers actively encouraging such talk.

Teaching a Novel

In the final example of small-group discussion, student teachers had been asked to consider how they might teach either *The Chocolate War* or *Catcher in the Rye*. Although students already had had preliminary large-group discussions of the novels, I explained that before we could consider how each might be taught, the small-groups would need to reach consensus regarding what each story was about. I initially allowed thirty minutes for the two-part task of locating themes and of planning initial instruction. By the end of the time—extended by ten minutes—few groups actually had completed the planning part of the assignment but through lively discussion each was well primed to consider pedagogy.

What kinds of talk characterised conversation across the different groups? Discussions featured five major kinds of talk: personal-response

statements; student-student questions; answers; text-based interpretation; and critical evaluations of statements. In students' talk about novels in contrast to poetry, I found a much higher ratio of personal-response statements in relation to text-based interpretation. I will consider
why at the end of the section.

To understand how these teacher readers made meaning, the high
number of personal-response statements proved a rich category for scrutiny. Responses drew deeply on personal history and prior experiences,
and they served to clarify and generalise understandings and to establish reading tastes across the group. For example, about the theme of
teachers' abuse of authority in *The Chocolate War*, Andrea asked, "Do
you think that could really happen in a school?" Cathy replied, "I don't
know. I went to Catholic school for a couple of years, and, boy, I got a
few yardsticks broken on my knuckles."

Her personal response then initiated a discussion of *Catcher in the Rye*
that considered the truth of stereotypical generalisations made about
the differences between how males establish power hierarchies in contrast to how females move more co-operatively. By going beyond
analysing features of the text, such discussion projected these teachers
into questions that enabled them to make connections with other course
readings as well as with contemporary social issues.

Predictably perhaps, discussion of the text itself focused on questions
of character and motivation. By resolving questions about the sanity of
narrator Holden Caulfied ("But he did have a nervous breakdown, didn't
he?"), interpretations also probed ways to teach the novel. Jerry explored
one such possibility:

> I think I'd try to go more from the perspective that it is possible to
> go against the grain. And like it is kind of a negative outcome that
> he does have a breakdown, and he does end up in the recovery place
> ... there's a way though that you can teach it in a positive outlook—
> that it's OK to be an individual, and it's OK not to want to fit into
> society.

By questioning the reliability of the narrator, another line of text-based
interpretation, teachers were able to construct and evaluate
collaboratively the actions of the Holden Caulfields that they constructed.

The student-to-student questions that occurred quite frequently during the conversation served not to test knowledge but to push understanding and to promote enquiry. "So how would you teach *Catcher in
the Rye*? Why would you teach it?" were real questions for new teachers
to think about. Only two-thirds of the student-generated questions received direct answers; questions often elicited further questions which
then prompted personal responses. Different kinds of talk alternated

and worked together as we might expect in a real conversation as opposed to a recitation about a book. Long stretches of discussion occurred without any questions at all. When evaluations of answers and responses did occur, they served to move the conversation forward by affirmations such as "That's a good thing to bring up because Holden is not trustworthy" or "I agree with you" and "that's true." Conspicuously absent in this conversation were the kinds of teacher-led question-answer-evaluation cycles of many whole-class discussions that invite me to initiate each new round or to wait out the inevitable silences.

What emerged in the discussion of teaching a novel, then, was a high degree of student-student interaction marked by frequent turn taking. Far fewer extended speeches occurred than in our whole-class discussions, which I mention here only to compare with small-group talk. Also evident was the same kind of interpenetration of personal response and text-based interpretation, found, though, to a much lesser degree than in the poetry reading activity. In part, this finding might be explained by the enduring belief that poems contain deep, hidden meanings that it is the students' task to locate. Although students also believe that novels contain symbols to interpret and themes to identify, students experience somewhat greater latitude in terms of the boundaries of acceptable conversation.

Another factor that might explain a marked increase in personal response was that the small-group work on the novel occurred after the poetry. I shared my findings with students, and together we raised issues for teaching. Conceivably, then, by the time students talked about the novels, our large-group reflections on classroom discourse had prepared and encouraged them to talk in a wide range of ways. Although not my intention, some students might have begun to provide more of the kinds of talk they believed their teacher valued. A time factor also deserves mention. Obvious perhaps to observe, student and teacher are likely to spend much more time working with almost any novel than with poems that are usually shorter in length; the extended time, then, allows for more discursive conversation.

Literacy as Conversation

At this juncture, I will move from describing small-group talk to raising theoretical issues and questions that go beyond the particularities of my own classroom. "Literacy as Conversation: Classroom Talk as Text Building," by Patricia L. Stock and Jay L. Robinson offers a rich conceptual framework to illuminate my own understanding of educational talk. Their essay shows how teacher-researchers can use discourse analysis to study how students use language to learn, to understand the oral processes of students' learning. The college population referred to in their study had been working together in a remedial writing course.

Stock and Robinson argue for the primary importance of social interaction, of conversation, in literacy development. Although my focus in this essay is on oracy as an independent mode of knowing and learning, in classroom practice I want to integrate and continually make visible the connections among reading, writing, talking, and viewing. For this reason, I would not teach any of the language arts in separate classes since to do so is to present a discreteness that works against students exploring the wholeness of language.

With the purpose of applying selected concepts from their essay, it will be useful to present three of the five axioms that inform these writers' thinking and from which my own work draws:

1. In attempting to characterize language and learning through language, it is not helpful to separate what is "social" from what is "academic." . . . Learning language is learning through language. Given the way we have organized ourselves into academic disciplines, genre blurring may be our only hope to capture what learning through language is.

2. Students' uses of language are ineradicably rooted in the concrete details of personal experience and in concepts that constitute their own personal knowledge—most of which are also rooted in personal experience. . . .

3. Students seem to know, and not only instinctively, that the private worlds of personal experience and personal knowledge must be explored if they are to form themselves into social communities in which the acts of text building—composition and comprehension—are made possible and enabled as something other than mechanical exercises. . . . Talk about persons and personal experience, even when it appears to be far from the immediate task at hand, is purposeful: not only does it build community among those who must learn to communicate, but it also provides common ground to which references may be made when students are working to make meaning of concepts already named and invested with meaning in the public world. (214)

The essay, itself a powerful and provocative example of interdisciplinary enquiry, has its roots in sociolinguistic and rhetorical theory drawing on such theoreticians as Frederick Erickson, Irving Goffman, Stanley Fish, and Lev Vygotsky. To understand "something as complex as human learning," Stock and Robinson argue that we need to be suspicious of the dichotomies that characterise much educational research, for example, an implied opposition between social and individual and between affective and cognitive domains. By grounding language learning in social exchange, each axiom affirms interaction as a precondition for meaningful education. In the Geertzian sense, we need to mix or "blur" genres in our analysis of talk, too. The truth of these axioms was confirmed when I listened to my students' initial exploratory talk about *Death of a Salesman* and what it means to sell. I wanted students to move immediately into those kinds of talk that led to analyses of character and situation and to work on the tasks that as teacher I had set. At first, I also heard David's memories of his own troubled family as a poignant but nevertheless off-task digression. Only as I made a transcript and used writing to understand the direction and purpose of the talk did I come to see how personal talk functioned as a more powerful mode of learning than had been discernible to me as a listener. When students' talk was transcribed, the writing allowed me to scrutinise each exchange before it disappeared into the next. What emerged was that the alternating movements between the students' talk about their own experience and their talk about the characters in the play were complementary and reinforced and extended each other.

We see this effect most immediately with David, whose talk shifts between himself and the play. The text offers a safe, public haven after he might think he has said too much or after what he has said finds no like response. Even after the initial cycle of personal discussion by all the group is over, he still continues to remember publicly his private life in disconnected statements that well up out of his past. "My father even got into organic gardening right before he died." David turns from his own connections with the play to analysing options for staging, including suggesting the double voices for Biff. Yet at the end of the performance, David concludes, "Willy is like Everyman," a universalising judgement that includes himself. If group members had moved directly to the planning work but without first personally identifying with character and situation, then their understanding and the performance itself might well not have been as engaging as it was.

In the example above, we can distinguish between personal talk and talk that serves to select the scene for staging. Although the two speech genres differ in form and function, they coalesce in interlocking exchanges. The two genres thereby support the group's shared larger purpose of collaborative learning in a classroom community. Citing Erickson, Stock and Robinson note that teachers and students who interact in classrooms "can be seen as drawing on two sets of procedural knowledge simultaneously: knowledge of the academic task structure and of the social participation structure" (173). In the rehearsal, though, if these students draw "simultaneously" on two sets of knowledge, they respond alternately and separately to each one.

What it means, though, to say that students "can be seen as drawing on two sets of procedural knowledge" raises issues critical for voice and empowerment, for what Douglas Barnes describes as the politics of oracy. If we value such appropriation as an active process, then we need to teach our students to tap consciously and deliberately into the social participation structure, a resource that clearly facilitates their learning. On the other hand, if we regard drawing on participation structures as a passive process that does not advance learning, then students likely will utilise this procedural knowledge non-consciously or even subversively. Although students might themselves value the social structures of learning, social talk becomes a sub-rosa form of discourse once we marginalise or suppress it for classroom use.

As teachers joining a group, how often have we observed our own students first becoming silent and then awkwardly shifting their footing back to the teacher-assigned task? For students and teachers to negotiate the politics of oracy is complicated yet further by situations in which small-group talk does not address the academic task structure. Except for an initial gesture to attempt the task, student talk can stall in personal or social realms. Teachers then often prematurely abandon group work in favour of direct instruction.

In order to promote communal text building, students must take significant risks in sharing details of their emotional life. For this to happen, though, students will need the full support of their small groups and the affirmation of the larger classroom community. In axiom three, Stock and Robinson describe the need for students to form what Fish terms an "interpretive community." Essential to the process is text building, a temporal process whose social and personal dynamics we are only just beginning to understand. The heart of this process is the construction of what Stock and Robinson describe as the "emergent text." The text is "composed by the interactions of members of the classroom community and from their transactions with written texts, and it is written in memory" (185). Time is a critical element in text building:

> But these texts are emerging, of course, in a present that includes among its realities both the selves—real and projected—of those persons who make up the community and the social relationships among these selves as these are projected and perceived: thus the references of language learning actions are always to a social present, even as they are simultaneously to past and future. Because they are characterized by dual references to a recalled past and an imagined future, and because they are realized in an enacted present con-

sisting of the relations among a set of actors presently engaged, we find these actions, realized in language, to be dramatizations not only of individuals' processes of learning but also of the community's emerging hermeneutics—its informing and patterned processes of negotiated meaning and values. (189)

Note here the double process of individual learning in conjunction with the social construction of community. Text building occurs through individual "recollections," themselves "language learning actions." Speakers relive or re-experience in the present the prior texts of their remembered past. Speakers also imaginatively project themselves into the emergent text formed by the classroom community:

Through recollection, members of the classroom community reconstruct for one another, in explicit language shaped for the occasion, prior texts that are stored in their individual memories. In doing so, they enrich and expand the context within which the emergent texts of the class and the emergent co-text of the course may be constructed; they make common ground. (195)

In terms of the teachers preparing to stage a play scene, the class members were involved in building text for a dramatic performance. The complexity of the process is compounded by requiring actions of two kinds: language learning actions and physical actions—themselves situated in time and space. Consequently, what we might construe to be a complete dynamics of group members actively negotiating and building a text cannot be fully rendered through talk alone. The learning that occurs exceeds what can be observed and subsequently represented in the form of a transcript which can recover only certain features of live talk but loses its performative dimensions.

Before the whole class watched the group act the scene, I was concerned that students had devoted sufficient preparation time to accomplish even a routine reading of parts, never mind to achieve a rehearsed, expressive performance that would reflect textual understanding and interpretation of a complex, challenging play. Yet as I listened to their reading to the whole class, I was very struck by a sureness of voice and a concentration of feeling that typically might come—if at all—only after several rehearsals. In Barbara's voice, I could hear the tension and frustration as she acted out the Biff who Willy could not or would not hear. In David's lines, I could hear and feel, too, the traces of his own memory of a father, who like the Willy he now acts, sees himself in the sons he has raised.

Tracking causal relations between these students' personal and social talk and their performance of a text would be hard to prove; the personal talk, though, would appear to have prepared the way. Such talk might have enabled each speaker to establish his or her own connection and commitment to a part in the play. The intimacy and trust generated in the group appeared to prepare students for a performance whose success outstripped the public, visible planning and rehearsal that I witnessed. By being free to talk in ways that I had not specified nor directed, students were able to take on and try out new and fluid identities as they projected themselves into the play. On this occasion, empathic responses did lead to understanding and a critical performance. I saw the results of students seamlessly integrating cognitive and affective domains in dramatic interpretations. Stock and Robinson would argue that such verbal improvisations are the foundation of all language learning:

> If educational talk, like conversation, is at all accurately described as a "sustained strip or tract of referencings," the units that compose it are open to memories of the lived and living lives of participants in the talk. Since educational talk, like conversation, is improvisation in which human beings project a self to establish relationships with other selves, it is subject to all the fluctuations and misapprehensions of human intention and human perception, even as it progresses toward the constitution of satisfying meaning. (183)

Timescapes of Talk: A Model for Teachers

From looking at examples of small-group talk from Stock and Robinson's perspective of text building in classroom communities, I next will consider how we might visually represent different kinds of talk in relation to time. Transcribing sounds into signs enables us to freeze and thereby to see talk, but by transforming it into writing we have changed the phenomenon and lost features of the original speech event. Unlike a still-life portrait, we need to view talk from what Young, Becker, and Pike refer to as a "wave perspective." Dynamic and evolving, talk unfolds in and over time evoking the past, inhabiting the present, and anticipating or imagining the future. If to represent the auditory medium of talk is difficult, to represent time and talk in relation to each other is even more so.

Gregory Bateson, quoting Korzybski, reminds us that "the map is not the same as the territory"; between the terms of a symbolic representation and what it intends to represent there cannot be a full correspondence (449). Time is no exception. As a basic frame or category of human perception, the concept of time has multiple referents including the familiar ones of clock and calendar that mark changes in experience and progression of events. We commonly represent time in terms of spatial metaphors and speak of time running out, of filling time and of spending time. The ways in which we construct time become significant when our representations determine how we measure in the quantitative terms of contact- and credit-hours, for example, the qualitative complexity of human learning.

I find it useful to view time not as a line but through the spatial metaphor of a countryside across which we travel. Recall for a moment the kind of large-scale topographical map used for cross-country hiking or cycling. Such maps do feature major roads and blue highways. Key information for the traveller, though, is represented by circular contour lines connecting land at equal heights above the ground zero of sea level. In planning a journey, these lines mark the shifting gradients that need to be interpreted.

In the timescape metaphor, each contour line represents a different kind of talk that students and teacher navigate together. To understand the different contours of students' talk, language teachers will need to map the different kinds of voice-tracks that students generate in classroom discourse. By reading their voice-tracks, we can see the range of conversational country they encounter in different kinds of classroom talk. We also can see the kinds of talk that students seldom practice or the kinds engaged in mainly by the teacher. Silences needs to be heard positively as the ground on which students learn how to listen actively to each other.

In Figure 1, I have drawn horizontal lines to suggest the contours of the different kinds of talk I recorded. (Teacher talk is indicated by upper case letters and student talk by lower case; for example, "A" in the timescape refers to a teacher answer, "a" to a student answer; "Q" to a teacher question, "q" to a student question, etc.) Our conversational movements through time, of course, are not straight lines but a series of circuitous backloops into memory and curve balls that carry and project us into the future. Conversation is seldom the shortest distance between two ideas.

I have rendered three timescapes: a lecture, a large-group discussion, and a small-group talk. Because I am using a time-space metaphor to describe talk, a timescape is not intended to have the representational accuracy or scale of a map. Although drawn on a computer, it is not generated by one. The explanatory power of a timescape, then, lies in its ability to get us to reflect on how different kinds of talk relate to one another and finally to encourage students and teacher to create metaphors that represent their own concepts of time and talk.

First, we need examples of talk from which to construct a timescape. With the purpose of getting preservice teachers to recognise the diver-

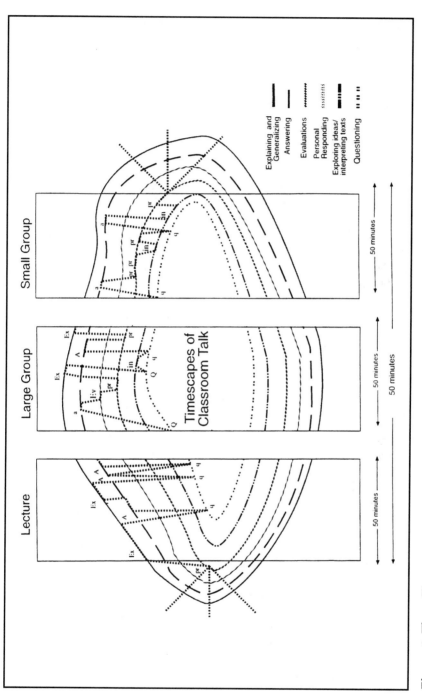

Figure 1. Three Timescapes.

sity of their own talk, they record and categorise examples of the different kinds of talk that they engage in over a week, a period that includes talk in school, at work and at play:

Kind of Talk	Purpose or Function	Context	Audience
questioning	clarify understanding	classroom	teacher
gossip	social contact	dormroom	friends
argument	change practice	workplace	supervisor

Second, students discuss how their own students can develop a full repertoire of oral skills both by structured practice and in the context of readers, writers, and talkers workshops. I am assuming here that although certain kinds of talk do "come naturally," other kinds, argument, for example, require extended practice for proficiency (Lofty). Representing different kinds of talk on a timescape reminds us of the genres of talk that students need to practice to develop a wide repertoire from which to make linguistic choices. For the purpose of comparison only, each timescape is drawn for fifty minutes—the traditional class hour. Block scheduling will allow more time for talk and make possible such different formats as pairs, small groups, and lecture. By comparing timescapes, we begin to see the different kinds of talk in which students and teachers engage.

Timescape of a Lecture

Lecturing continues to be one very appropriate means of presenting certain kinds of information in English classes. In my own teacher-education classes, pair-, small-, and large-group work are the formats we most frequently use. If we can risk speaking of the event of a "typical" lecture, the prior diagram might lead us to expect to hear the teacher engaging students in extended stretches of some kind of explanatory talk—the "Ex" contour on the diagram—whose purpose would be to impart or deliver information and knowledge needed by students.

The term "interruptible lecture" itself suggests that questions or comments—"q" contour—from students distract or disrupt the otherwise normative flow of a teacher speaking while the students listen and take notes. Obviously, Socratic-style lectures would be much more dialogic and show many more alternations between the explaining-questioning-answering contours. Certainly, lecturers do use personal and anecdotal material to illustrate the ideas, concepts, and practices they explain. The practice of sharing taped lectures or borrowing notes indicates that many students believe that to learn from this kind of direct and directive talk, interactions between teacher and student and student and student are neither essential nor often desired.

Timescape of a Large-Group Discussion

Because conversations between students and teacher publicly occupy "the floor" or space in which we speak, the frequency and duration of exchanges become an important indice of time. From the transcript of one thirty-minute conversation, I counted thirty-five turns that as teacher I initiated. In a forum designed to explore students' thinking, for teacher talk to occur on average twelve times more often than student talk would seem inappropriate. In this particular class, half the students spoke on average three times. Issues of gender also emerge. In a class of twenty-four women and six men, Hillary led the women speaking four times in contrast to Michael speaking ten and David nine times.

In the timescape above, we see the commonly found Q-a-Ev pattern of the teacher asking a question, the student providing an answer, and the teacher then evaluating the answer. Teacher explanations continue to be a dominant feature, although not so extensively as in the timescape for a lecture. Although personal responses certainly were evident in our large-group discussions about literature, they were neither as frequent nor as developed as in small-group work. Furthermore, they came more often from students than from myself—an observation with clear implications for teacher modelling, for example: Ev-pr-pr-interp-pr-ev-interp-pr-q. One common contour of large-group talk was the teacher giving explanations and answers to students' questions as in a lecture, for example, Ex-q-a-Ex.

If students are to explore ideas through talk, this kind of a profile again would be inappropriate. But it was not until I transcribed several of my own large-group discussions that I was able to see the kinds of talk commonly practised. I had believed that in relation to students I was speaking much less than in reality I was. I also had thought that students were initiating and facilitating more of our talk than the transcripts revealed. Once I saw the patterns of actual talk and compared them to the patterns I believed are appropriate to seminar-style learning, I was then able to monitor my own role in the group.

When questions both from students and myself were on the floor, I learned to wait much longer before speaking so that ideas could be explored through student-student interactions: q-a1-a2-a3-A-ev. In this chain the teacher's answer is then evaluated by a student. Although I had been very aware of the need to listen more and on occasions for teachers to sit outside the discussion circle, reading and discussing sample transcripts provided both the class and myself with clear information and motivation to re-attune the timescapes of our large-group discussion to the learning through talk we had planned. The reflective exercise also provided teachers with a simple technique to monitor their own future classroom talk and avoid obvious pitfalls.

Timescape of Small-Group Talk

As we might predict from the above discussions about small-group talk of poetry, fiction, and drama, the timescape for this talk features stretches of personal response alternating with some kind of text-based commentary or interpretation: pr-pr-pr-interp-pr-q-a-ev-interp-interp-q-a-pr-pr-interp. One explanation of this kind of a sequence would be that personal response and interpretation trigger each other; it matters (to me) less whether one kind of talk is a cause and another an effect. What is important for teachers to address is that talk about task and talk about self are both valuable and appear to elicit, support, and reinforce each other. Stock and Robinson would add that both are critical to text and community building.

If exchanges that feature personal response enhance performance, as appeared to be the case with students preparing to stage a scene from *Death of a Salesman*, then we must allow time for it. The three-and-a-half-minute segment of transcript shows the kinds of talk engaged in by students:

> response - response - response - response - response - response - exploring - interpreting - response - question - response - explaining - exploring - interpreting - interpreting - interpreting - reflection - planning - question - answer - observation - question - answer - response - laughter - planning.

Personal response served as a powerful springboard to kinds of talk other than interpretation, namely, analysis, planning, and solving staging problems. Had I nudged this group to move directly into planning talk, then my guess is that the performance would not have been as successful as it was; talk crucial to building the individual text and the emergent text of the classroom community would have been omitted. On another occasion, though, one group never moved itself into text-based planning talk. Consequently, we need to explain to students the value and function of each kind of talk so that neither appears gratuitous to meeting all of their language needs.

In the spirit of Jay Robinson's work, I will close with questions, raised both by his work with Patricia Stock about classroom talk and by this essay:

> What have we created in this vision of ours of classroom talk and classroom learning? What have we not seen? Which conventions have we followed and which have we challenged? What genres have we blurred and to what purposes? (214)

What kinds of timescapes can best serve the acquisition both of oracy and literacy? How do we enable ourselves and our students to move beyond those learned experiences of time that do not enable students to develop and use a full repertoire of different kinds of talk?

Works Cited

Barnes, Douglas. 1988. "The Politics of Oracy." In *Oracy Matters: The Development of Talking and Listening in Education*. Eds. Margaret Maclure, Terry Phillips, and Andrew Wilkinson. Milton Keynes: Open University Press. 43—54.

Bateson, Gregory. 1972. *Steps to an Ecology of Mind*. New York: Ballantine.

Becker, Alton L. 1995. *Beyond Translation: Essays Towards a Modern Philology*. Ann Arbor: University of Michigan Press.

Britton, James. 1969. "Talking to Learn." *Language, the Learner and the School*. Ed. Douglas Barnes, James Britton, and Mike Torbe. 4th ed. Portsmouth: Boynton/Cook–Heinemann. 91–130.

Lofty, John. 1996. "More than Lipservice: Oracy's Coming of Age in Britain's National Curriculum." *English Education* 28: 4–38.

McCormick, K., G. Waller, and L. Flower. 1989. *Reading Texts: Reading, Responding, Writing*. Lexington: Heath.

National Education Commission on Time and Learning. 1994. *Prisoners of Time*. Washington, D.C.

Probst, Robert. 1988. *Response and Analysis: Teaching Literature in Junior and Senior High School Years*. Portsmouth, NH: Heinemann.

Robinson, Jay. L. 1990. *Conversations on the Written Word: Essays on Language and Literacy*. Portsmouth, NH: Heinemann.

Rosenblatt, Louise. 1976. *Literature as Exploration*. New York: Noble Books.

Stock, Patricia L., and Jay L. Robinson. 1990. "Literacy as Conversation: Classroom Talk as Text Building." Jay L. Robinson. *Conversations on the Written Word: Essays on Language and Literacy*. Portsmouth, NH: Boynton/Cook. 163–238.

Young, Richard, Alton Becker, and Kenneth Pike. 1970. *Rhetoric: Discovery and Change*. New York: Harcourt Brace & World.

Index

Editors

Cathy Fleischer is associate professor of English at Eastern Michigan University, where she teaches courses in English education and literacy and directs the Eastern Michigan Writing Project. She is the author of *Composing Teacher Research: A Prosaic History* and a number of articles about literacy and teacher research. Her current research looks at teacher advocacy, connecting teacher research to community organizing strategies and theory. In addition to studying with Jay Robinson, Fleischer has both co-taught with him at the University of Michigan and collaborated with him and a number of teachers and students under the auspices of the Center for Educational Improvement through Collaboration.

David Schaafsma is assistant professor of English education at Teachers College, Columbia University. He is the author of *Eating on the Street: Teaching Literacy in a Multicultural Society*, the co-director (with Patti Stock and Janet Swenson) of the Write for Your Life Project, and editor (with Ruth Vinz) of the journal *English Education*. His interests in community-based writing programs and narrative inquiry stem from working with Jay Robinson and a number of students and teachers in Saginaw and Detroit.

Contributors

Todd DeStigter earned his Ph.D. from the University of Michigan in 1996 and is now assistant professor of English at the University of Illinois at Chicago, where he teaches courses in English education and literacy. His research interests include educational ethnography and the literacies of Latino students. Todd was a student in several of Jay Robinson's graduate seminars focusing on rhetoric, literacy, and educational philosophy, and they recently worked together on a review of Michigan's Secondary English Certification program.

Colleen M. Fairbanks is associate professor in the Department of Curriculum and Instruction at the University of Texas at Austin. Her research and teaching interests include the social contexts of literacy learning, teacher education in the language arts, and the uses of narrative in research and teaching. These interests have grown out of the three years she spent as a teacher researcher under Jay Robinson's supervision in the Saginaw Public Schools.

Roberta Herter teaches English at Henry Ford High School in Detroit. Her research interests include school/university collaboration, writing instruction and assessment, and cultural studies of literacy. She is grateful to Jay Robinson for the commitment he inspires in public education, and for showing her both how democratic classrooms work and the difference they can make in the lives of students and teachers.

John S. Lofty is a former classroom teacher from England, associate professor of English education at the University of New Hampshire, Durham, and the author of *Time to Write: The Influence of Time and Culture on Learning to Write*. He studies classroom discourse and the contextual influences of time on learning. Like many contributors to this book, Lofty first met Jay Robinson in the English and Education program at the University of Michigan, where Jay later served as his dissertation chair. Lofty says that Robinson's greatest influence on his work was to teach him to ground his observations of classroom life in the local context.

Thomas Philion is assistant professor in the Department of English at the University of Illinois at Chicago. Articles he has written have appeared in *English Journal*, the *Illinois English Bulletin*, and several collections published by NCTE. He dedicates his essay to three people: to Jay Robinson, for intellectual grounding with regard to the notion of self-reflection; to Cathy Fleischer, for editorial assistance in writing self-reflectively; and to Ginger Brent, for modeling self-reflection in teaching and life.

Sylvia G. Robins teaches composition and basic reading and writing at Delta College near Saginaw, Michigan. She is enrolled in the English Education Ph.D. program at the University of Michigan. It was a 1988 conference panel led by Saginaw High School English teachers and including Jay Robinson which convinced her that there might indeed exist a university program which honors teachers and permits them their voice. She subsequently took two courses from Robinson, gaining from them intellectual approaches that would foster respectful, responsive ways of reading student texts.

Laura Roop, former director of the Oakland Writing Project, is currently working with teachers and administrators in a number of Michigan school districts as they attempt to revise classroom literacy practice and curricula. She spent three years collaborating with Michigan educators to create English language arts content standards and benchmarks. With Anne Ruggles Gere, Colleen Fairbanks, Alan Howes, and David Schaafsma, Roop co-authored *Language and Reflection: An Integrated Approach to Secondary English*, winner of NCTE's Richard Meade award. She says her mentor and friend, Jay Robinson, has inspired his students to become pragmatic dreamers, practicing education theorists who choose to straddle the worlds of K–12 schooling, universities, and the larger community for the sakes of young people.

Jacqueline Jones Royster is associate professor of English and Vice Chair for Rhetoric and Composition in the English Department at the Ohio State University. Her research interests include the rhetorical history of women of African descent, the development of literacy, and delivery systems for the teaching of composition. She has published extensively in both literacy studies and women's studies. Since the days when Jay Robinson graciously served as her teacher and advisor, she has benefitted from his wisdom, his example as a researcher and scholar, and from his friendship.

Carol L. Winkelmann is associate professor of English Language and
Literature at Xavier University in Cincinnati, Ohio. She teaches linguistics, electronic literacy, and a course on women and violence.
Winkelmann completed her graduate studies at the University of
Michigan (1992) where she studied with Jay Robinson. She currently
researches in the areas of women's language practices and the politics of literacy.

This book was typeset in Palatino by Electronic Imaging.
Typefaces used on the cover were Futura and Garamond.
The book was printed on 60-lb. Arbor Offset by Edwards Brothers, Inc.